Appetite
for
Destruction

By the same author

No One Here Gets Out Alive
(with Jerry Hopkins)

The Doors: The Illustrated History

Wonderland Avenue: Tales of Glamour & Excess

The Doors Complete Illustrated Lyrics
(Editor)

APPETITE

DESTRUCT ON

DANNY SUGERMAN

THE DAYS OF GUNS N' ROSES

FOR

ST. MARTIN'S PRESS

NEW YORK

Dedicated to
Johnny Thunders
and
Stiv Bators
R.I.P.

Design by Jaye Zimet.

Library of Congress Cataloging-in-Publication Data

Sugerman, Danny.
    Appetite for destruction : the days of Guns N' Roses / Danny
Sugerman.
        p.   cm.
    ISBN 0-312-07634-7 (pbk.)
    1. Guns N' Roses (Musical group)   2. Heavy metal (Music)—History
and criticism.   I. Title.
    ML421.G86S9   1991
782.42166'092'2—dc20
    [B]   90-26940
                                                                              CIP

First Paperback Edition: May 1992

10 9 8 7 6 5 4 3 2 1

CONTENTS

PART 1—THE BATTLEGROUND

Chapter 1—Roses and Stones   3

PART 2—WELCOME TO THE JUNGLE

Chapter 2—The Return of Dionysus   21

Chapter 3—Arrival of the Beast

Chapter 4—Imitating the God

PART 3—DEATH, DRU
RO

Chapter 5—

Chapter 6—

PART 4—TECHNICIANS OF THE SACRED

Chapter 7—Back to the Garden   173

Chapter 8—Initiation Rites   201

Epilogue   215

Postscript   227

Acknowledgments   251

Index   255

CONTENTS

vi

THE BATTLE-GROUND

PART 1

ROSES AND STONES

Guns N' Roses had no sooner hit the stage when the band started to fall apart in front of 83,000 people. It was the fall of 1989, onstage at a monstrosity more often used for and better suited to football games. Axl Rose stepped right up to the microphone, not to sing, but to speak. "Before we start playing I want to say I'm sick of all this publicity about our song ["One in a Million"]. I'm not a fucking racist . . ." and he went on to state that not all "black men are niggers" but if someone is "acting like a fucking nigger" then he'll call it as he sees it. And the same thing goes "for fucking faggots." And, "if you still want to call me a racist, you can shove it up your ass."

What was both shocking and impressive was Axl's total obliviousness to the fact that these words offend, of and by themselves. And this was just to begin the set; before it was over he would again choose to speak instead of sing, perhaps figuring, "They're my words anyway, what's it matter how

3

they're delivered, sung or spoken." Or maybe he just had the urge to talk. This is what he said: "I don't like to do this onstage, but unless certain people in this band start getting their shit together, this is going to be the last Guns N' Roses show." The crowd didn't cheer, they didn't clap, they didn't boo; they mumbled, obviously confused. It did seem difficult to believe that a band at the crest of their musical power would call it quits. Then Rose clarified his ire: "I'm sick and tired of too many people in this organization dancing with Mr. Brownstone." He was referring here to two things: the song "Mr. Brownstone" and the drug Mexican rocks, a.k.a. heroin. For all the criticism heaped on him for being irresponsible about glamorizing drug use, Axl Rose is the only name who has stood live onstage in a concert setting and delivered a provocative antidrug lecture.

Before the set ended, Axl took a tumble ten feet off one of the ramps, picked himself up, and rocked some more. When returning for the encore, "Paradise City," he announced, "There's no need to look for a fucking Paradise City 'cause none exists." Then he ripped through the song with a vengeance—anger, angst, rage, and more passion than all the rest of the set combined. He delivered, the musicians delivered, and almost in spite of themselves they ended on a note of triumph. Teetering on the edge of disaster, but triumphant still the same.

In the *Los Angeles Times* a day later, in his concert review, Robert Hilburn fueled the issue of racism further and then commented, "Like Jim Morrison, Rose exhibits a fierce independence that sometimes leads to errors in judgment as he races in a somewhat romantic pursuit of artistic truth. He also shares Morrison's duality: exploring the dark side of man's nature while also possessing an almost old-fashioned yearning for innocence." He went on to say, "The most striking similarity with Morrison in Rose's tendency onstage to act on raw impulse and emotion. He is someone you can't take your eyes off. There is a sense of genuine involvement."

After months of speculation and continuing rumors that Guns N' Roses would be opening for the Rolling Stones through their U.S.A. tour, four Los Angeles dates were, in the end, all that emerged. It appeared to everyone that the Stones themselves were giving credence to all that hype about Guns N' Roses being the new Stones by inviting them to share the bill with them at their Los Angeles engagements. What was it? Were the Stones in fact acknowledging a passing of a torch? Or were they simply being the astute capitalists they are by making something happen that the public so obviously desired? Or were they really challenging the young upstarts? The young guns versus the old guns, a sort of rock 'n' roll late eighties Pat Garret meets Billy the Kid affair? The Stones as the older Garret, once wild, now tamed, part of the Establishment and representing authority and civilization; Guns N' Roses as the younger and recalcitrant Billy, symbolic of the wild and free West.

Although he called LSD "a new kind of wine," Jim Morrison preferred alcohol, a regular rock 'n' roll Dean Martin. Morrison was also the first to consciously integrate rock and shamanism. *(Courtesy* The Doors: The Illustrated History*)*

Axl Rose has made it clear that when the band does something for the money, disaster strikes. Not long before the Stones engagement was booked for Guns N' Roses, Axl told an interviewer that

> we learned a long time ago we can't really do things for the cash. Whenever we've tried to do something that we really didn't want to do, but it was a good money move, and we weren't really into it, we'd go onstage, and it turned into a disaster because nobody's heart was really into the playing. We're doing it because we thought we were being smart businessmen, and it was the right move, and we were advised to do it—you really didn't want to play, but it's a smart move, and it can pay off some bills, we've gone in and done the show and had nothing but a chaos hit.

Yet beyond the possibly irresistible invitation to appear on the same bill as one of their biggest influences, there can be no other reason besides money for their agreement to appear with the Rolling Stones on that band's Los Angeles dates. They had no new LP out to promote and in fact, spent precious time away from the recording studio where they should have been hard at work on their new album. Instead they had been playing selected club dates around town to warm themselves up for the Stones appearances, which were then being hailed as a heavyweight rock 'n' roll title match—sort of a Battle of the Bad Boy Bands.

The Rolling Stones' reasons for inviting the band, industry people speculated, were both simple and complex. Perhaps they were seeking to diffuse the comparison by bringing it into focus and putting the upstarts in their proper place. Others felt it was for no reason more mysterious than the added bodies and dollars the billing would bring. As to why Guns N' Roses agreed, the only logical reason for their willingness to appear, unless they took all that hype seriously and actually thought they stood a chance of winning by blowing the Stones away, was the money, reported to be $250,000 a *night*. In actually, they were offered and contracted $400,000 for two nights. When those two shows sold out and two more nights were put on sale, the band demanded,

Axl Rose. On the verge of disaster, or bliss, or both. *(Courtesy Larry Busacca/Retna Ltd.)*

and received, an additional $600,000. They no doubt earned this amount and they were worth every penny. It's also just possible the Gunners agreed to the invitation to appear for no good reason at all save their love of playing live. Which is, after all, what a great rock band does and what this band, in particular, does extremely well. In the end it might have been the Stones songs the audience was humming, but Guns N' Roses was the band name on everyone's lips. Last, but not least, there was the matter of all the irresistible publicity attendant to the event—and *who* could pass that up?

When the Rolling Stones' machinery gets into gear and starts rolling, it is one of the most awesome rock 'n' roll spectacles you've ever seen, the biggest and best of everything, from the stage to the travel accommodations to the money that's being made to the show you see on the stage. It takes a lot for anything, especially any single event, to take away the focus, which is squarely on the Rolling Stones.

It was certainly nothing new for the Stones to feature an impressive opening act. In the past critical faves such as Ike and Tina Turner, Stevie Wonder, Iggy Pop, and Prince have opened Rolling Stones tours. They never had invited anyone with the commercial clout Guns N' Roses had already demonstrated, and certainly nobody has ever opened for the Stones who has drawn as many comparisons to them as Guns N' Roses.

As the rumor mill was churning out bits and pieces of hearsay, intense behind-the-scenes discussions were going down between the Stones camp and Guns N' Roses management, the Stravinsky brothers. The Stones *had* invited the Gunners to accompany them as special guest stars on the entire tour, apparently unafraid of any inevitable comparisons, but the Stravinsky brothers did not see why their act, at that moment the hottest act in the country, should allow themselves to be used to help pack stadiums for anybody, the Rolling Stones included. After all, Guns N' Roses had just finished a prolonged period opening for other headliners such as Aerosmith, Mötley Crüe, and the Cult. Now that they were out of those obligations, why should they return to such a second-string position?

At first, it was only rumored that Guns N' Roses would be

joining the Stones onstage in Los Angeles for their two Los Angeles Coliseum dates. But it was a rumor that was trumpeted by not only the local media but the national media as well. Living Colour had been the official opening act for the tour, having obtained a direct lien to the Stones via Jagger himself: he had been involved in the band's demo, which led them to a Columbia Records recording contact. Jagger had also gone on to produce a track on their debut LP. There hadn't been any other opening acts during the tour; why should Los Angeles be different? It seemed—and the rock world was buzzing with the news—that Guns N' Roses would indeed share the stage with the band to which they had been so consistently compared. Even before the tour got started, the Gunners were rumored to be the opening act for the Stones. But then that rumor was squelched when the Guns N' Roses management issued a terse statement denying the whole affair. Then came the new Los Angeles rumors.

As quickly as the engagement was officially announced, an additional two nights at the Coliseum were added. There was a feverish excitement about the engagement with the local media speculating and comparing what they felt was going to be the upcoming battle between the two bands. The *Los Angeles Times*, in particular, emphasized this aspect with an almost slavering zeal, indicating the dates were more than what they appeared to be, more than simply an exciting and full evening of the best of the old and the new that rock 'n' roll had to offer. As the engagements loomed closer, the louder the beating of the drums announcing the imminent clash became. When it finally reached a sort of volcanic crescendo, it was showtime.

The day before the first of four shows, warm-up act Living Colour's lead guitarist, Vernon Reid, did a radio interview. A caller asked about the Guns N' Roses controversial song "One in a Million," which contains the words *niggers* and *faggots*. Reid, who is black and a member of the Black Rock Coalition, said he liked Guns N' Roses but he took exception to some of the words and sentiments in that particular song. There was some expectation that Reid might voice his feelings onstage during their set that first night.

A bearded Axl Rose and hooded-eyed Slash: the Toxic Twins of GNR. *(Courtesy Retna Ltd.)*

When Mick Jagger was informed of the impending confrontation, he said, "That would be great." But during his first set, Vernon Reid let his music do the talking.

There was some additional expectation, although slightly less, that if Reid said something, then Axl might say something, and if Axl started to speak—well look out, that would be something to see. While Reid was known for speaking out on behalf of black rock, Rose was known for saying almost anything. On his way to the stage for his band's set, Axl pressed his face close to the Living Colour's bassist's face and challenged him, "I heard on the radio that you guys got a problem with some of the things I got to say." Axl launched into his own defense claiming he never thought of "you guys as niggers." Which I have to admit took guts on Axl's part. One of the Guns N' Roses management team ran up to Will Calhoun, Living Colour's drummer, and tried to play the incident down: "Axl's from Indiana and he doesn't know any better." It is not known whether Axl heard the words to his defense or, if he did, what he thought about being excused by his own team on account of being ignorant and insensitive. Then again, does *anyone* ever admit to being a racist?

At the second of the four shows, wearing a Betty Ford Clinic T-shirt, Slash (the apparent target of Axl's earlier anti-heroin wrath) stepped up to the mike before a note was struck; now he too had something he wanted to say. "Over the years rock 'n' roll has lost a lot of great ones." He named Elvis, Janis, John Bonham, and rambled on.

> Rock 'n' roll and excess have become synonymous. There has been a lot written about this band and drugs. A lot of it is bullshit. A lot of it is true. Last night you almost saw the last Guns N' Roses gig. I remember coming here as a kid to see Aerosmith and Van Halen and the Stones, dreaming of being up here. Last night I was up here and I didn't even know it. Smack isn't what it's all about. No one in this band advocates the use of heroin. That's not what it's all about and we're not going to be one of those weak bands that falls apart over it.

He went on to say that none of the people in the band did it. He must have been referring to a very recent decision, because ten minutes after the first show, Axl Rose was overheard remarking to singer David Lee Roth that "three out of the four musicians in the band were smacked out of their minds for the show and," he remarked incredulously, "everyone thinks *I'm* the junkie." Word on the street was that Slash had stopped each night on his way to the Coliscum at his dealer's house to fill up before showtime. That is the problem with heroin; it is, after all, hard to give up. After Slash's confessional address, Axl stepped forward and apologized, "I just don't want to see any of my friends slip away." They embraced as the band began "Patience."

What hadn't been revealed was that two weeks earlier Slash's grandmother, the Hudson family matriarch with whom he had enjoyed an especially close relationship, had passed away, dealing the introverted guitarist a devastating blow and sending him reeling into a chemically induced tailspin.

Rose meanwhile had been dealing with his own domestic crisis. In a good-natured and spontaneous display of generosity, Axl invited several close friends and family members from Lafayette, Indiana, out west to partake of his success and enjoy an irresistible front row—or better yet, backstage —vantage point for the Rolling Stones, as well as the Gunners themselves. Trouble erupted, however, as long suppressed anger, resentment, and ingratitude broke out. Exact details of the infighting were kept under wraps, but it doesn't take much to imagine the expectations his family and friends nursed toward their newfound benefactor and longtime favorite son/friend—who better for him to share his recent good fortune with? Of course he would want to express his gratitude for their faith and support and would want to reward them, to share with them the fruits of his labors; afterall, didn't they believe in him all along?

And it's not difficult to imagine Axl's reaction to such expectations, whether expressed or suppressed. What the fuck did any of them *ever* do for him? If they believed in him so much and took such great care of him, then why'd he have to run to L.A. in the first place? Now that they were out here, where he'd originally run to get away from them, brought out here on his tab, what else did they have a right to expect? It doesn't take a psychic psychiatrist to imagine the havoc all of this played on Axl's eager-to-please/difficult-to-be-pleased demeanor.

One thing is certain, it was not a joyous reunion. By the time Axl was due to commence his singing engagement on the Stones bill, while Slash was going through his own poignant anguish, Axl had thus far been awake, non-chemically induced, on the natch, although one can only speculate as to what spontaneous combustion his brain matter was churning out, midway into a manic downswing. In other words, the emotional turmoil of all the attendant dramas combined to produce a state of total insomnia and by the time Axl stepped on stage to sing he had not slept in more than forty hours. He would sleep only sporadically until family, friends, and Stones were all well on their way out of town.

Seen in this light, not only does the reason for Axl's outbursts seem clear, so does the motivation for his plea to his fellow band-members to clean up become more understandable—having forsaken his family, his reliance on his band becomes intensified. Maybe he could get by without one and not the other, but to be so close to losing both band and family must have been chilling.

At the third show, the band performed two songs including "Mr. Brownstone," which, on this particular night, took on ominous overtones. The Guns N' Roses' soap opera then continued as Axl went after Mr. Hilburn—not by name, but by implication in an angry diatribe, informing the audience that someone had woken him up that morning and handed him a concert review that brought up the whole racist issue *again*. Of course, Axl felt compelled to point out again that "I'm not a fucking racist. And don't compare me to people that have been dead for twelve years [referring to Jim Morrison who'd been dead for nineteen years at concert time]. . . . This is fucking art, this is how I feel. You don't like it—don't fucking listen. It's real easy." Then as an aside he said to the rest of us, "Fuck 'em 'cause I'm on this stage tonight."

Which turned out to be the truest thing he said all week. Every time he steps on that stage it is a victory for him and a blow to his have-been and would-be oppressors—from parents to authority figures to critics. His enemies are vanquished and rock 'n' roll is triumphant. "I write for you, not them," he told the crowd. And the pact is renewed between singer and audience, stronger than blood, made in spoken words; the bonding, already established, that is forged with their records and videos is made official, irrefutable. The band then launched into "Night Train" and kicked ass from the stage at the first yard line to the goal posts, up to the last row. It was heroic.

Jagger once said that "the best rock 'n' roll music encapsulates a certain high energy, an angriness. Rock 'n' roll is only rock 'n' roll if it's not safe. Violence and energy—that's what rock 'n' roll is all about." It sounded to me like he would be among the very first to champion what Guns N' Roses were trying to do. I didn't think I'd have the opportunity to talk to him about it, but as things turned out, I did. Backstage after the Guns N' Roses show and before the Stones began their set, I asked Mick Jagger if he'd caught the GNR show the night before. He had. So what about this sense of danger and threat that he himself admires in a band and that Guns N' Roses allegedly have that's prompting everyone to compare them with the early Rolling Stones?

"Well, I don't know about that," Jagger said. "They're much more heavy metal." He laughed, not as if he couldn't bother to take their threat seriously, but as if he'd simply grown beyond caring about such trivialties. The implication was that he was Mick Jagger—and Axl Rose has a long way to go. I got the feeling that going the distance was the only way Jagger was going to judge this band, and for that it was still too early to tell—it was therefore irrelevant.

The implied understanding was that energy and danger are fine elements for a band to possess, but without a sense of survival all is for naught. "It's like the Clash isn't it? Or the Sex Pistols? Not the music, but that other thing, like they're set on self-destruct."

"A self-fulfilling doom prophecy," is what I said and mentally jotted down simultaneously.

"Exactly." Jagger smiled. "A built-in obsolescence. They can't last like that. They will simply self-destruct."

"Chemically?" I suggest.

"Yeah, but is that a symptom or the cause?" he asked back with a devilish grin. "It doesn't matter does it?" he finished. He was referring to a band that just one night before was literally falling apart. He didn't seem too impressed. But like I said, he didn't seem to care that much at all, one way or the other, although he was unfailingly polite.

The last thing he was asked before going on stage was,

"Does it make it hard for you to follow them after a set like tonight?"

"Well, it makes it harder to say anything!" He laughs as if he's seen all this before. Which he has; he's seen 'em come and go, and it's safe to say he'll see a few more. In the end, though, Mick Jagger is not your typical Guns N' Roses fan. Even the first- and second- and even third-generation Stones' fans are not your current or future Guns N' Roses fans. But, it is true; the audience Guns N' Roses have is almost identical to the Stones' original audience twenty years ago, in terms of social outlook. I think what Keith and company represented yesterday, Guns N' Roses symbolize today. The Guns N' Roses audience is newer and younger, harder to shock yet easier to please, and they need their own Rolling Stones and all that the group represents. I didn't see or sense a torch being passed any of those nights. It felt more like a stick of dynamite, and then it was being dropped. Keith Richards, who had previously slagged off the band, reportedly was not all that impressed with the Gunners' stage behavior either. Slash, however, did venture the opinion that "Jagger should have died after he made *Some Girls*."

As for the alleged battle of the bands—it never happened. It was no contest. The Stones had more ammo and more powerful artillery. The Stones' professionalism (despite a pronounced lack of spontaneity), and a truly spectacular backlog of classics, fused past and present to make a presentation of awesome proportions if not transcendent moments. For all that, it was the name Guns N' Roses that was most spoken in the days to come. The Stones had the songs and even the show and entertainment—but Guns N' Roses had Axl Rose and he possessed the spontaneity, the spark, and the fire. No other band could have upstaged the Stones to the degree Guns N' Roses did. Certainly not Living Colour, whom 86 percent of the crowd had chosen to miss. By the time Guns N' Roses hit the stage nary a seat was unfilled.

It is surprising how oblivious, at first, Axl was to the reasons why he'd been called a racist. In defending his use of the words *nigger* and *faggot*, he argued that what a person feels and says *together* can be considered racist, but words alone should not be considered so. He appeared not to understand that the words are offensive and can hurt regardless of the user's intent.

It's not the word, it's the meaning, he seemed to say. If you hate African-Americans and call them by their slang derogatory names, that's racist—but, just saying the words doesn't make you a racist.

Apparently, not many people agreed with him, especially Robert Hilburn of *The Los Angeles Times* and Vernon Reid of Living Colour. At one point, Reid said, "If you don't have a problem with gay people, don't call them faggots. If you don't have a problem with black people, don't call them niggers." Clear enough.

While Axl has probably become enlightened by the controversy, he has not backed down in defending his intentions. "That's not what I mean!" he declared in an attempt to clear the air. It takes a particular innocence to repeatedly insist on his intentions, a perverse sort of stubborn pride and an exacting sense of honesty especially when his lead guitarist, Slash, is half black.

Edgar Allan Poe once said, "Any man who dares to write a book with complete frankness and utter honesty would then produce a masterpiece." The same no doubt applies to writing (recording and performing too) today.

Axl Rose possesses such an honesty, if not genius, which was what Poe was speaking of. Guns N' Roses have a type of crooked nobility that only the five of them really understand, but which a worldwide audience of nearly 20 million has responded to with dollars and soul. Perhaps it is unspoken, perhaps it is even unconscious, but it is real and it is heartfelt. It is harder to defend than it is to capitulate, apologize, or recant. It would be easier for Axl to say "I'm sorry" than to fight continually to give a clearer presentation of his intentions.

It would *appear* to be easier at least. To be false, to compromise, is clearly not easy for him or any of them, because it means to betray their hearts and it is their hearts that got them where they are; it is their hearts that they must follow.

What's really surprising is that Axl Rose is talking about all this onstage in front of 83,000 people. It's exactly that quality, that devotion to their own outlaw code, their insistence on being true to their instincts, that gets them in trouble but also makes them so exciting. Axl had taken a fall off the stage the first night. Will he take a fall again, but hurt himself this time? Will he be more careful? Was he drunk, stoned? What's he going to say tonight? Whatever happens, you know it will be different from the show before, not just a different song here and there. Anything can happen. They allow the unknown to occur, promote it when it arrives. Who knows where it will lead? Their purpose is to follow it. The arrival is redundant. If it works, great. If it doesn't, that might turn out to be less great but more exciting and therefore even greater.

It is this possibility of danger that we all find stimulating; thrilling, part fear, part joy. To be truly effective, some violent, but attractive, action must be unexpected, yet somehow subconsciously willed. The excitement comes in the expectation of the unexpected, unplanned, and/or ecstatic explosion, increased combustion—watching them onstage, whirling like musical dervishes worshiping at the holy altar rock 'n' roll has erected, on the verge of spinning out of control—now *that's* exciting. Witnessing them on the precipice of chaos, so hot they're steaming, on the verge of disaster, or bliss, is truly a rare and wonderful experience to behold. The actual spin-out is by its very nature anticlimactic. Wanting the impossible, expecting the unpredictable, sensing its imminent arrival, building to the highest possible peak, teetering on the precipice, right up there against the edge, and then leaning there, and the band is not even in control of this because something bigger is controlling the band—they are merely, yet incredibly, the vehicle. That's entertainment as it should be. Or at least as it could be. The band is out of control. Right where they want to be. Of course, this can (and has) produced impossible expectations.

Back to the show. On the third night, two songs after Axl's attack on the press, he introduced the band, ending with Slash who "has a few words to say. And then he's gonna play for you." Slash sauntered up to the microphone, casually lit a cigarette while 80,000 people watched in silence. There was no tension, no electricity, nothing. Then he spoke. He rambled on for four or five minutes about what "a great fucking town Los Angeles is." A five-minute diatribe, a variation on what most bands express in four or five words (such as "Alright, Los Angeles!" to the cheers of said city's audience on this planned-to-appear-spontaneous exclamation).

Then he stepped back and played a guitar solo. That went nowhere and did nothing outside of meandering into what sounded like an instrumental version of Alice Cooper's "Only Women Bleed" and then into "Knocking on Heaven's Door." Suddenly, the band kicked in and soared to the heavens and were immediately forgiven. Slash playing at his very best, as if to compensate for the previous lull. Axl dancing, as if possessed, a rare combination of danger and innocence; part child, part man. Does it really matter what they have to go through if it gets them to this point? Do they need all the attendant distractions and destructions to get there? Is what makes them great the same thing that eats them alive? And which are *we* really interested in? And, how come the people, the artists, we love the most are so often the same ones destined to live the shortest?

WELCOME TO THE JUNGLE

PART 2

CHAPTER 2

THE RETURN OF DIONYSUS

There are certain descriptive words and phrases that a writer can amass that give a stronger and better impression than any biographer's marshaling of facts can convey. One of my favorite such gatherings about Guns N' Roses was from the hard rock journal *Kerrang!*: "Rowdy, raunchy, gut-level rockers who lived on the streets of Hollywood and put their experience to music. Delinquent, delicious, decadent, Excess All Areas Rock, Guns N' Roses stalk through every silk scarf fantasy and rub you raw like Piranhas in a Jacuzzi." Which is as good a description as you're likely to find. But it isn't nearly enough and it doesn't tell us *why*.

Why, in an era when drug use is regarded as not only foolish and destructive, but unattractive as well, is this group who flaunts its substance abuse with blatant disregard for anyone's opinion, nevertheless so extremely popular?

It's not because of the songs, which are certainly good but not consistently great, although some definitely are; it's not because the musicianship within those songs is so spectac-ular, because while it's good, it's not ground-breakingly unique.

It's not because they play the music business game with such savvy. The week their first album was shipped it was recalled in many places; record outlets refused to stock it because the cover artwork was, in their opinion, not ac-ceptable.

There are many who feel everything about this band is unsavory. To be sure, they are every parent's nightmare. They are the essence of what teachers are referring to when they talk about "bad attitude." And the band knows it. In the liner notes on their first LP, *Appetite for Destruction*, after they give thanks to a hundred friends and allies, they end with a bitter bow to "the teachers, preachers, cops, and elders who never believed" in them.

No, they're not successful because they're great musicians, or brillant songwriters, or because they are cute boys next door, the brother you never had, or exceedingly handsome, or especially diligent businessmen.

On the contrary, it appears they do everything wrong; they're fuck-ups of the first magnitude, which their prolonged inability to record their follow-up album demonstrates. They're even failures at success, which they're not handling all that well. Clearly, they don't appear to give a damn. These kids, it appears, are not all right. They're perennial outsiders, outcasts, misfits . . .

And yet . . . and yet, they've got *it*.

Whatever rock 'n' roll is, Guns N' Roses personify it today like no one else. No one else even comes close.

"As amazing as it seems," Slash has observed regarding the bands meteoric rise to stardom, "in this drug-free exercise-and-health age, there's a bunch of us who are still clinging fast to the late sixties and early seventies." No shit. A *big* bunch. It's not so amazing either that Guns N' Roses success coincides with the rise of Classic Rock radio and it shouldn't be difficult to see that what the young audience sees today in the music of that era is the same thing that makes Guns N' Roses so immensely popular.

Clockwise from bottom: Steven Adler, Slash, Izzy Stradlin, W. Axl Rose, and Duff McKagan. An early publicity shot. *(Courtesy Geffen Records)*

Alternately referred to as Lines n' Noses or Wine n' Poses, Guns N' Roses have been hailed as "the only real rock 'n' roll band to come out of L.A. in the last ten years." They have been credited with single-handedly bringing rock 'n' roll back to life. They are to the eighties and nineties what the Sex Pistols were to the seventies, or the Stones to the sixties. They bristle with their own brand of rage and outlaw irreverence. Their music is rock stripped down to its absolute fundamentals; it's no-bullshit hard and lean; all muscle no fat; strong and sinewy. It confronts you, it hits hard as well as home and its message is simple: love or let us run wild. . . . We're who we are, now what are *you* going to do about it?

As one British writer put it, their music is primeval with the emphasis on "evil, relentlessness and paranoia, all: 'They're out to get me—I'm innocent,' or 'The world is fucked up and so are we.' " They express the angst of teen isolation and despair with an unerring sense of honesty and directness.

The Romans transformed the Greek god Dionysus, a symbol of intoxication and creation, into Bacchus, the god of drunkenness—an entity from which we derive our term "Bacchanalian."

There is so much more. At times they demonstrate a genuine sense of vulnerability, innocence, and even nobility and grace. Then there is their devotion to the ecstatic omnipotent state of rocking. All of which is a combination that the very best rock 'n' roll should have to offer.

The constant comparisons with the Sex Pistols and the Rolling Stones—and there have been literally dozens—begs a question that has never been satisfactorily answered: what's so good about *bad?*

According to their critics, Guns N' Roses are "Common, noisy, gross, selfish, irritating, irresponsible, offensive, racist, white trash, reprobates, scoundrels, uncouth, and loathsome street rats," and to sum it up in a word, "vulgar." They are. They're damn difficult to defend. The entire picture, however, is not quite so simple. In most of these portrayals, such negative responses and accusations and lamentations only serve to prove and underscore the vitality of this still incredibly young band. If vulgarity can be defined as the absence of cultivation, then Guns N' Roses are vulgar. If lack of cultivation is the inward mark of vulgarity, then delicate authors agree that the outward and indicative sign of this deficiency is noise. ("Let the tongue be silent!" admonished Horace.) If this is so, Guns N' Roses are loud and vulgar.

Besides, rock 'n' roll recognizes no class boundaries, in the egalitarian spirit of vulgarity. Guns N' Roses appeal to the English heavy metal head banger, to the CD buff in Harvard Square and the rebel hick in Tallahasee, as well as the jaded rock heavies in New York City and Los Angeles, and the sixties renegades living in Amsterdam. In 1859, British writer John Ruskin invoked the term *vulgar* to characterize the seventeenth-century painters, and to describe what had happened to refined Western culture since its fall during the Renaissance. He criticized artists such as Rembrandt, with his paintings of low-life characters, complete with pockmarked faces and red noses, who inhabited seedy taverns painted with browns and grays, as betraying a sensibility "absolutely careless of all lovely living form." According to Ruskin, vulgarity is the opposite of that quality which defines a gentleman.

Ruskin, a leading art critic of his time, although speaking

Axl. *(Courtesy Larry Busacca/Retna Ltd.)*

on behalf of many at the time, was wrong. Vulgarity isn't an absence of, so much as an indulgence in, passion. Oscar Wilde noted, "Live! Live the wonderful life that is in you! Let nothing be lost upon you. Be always searching for new sensations!" In Romanticism, restraint was gone. In a world and age full of conflict and confusion, as Nietzsche and the Romantics testify, the senses don't lie. It was true during the industrial era of the Romantics and it is truer in today's computer and neoindustrial age, as it is expressed over and over in the so-called vulgarities of rock 'n' roll.

The art of Shelley and Tennyson, of Picasso and Van Gogh proceeded from the same impulses that fueled Elvis Presley, Mick Jagger, Jimi Hendrix, Jim Morrison, Johnny Lydon, and now Guns N' Roses frontman Axl Rose. Axl Rose is to Guns N' Roses what Jagger is to the Stones and Morrison to the Doors: the centrifugal force behind the magic. He has the vision and the band has the underappreciated and underrated job of implementing and complementing those words and that vision.

The romanticism that longs for the primitive and the urgent is alive today in rock 'n' roll, and most apparently, vividly alive in Guns N' Roses. Cultured people who despised the sound of real life then, still hate this sound today. In the best possible rock 'n' roll, the kind of rock 'n' roll Guns N' Roses plays, the same yearnings expressed by the Romantics are to be found once again. Who would have guessed? As Shelley so carelessly and cockily wrote, the poets really are the "un-acknowledged legislators of the future." Or as Rimbaud said: "Priests of the invisible."

Rock music has breathed life into the notions so long ago expressed by the Romantics. Oxford professor Walter Pater once advised his followers (among them Oscar Wilde), "To burn always with this hard, gem-like flame, to maintain this esctasy, is success in life." This is the ecstatic risk: the only thing worth living for; the only thing worth dying for. It offended refined sensibilities then and it still does now.

Reaching up underneath to join with this powerful, urgent mentality is the foundation upon which the romantic credo would rest: the noise itself. Rock music's roots are based on the imposition of Romantic myth on a backdrop of black Southern music. If the brain and emergent spirit of rock 'n' roll originates from the Romantics then the body and the (heart)beat comes from Africa. You don't have to be a student of African or American history to know how repulsed white society was by this people's animalistic, savage, jungle music.

If we had to look for an even more offensive movement on which to graft the Romantic sentiment, there is none better than black Southern music by way of voodoo. Of course, cultivated members of society today are still offended by what became rock music. That means the music itself is working and real. That's what it's supposed to, and meant to do. It is a testimony to its authenticity.

In 1958, the *Music Journal* noted rock music as "this throwback to jungle rhythms" that incites youths to "orgies of sex and violence. Teenagers use it as an excuse for the removal of all inhibitions and the complete disregard of the conventions of decency." From Ruskin's condemnation, to this fifties' attitude, to today's fears, attitudes on liberation have simply not changed all that much.

To their fans, Guns N' Roses are the most exciting and true rock 'n' roll group to emerge from anywhere since the Rolling Stones emerged over twenty years ago to play the shadow to the Beatles' sunshine. Guns N' Roses are every bit as mad, bad, and dangerous to the parents of today as the Stones were in their heyday or for that matter, Byron and Shelley were in theirs. Wantons, seducers, defilers all.

Their first album, *Appetite for Destruction*, remained in *Billboard*'s Top 10 for over a year. It has sold in excess of 10 million copies around the world and is the best-selling debut LP by a band *ever*. A more recently issued EP, *Lies*, recorded before the LP and released months later, stormed up the charts to join *Appetite* and then both sat there within the Top 10 for a few months, selling steadily. In a typical week, during this period, Guns N' Roses sold in excess of 200,000 pieces of product. Not bad for five supposedly alienated youths who set out only to blow away all the other L.A. club bands and to show the posers and wanna-be's how it was really done. To be entirely true, to do it up right in the true spirit of rock 'n' roll romanticism, they should have then walked away, split up, and/or died like the Sex Pistols or the Doors. Luckily, that wasn't the case. Instead, after having fought their way out of the trash heap of L.A.'s heavy metal Sunset Boulevard scene, they've gone on to be heralded and knighted as the avatars of eighties rock, pop, heavy metal, and even punk (as much as punk was always more attitude than music). They've been attacked by the rock press as well as the straight press as much for the style of life they lead as much as they have been for their music. Guns N' Roses attract controversy wherever they go for almost anything they do. Their life-styles are reflected in so many of their songs—not necessarily celebrated, but presented without apology still the same. They walk it like they talk it. What they're talking about is making some people very nervous.

The notion of wine, women, and song is nothing new. The holy (or unholy) triumvirate has been united for eons, a celebrational haven for some cultures and the ruin of others.

Bassist Duff and ex-wife Mandy, in happier times. *(Courtesy Michele Matz/Retna Ltd.)*

It is either loved and indulged or despised and avoided, creating a sort of ying and yang of life attitude—can't live with it, can't live without it. In the past few decades, only the names have changed: sex, drugs, and rock 'n' roll was a 1950s sin, a sixties credo, and a seventies cliché; and in the current political climate of Reagan/Bush, Just Say No, and AIDS, it's become big bad news once again. Some critics howl and say that it is this championing of excess that really fuels Guns N' Roses celebrity, all show and no go. Their record company, Geffen Records, in response to the claims of irresponsibility, says it's an act and they're just selling records. The boys in the band maintain they're just being themselves. But the little girls, they understand . . . and in this case so too do the boys. The members of the band are young, foolhardy, stubborn, cynical, proud, impatient, uncompromising, insolent, conflicted, and very honest and up front about their faults. They believe in themselves, as well they should. They *are* good, as defined by the hard rock world of values, the only true forum in which they should be judged, in relation to their peers. They are a band in the best sense of the word, a rock 'n' roll gang, a family joined at the hip by something richer and deeper than blood or reason and they hang together because, one suspects that without each other, they'd hang apart.

In a culture where half the population elevates rock stars to deities and the other half damns them to hell, it really shouldn't come as too much a surprise that the two forces would be in conflict and produce a bastardized jewel that as a whole society both wants and deserves, loathes and judges, elevates and condemns to eternity.

Western culture has, in different temperatures and different times, exploited and celebrated, supported and suppressed the rock culture since its birth. Rock 'n' roll remains the entertainment industry's billion-dollar wayward son. Rock 'n' roll as an art form has never been truly accepted, regardless of its profit-producing abilities. Tolerated, maybe, warily; most often condemned and repressed.

The Judeo-Christian age, since the industrial revolution, has been moving full speed ahead into the computer-robotics age, and has worshiped and continues to worship the god of logic, a.k.a. the Greek god Apollo. The intuitive and wild Dionysus has been pushed progressively further and deeper into our collective unconscious, ignored and repressed. Not Bacchus, Dionysus's Roman incarnation, the god of drunkenness and bacchanalian revelry, but of the original Greek Dionysus—the liberator, the bringer of ecstasy or madness, the representative of the marriage of man and his true nature.

When the Greeks proceeded to elevate Apollo, god of light, logic, and reason, they simultaneously made Dionysus, god of dark, creative, illogical impulsiveness, his counterpart or his opposite. Apollo was up there in the sun, clear, pristine, and it stood to reason Dionysus, as his opposite, became the enemy, down there, dark and evil. Christianity took the lead and made the capricious nature of Dionysus, represented by the goat, into the horns and cloven hooves of the devil. And from the hairy flanks of Pan, the god of music, the devil received his loins, courtesy of the church. In other words, they took the recklessness of Dionysus and the animal powers inherent in the music of Pan and made them a pure and simple sin, punishable by horrific, if not always swift, retribution. The church also, in their bid to stamp out the drunken pagan worship of Dionysus, usurped the honoring wine ritual and made it their own, a symbol of Christ's blood. Orphism had made a similar move on the Dionysian cults in the sixth century B.C. The Moslems simply banned outright the use of wine—in any context. In the Koran, it is written, "They will ask thee concerning wine. Answer them, 'It is a great sin.'" Elsewhere in the Koran, in the Chapter of the Table, it is said, "Surely wine is an abomination and the work of Satan. Therefore avoid, that ye may prosper. Satan seeketh to divert you from remembering God thusly, therefore, abstain." Collectively, as a series of societies, we've never really looked back. Even today the major religions of the West continue to preach negation of life and extirpation of the passions. It's okay to make yourselves miserable in life, the reasoning goes, to spend eternity (i.e., death) in grace (i.e., heaven). If not, the logic goes, to enjoy the physical, sensual passions of earthly life, one must prepare to spend eternity paying for it in hell. Eastern religions on the other hand, often utilize the physical nature of the body through yoga (from the Sanskrit word *yuj* meaning to join or to yoke, as man to his nature). When we in the West do honor our physical self, it is more often than not with guilt and anxiety rather than grace. The Jews fare no better than the Christians in honoring the physicalities as honored through Dionysus, a.k.a. the God of ecstasy. An old Yiddish proverb observes whatever legitimate pleasure we deny ourselves on earth, we are freed of that desire in heaven. Yom Kippur, the Day of Atonement, is when all the sins of the people were heaped on the back of the *goat*, which was then delivered into the wilderness, taking all evils with it. Yeah, the original scapegoat; the wilderness where it belonged.

A popular theory gaining increasing acceptance these days among psychologists and intellectuals is that while the ancient Greek gods no longer dwell on Olympus, that does not mean they have ceased to exist as archetypes. This is not a new or radical theory. Both Carl Jung and Friedrich Nietzsche utilized the symbols of Apollo and Dionysus specifically to represent the two major warring factions of man's existence. They became the primal (or Dionysian) urge, the "I want" of the id and the cultural (or Apollonian) "thou shalt not" of the superego.

Jung believed that since we do not believe in the reality of Olympus so the ancient gods of Greece live on for us today as symptoms. We no longer have access to the divine ecstasy of Dionysus; we are consumed and pestered by addictive behavior and cheap thrills. Rock 'n' roll is the juncture where the real thing and the cheap thrills meet.

Dionysus, as much as he was despised, could not be killed or even suppressed. When King Lycurgus drove the armies of Dionysus from his country, he thought he had gotten rid of the troublesome and threatening god for good. But Dionysus had merely gone into hiding deep beneath the sea. When he reemerged, he manifested as violence, terrifyingly powerful violence; it was the other side of his other equally powerful quality, ecstasy. The harder we push Dionysus away and downward, the harder he simply returns. As Carl Jung argued, and as the mythology of Dionysus' demonstrates, if an impulse arises and is not dealt with, then it goes back downward and develops antihuman qualities. Dr. Frederick Pearls founded his Gestalt Therapy on the necessity of fully experiencing one's own emotional life. If not, one's experience of life is impure, indirect, and confused, one's behavior destructive or negative. With this in mind, what happens then if society as a whole continues to condemn all of its sensational impulses generation after generation, while simultaneously engaged in a ceaseless, tireless quest for yet greater and greater means of satisfaction and satiation? What you get is today's rock 'n' roll kids, desperate for and loyal to anything that brings them in touch with themselves. So, what if a society tries to forbid these kids that music, that experience of unity and transcendence that their collective souls demand? Heavy metal kids, Megadeath, crack addiction, teenage alcoholism, devil worship, aborted ecstasy, and yes, Guns N' Roses and madness.

The quintessence of Dionysus is just this madness. And as the myths tell us, it is easy to pass beyond the bounds of rapture into a dangerous wildness and on to destructiveness; from sacred to profane. The gateway to Dionysus is intoxication. The god of creativity and destruction and the god of wine are one and the same.

And we also know Dionysus (and his counterparts) demanded a sacrifice and that sacrifice was to be made of the flesh and blood. If it wasn't offered willingly, it would be taken, tragically, nevertheless.

Although Guns N' Roses had been transubstantiating the light and energy of life into the immortality of music, the day was soon coming when Dionysus would require a more substantial demonstration of loyalty in exchange for his blessings.

For Guns N' Roses there would be a time and a place: 1988, Castle Donnington, at the "Monsters of Rock" festival. "I saw it," Axl reported, still finding it almost impossible to believe.

> I saw it go down. Right from the stage. I saw these two faces go up and then go down. They went down and then they came up again and went back down and then they didn't come back up. The audience was going crazy, we brought that out in them. We didn't make 'em do what happened, we stopped the show three times to try and cool things out. The security didn't help. I knew if I went down there, there'd be a riot. I think someone could've gone down there and helped those people. . . . I don't know what really to think about it.

Two teenagers, eighteen-year-old Alan Dick and twenty-year-old Landon Siggers, were trampled to death midway into Guns N' Roses' performance before a crowd of 107,000 sweating, dancing, entranced celebrants. Bassist Duff McKagan had earlier expressed, just prior to the festival, that "You're making history if you play Donnington." He was right. As soon as the band climbed the stage, fans surged forward and crushed audience members in the stampede and crunch to the front. You can see the hundred thousand move as one in the video used to promote "Paradise City," their third and last single off *Appetite*. It is a fine yet also terrifying example of what is so great and special about this band.

Slash gave a detailed eyewitness account immediately after the show. "It was real scary. . . . It was kids piled on kids piled on kids, horizontal on the ground. They were unconscious and more people kept falling on them. I saw them. It took about two minutes to get everybody out. We stopped the show a few times and they finally pulled the last couple of people out and I think they were dead. It was really weird. I saw no life in those bodies at all."

Slash opined that "American crowds are really cool. British crowds tend to be more hectic, more insane. That's the big difference. I think Brits are more starved for it. They have to go through more hell with life in general. In America, everybody just gets into it because they want to have a good time. In England, they're desperate for it because the rest of life is pretty dismal. I was born here and I know what it's like. . . ."

But it can happen anywhere. It happened at the Who concert in Cincinnati, before the music ever started, in the mad anticipatory rush to get inside the auditorium and to the best unreserved seats. It happened to the Doors in concert when an audience member stood up along the ledge of the second auditorium tier and with a blissed-out expression extended his arms into a martyred swan dive and dove with a sticky *plat* onto the asphalt floor as the Doors finished the inflammatory introductory chords to "When the Music's Over." And it happened in Alamont Speedway, when the Stones were performing the opening of "Sympathy for the Devil," prompting Jagger to crack (unknowing of the severity of the rustling of bodies out front) "something weird always happens during that song."

In summing up the band's frustration and anger over the accident, Slash inadvertently put his finger squarely on the dilemma the band faces: if everything is arranged and planned out in advance, the gig's a drag, and if too much is left to

chance, accidents can happen. Fortunate accidents, and un-
fortunate accidents like the one at Donnington.

> When kids die at a gig, that's a little . . . The screwed up
> thing about it is it's a sort of catch-22, because you want to
> have that element of danger and chance, and you want to
> have that sort of chaotic you-don't-know-what's-going-to-
> happen-next kind of thing happening, but then when people
> really do get hurt, or somebody dies from it, then you feel
> responsible, and you just hate to, because a rock 'n' roll show
> is really supposed to be about having a good time and that's
> what we try and provide. It was originally supposed to bring
> people together. So, it just sort of blows the whole thing. It's
> great to go out there and really kick ass, but then that kind
> of energy that you're putting into it also sort of generates a
> stronger kind of energy, and before you know it, you can't
> control it.

Axl also feels some of the responsibility, but not all of it.

> Yes, we're part of what happened 'cause we're there. But I
> don't feel like we're responsible for what happened. We
> didn't tell people to smash each other until they couldn't
> breathe. We didn't tell people, drink so much alcohol that
> you can't fucking stand up. I think everybody who was there
> that day is responsible in some way. Don't get me wrong,
> people getting hurt was very tragic, the deaths, those were
> tragic, no way around it. But we had the best fucking response
> of any goddamn band that day.

Which he has every right to be proud of. It was the biggest
crowd they had thus far played for and a lot of the audience
was there for someone else, although the Gunners pulled in
an extra large, unanticipated number of people that day, and
they went out there to blow the headliners away, to give the
show everything they had so the last person in the back of
the concert area would be blown away as well. And they
succeeded. "Banners, signs, singing, dancing, everything," Axl
remembered. "It was insane."

Still onstage, before he had been informed anyone had died,

Axl told the audience, "Have a good fucking day and don't kill yourselves." But it was too late. Dionysus can express ecstasy or madness to his followers and much of the time one becomes the other in the blink of an eye; or one and the other become the same.

One thing is for sure. It was a difficult, painful test for a band still so young—a young band who had been tested so much already, and who would continue to be tested in the weeks and months to come.

The Dionysian parallel here is that if we refuse an immortal god or an archetype it will not disappear; it may go away, underground or into the sea (of unconsciousness), but it will return, perverted, and stronger than ever. In other words, when you suppress a god, you get a demon. Those who accept him achieve ecstasy, those who oppose are damned.

The madness or mania spread by Dionysus attacks and affects a great number of people. Whenever suppressed or opposed, Dionysus takes on epidemic proportions. The deities most revered in antiquity were the migrant, roving gods—Orpheus, Pan, Hermes. These gods had their seasons; people invoked their presence; hymns were sung to them. Dionysus, among the gods, was the most desired, the most feared, and the most revered. When Dionysus was given his due, he left after honoring those who favored him. The important thing to note is that Dionysus is always on the move, and has been referred to as the sovereign master of the spontaneous and sudden, appearing in a surge of natural energy, the "prince of immediacy." He cannot be stopped, and when an attempt is made to do so, the incipient action of the god reverses. It does not quit or go away. For every opposing action there is a greater reaction.

Today, the madness of Dionysus is more evident than ever before. He is on the loose and larger and more powerful and destructive than ever. The problem King Lycurgus experienced was a microcosm of the problem we face today with the epidemic of drugs. And, it is interesting to note, *epidemic* was originally a word used in talking about a "sacrifice to the gods."

The thought of appeasing and making a place for Dionysus

was as abhorrent to King Lycurgus in his kingdom as the thought of legalizing drugs is to the policy makers of today (even though as of this writing former Secretary of State George Shultz has come out in favor of legalization: "We tried to stop it at the source, that didn't work; we tried to stop the demand, that didn't work. It's [legalization] the only answer. There isn't enough jail space in the world to contain one-tenth of this country's drug users"). Just as Dionysus returned with three times his force and fury, so does the drug problem continue to exact its price. In the same suppressive manner, whenever "they" try to cancel a concert, rate a record, or try to take away, ban, diminish, or attempt to legislate our music in any way, it will ultimately backfire on "them." Every time "they" try to legislate against people's tastes, the desire for transcendence or intoxication, Dionysus will continue to counterattack.

After three decades of repression, rock 'n' roll appears to have been embraced by the mainstream population. Watch television and see how many Madison Avenue creations now utilize the soft side of rock as their mesmerizing, emotion-enticing backdrops. Despite such popular acceptance, rock 'n' roll will always produce an outlaw fringe uninterested in mere entertainment. To them rock 'n' roll is an attitude, a stance, a life-style, or, if you will, a religion. How do the parents of today feel about their sons and daughters worshipping at the altar of these outlaws? The same way the fathers and mothers of Thebes felt when their offspring refused to honor the family's traditional ways and ran off to join Dionysus and his tribe in their ecstatic revelry. Patriarchy seeks to stop the exodus; end the madness—deny the god. The parents feel furious, possessive, protective.

Today, there are laws being drafted at both state and federal levels designed to create a rating system for records similar to the film world's *X, R, PG*, and the recent *NC-17*. It is an attempt to temper the power and appeal of the music. The attempt will backfire and the more severely a record is judged the more intense will be the kids' reaction and desire to hear and own it. Witness the public reaction to 2 Live Crew's suppression in 1990. Record sales quadrupled. The songs and

Lord Byron: mad, bad, and dangerous to know.

music of Guns N' Roses, you can be assured, will be among the first sought to be controlled and contained. In some states, their records have already been marked and tagged as containing "potentially offensive language."

It is no accident that the powerful emotion the Beatles ignited in their worshipers was called Beatle*mania*. Mania is the exclusive realm of Dionysus. Just as the Beatles were Dionysus arising in response to the suppression he endured during the white-bread, Eisenhower fifties, so is Guns N' Roses creating a mania, but in terms of sheer sales, they are even bigger than the Beatles. They are beyond successful. They are a phenomenon—a *mania*. Significantly, madness or mania was regarded by the Greeks as an impurity. It could be cured only by a purification ritual conducted by either a soothsayer or a magus. Dionysus himself was purified by his grandmother Rhea after his jealous stepmother aimed her rage and fury at him. He wandered throughout Egypt and Syria until Rhea, mother of the gods, saved him from his mania.

This process also echoes the experience of the ancient shaman who must by necessity become wounded before he can heal. He must suffer before having the power to cure suffering. The power again is Dionysian. A rock concert in rare instances can produce a similar profound experience, addressing the spiritually wounded or physically scarred adolescent audience and healing them with the power of music. Guns N' Roses are among that sacred class able to effect such change because they in essence have in the past been scarred.

Axl, Slash, and Duff: "Noisy, gross, selfish, irritating, irresponsible, offensive reprobates, uncouth scoundrels, and in a word, 'vulgar.'" *(Courtesy Larry Busacca/Retna Ltd.)*

Guns N' Roses are the bruised angry heart howl of a generation malled-in, cinemaplexed, media-manipulated, under-educated, spiritually undernourished, self-disgusted, and cut off from the wellspring of a dynamic inner life.

Even the name Guns N' Roses is symbolic of Dionysus's dual nature; ecstasy or madness; creation or destruction; violence and romance; beauty and ugliness, a kiss or a kill. The tattoos all the members of the band wear are also symbolic. In addition to being a form of self-destruction, the tattoo seals the wearer off from the rest of normal society forever. It's not all that surprising to note that the largest number of tattooed in Japan belong to the underworld, and in America tattoos are most prevalent either in jail or hard rock bands. The tattoo also represents another paradox: beauty created through brutal means, "the glorification of the flesh as a means to spirituality" (Diane Ackerman from *Natural History of the Senses*). Axl personifies perfectly the duality with his innocence as represented in a track like "Sweet Child o' Mine," and impulsive fury as heard in "Welcome to the Jungle." It's even appropriate that Axl's last name figures in to the title of the band. The rose, beauty with thorns. "Welcome to the Jungle" is in fact a double metaphor—the jungle as a city, yes, but also the jungle of primitive, powerful emotions such as fight or flight; the Dionysian urge to be ecstatic or go mad trying.

The argument has been posed, in the continuing debate on why the law cannot seem to succeed in legislating human taste, that the desire for intoxication is in actuality a fourth drive. In his book *Intoxication*, Dr. Segal explains:

> Recent ethnological and laboratory studies with colonies of rodents and islands of primates and analysis of social and biological history suggest that the pursuit of intoxication with drugs is a primary motivational force in the behavior of organisms. Our nervous system, like those of rodents and primates, is arranged to respond to chemical intoxicants in much the way it responds to rewards of food, drink, and sex. Throughout our entire history as a species, intoxication has functioned like the basic drives of hunger, thirst, or sex, sometimes overshadowing all other activities in life. *Intoxi-*

cation is the fourth drive. Drugs have also given humans sights to see, voices to listen to, thoughts to ponder and altered states of consciousness to explore. It has generated global conditions that can only be described in terms such as *ecstasy* or *madness.*

We consume drugs, the poet Baudelaire wrote, "to ape the angels, only to become animals."

Jean Cocteau, the addict-writer-painter-filmmaker, described the animal attraction to intoxication:

> Animals are charmed by opium. Addicts in the colonies know the danger of this bait for wild beasts and reptiles. Flies gather round the tray of opium and dream, the lizards with their little mittens swoon on the ceiling and wait for the night, mice come close and nibble ... the cockroaches and the spiders form a circle in ecstasy. [*Opium: Diary of a Cure*]

If both animal and man have a perfectly natural need to seek altered states of consciousness, it puts the whole legislative attitude and forbidding tone of patriarchal moral supremacy in its place. Dionysian behavior cannot and must not be outlawed. It will not be stopped because it *cannot* be stopped. As Greek mythology makes clear, resistance to this force will only bring continued and increased persistence. Dionysus did not only represent the dual forces of intoxication and madness, however—the great god also danced, and equally important, he made music, and he had his followers, the maenads, the first rock fans.

The divine essence of Dionysus is madness, but the madness that is called Dionysus is no sickness, no debility in life, but a mere companion of life at its healthiest. It is in the words of Walter F. Otto, the "churning up of the essence of life surrounded by the storms of death. Since such tumult lies waiting in the bottommost depths and makes itself known, all of life's ecstasy is stirred up by Dionysian madness and is ready to go beyond the bounds of rapture into dangerous wildness." It is the primal unreasonable madness inherent in the womb of the mother that attends all moments of creation, constantly changes ordered existence into chaos, and ushers in primal salvation and primal pain—the primal wildness of being. . . . The deep emotion with which this madness announces itself and finds its fullest expression is in intoxication, music, and dance.

Trancelike states or madly whirling were forms of possession that overtook the maenads as they became captivated by the sound of Dionysus. The transforming paradox of craziness and creativity takes us right up to the edge and then down into the abyss. From those elemental depths comes madness that threatens to destroy all sanity through loss of control and/or fear of death. From the primal wilderness within arises also the strange and uncanny, which breaks through the security of daily life and can bring inspiration, ecstasy, and the prophecy of new life. Dionysus is the divinity that personifies these contradictions.

> All earthly powers are united in the god; the generating, nourishing, intoxicating rapture; the life-giving inexhaustibility; and the tearing pain, the deathly pallor, the speechless night of having been. He is the mad ecstasy which hovers over every conception and birth and whose wildness is always ready to move on to destruction and death. He is life which, when it overflows, grows mad and in its profoundest passion is intimately associated with death. [Walter F. Otto in *Dionysus: Myth and Cult*]

This is the Appetite for Destruction.

The world of sunlight is the domain of Apollo. Where life is kept at a distance. Dionysus is the alternative—the world of night, complete and immediate. Apollo preserves where Dionysus destroys. Apollo is the god of form, not instinct. When these two archetypal energies are out of whack, addiction—whether to love, to power, to substances, or to activities—fills the gap and obscures the danger. Only by uniting these energies can longevity, creativity, and results flourish. An artist needs contact with the dark world of creativity, but he also must have the disciplined logic represented by Apollo to put that creation forth. In order to survive a long productive balanced life, we need to experienced both worlds with impunity. But longevity is not a concern of the rock 'n' roll primal force. *Now* is all that exists. The intense now.

When Paul spoke to the Athenians, he tried to explain the unknown God: "It is God who created us to seek through shadows of our ignorance, and find God." And, of course, God promised a response. "When you seek me with all your heart, I will let you find me."

Carl Jung pointed out that it was no accident that alcohol is also called "spirits" and said that the alcoholic's thirst for alcohol is equivalent to the soul's spiritual thirst for the "union with" God.

"Alcohol in Latin is *spiritus,* and you use the same word for the highest religious experience as well as for the most depraving poison. The helpful formula therefore is: *spiritus contra spiritus.*" It's an alchemical formula. It means, in the words of a letter Jung sent to the founder of AA, Bill Wilson, that it takes spirit to counter spirit—fire to fight fire, in other words.

Jungian analyst Marion Woodman elaborated years later: "Looking at alcoholism and addiction as a longing for spirit might mean that something very different is going on in our society than at first appears. One might say that we don't have a crisis with alcohol and drugs as much as we have a spiritual crisis."

Freud insisted that our civilization at large is a repressive one. There is a conflict between the demands of conformity and the demands of our instinctive energies, what Nietzsche called Dionysian, and what Freud called sexual. And we seek to slake our natural thirst in any way possible.

Author-humanist-philosopher R. D. Laing wrote in his book *The Divided Self* that "our civilization represses not only the instincts, not only sexuality, but any form of transcendence. Among one-dimensional men, it is not surprising that someone with an insistent experience of other dimensions, that he cannot entirely deny or forget, will run the risk of either being destroyed by the others, or of betraying what he knows and needs, or, destroying himself."

We seem to displace our longing for God with other things; we cathect with them instead of God. We seek satisfaction, achieve it, but sooner or later, we are disappointed. If this is true, it certainly shows us why God's appearance, a spiritual awakening, appears to be the only thing that can make an addict well. The only thing that can be done is to replace the drug with God, the original intention, that is, to undergo the purification ritual. God enters, as in shamanism, through the wound.

Even the phrase "getting high" is a giveaway and betrays its spiritual aspirations. Moses received the Ten Commandments from up high on a mountaintop, the gods and goddesses of Greece dwelled atop Mount Olympus. Heaven is "up there," ethereal. Hell, of course, is "down there," earthbound, material.

The world of drugs and music can be seen as a restless culture seeking initiation. Archetypal needs that have not gone away with the passage of time.

In the 1930s, Dr. Carl Jung commented about the rise in alcoholism among his patients: "About a third of my cases are suffering from no clinically definable neurosis but from the senselessness and emptiness of their lives."

The emptiness that Jung refers to hasn't diminished. If anything, in today's society, it's increased. So much so that Dr. Rollo May, a prominent New York psychiatrist, wrote in 1969, "It may seem surprising when I say on the basis of my own clinical experience that the chief problem of the middle decade of the 20th century is emptiness . . . while one might laugh, boredom extends to a state of futility and eventually despair which, at best, only holds out as an attraction the promise of dangers."

"The archetypal need to transcend one's present state at any cost, even when it entails the use of physically harmful substances is especially strong in those who find themselves in a state of meaninglessness, lacking both a sense of identity and a precise society role," the author of *Drugs, Addiction & Initiation* writes.

Drug use, seen in this context, is not so much an escape

from society as a desperate attempt to fit in anyway one can, as well as a "naive and unconscious attempt at assuming identity and role negatively defined by the current values" (i.e., being an outsider is better than being nothing at all).

The author concludes that young people of today are desperately in need of a chance to "participate fully in a total confrontation, like that between death and living, something once provided by rites and rituals" and now provided by the world of drugs and music.

We run from one event to another, driven from devotion to devotion, to one object to another and again on to another, because the meaning of each quickly vanishes and the creative eros is transformed into indifference or aversion. Everything is tried and nothing satisfies. Anxiously one turns away from all concrete solutions and starts looking for an ultimate solution, or at best some meaning, only to discover that there is a pervading sense of meaninglessness and despair. Everything around us promises relief—but nothing works.

From the time we can speak, we are bombarded with the message that we alone are not enough: take this; buy this; have this; feel better, stronger, safer, sexier, more desirable, more secure, more powerful, and none of it works because it's never enough, and it's not enough because we're looking in the wrong place. The primary religion of America is consumerism; capitalism is not a system, it is a way of life. We have been given gargantuan buildup, a sales campaign without peer, with one relentless message: *Buy, consume.* The merchandise we're sold is faulty because of its built-in obsolescence: It doesn't work because the values are inverted. We are led to expect gratification and it never happens. We are dying of a thirst and the buckets all have holes. When the goods fail to satisfy us fully, and we know it, it's then that we turn to drugs and music. Many of us discover that they work. We pay for something and voilà! It changes how we feel, under our skin where it matters, where we live. It works. The goal is achieved: we feel better about ourselves—different, special, stronger, just like we've been told we should, but that nothing else ever accomplished. Drugs and music, seen in this context, are only the most available (and temporarily effective) solutions to a rampant spiritual malnourishment.

Indulgence in or addiction to "wine, women, and song" is a way of transcending the self, the critics complain, without really doing so. As if the work ethic applies here—as if it's wrong to sneak into paradise through the back door without paying the price of admission, when in reality we have paid and paid and the problem is no one knows where the front door is. The soul is constantly searching for transcendence, for some sort of escape from the drudgery of its own self. Intoxication, it appears, is better than nothing at all. If we can not acheive transcendence legitimately, we will do so illegitimately.

Nietzsche, as the heir apparent to the Romantics, defended the cult of intoxication in *The Birth of Tragedy Out of the Spirit of Music* saying, "A feeling of plenitude and increased energy visit the participants—where the entire emotional system is alerted and most alive, as in the intoxication of spring, or into the opposite, intoxication in destruction. And under the influence of alcohol and narcotics." Baudelaire believed intoxication was absolutely essential to creativity and the source of that intoxication was irrelevant: "Always be drunk. That is all."

Clearly, rock 'n' roll today in general and Guns N' Roses specifically, personify the zeitgeist and in that process echo the feelings and philosophies of the Dionysian spirit and the romantic sentiment. But now enter the other side—the church, the self-designated authority, the so-called moral majority, the defenders of decency, various municipalities, Tipper Gore and her PMRC (Parents Musical Resource Committee, a censorship campaign harassing the entire music business), authors, critics, preachers, mothers, the PTA, fathers, and any one of a number of potential saviors or self-appointed custodians of man and his tempered spirit. Allan Bloom in his best-selling book *The Closing of the American Mind* pretty much blames hard rock music for the decay of values in the American youth. As an extreme representative of that music, Guns N' Roses are then, one must assume, the worst defilers and corrupters of the lot, according to Bloom and his rock-as-cause (rather than effect) theory.

In a U.S. government pamphlet called "The Downbeat Effects of Rock Music on an Upbeat Generation" compiled by something known as "The National Committee on Music" in 1988, hard rock is accused of arousing the sex drive by "changing the cerebrospinal fluid, disrupting the function of the pituitary gland, throwing off the balance of sex and adrenal hormones circulating in the blood, in turn causing changes in blood sugar and calcium levels," which in turn affect the brain. Since "the brain is nourished exclusively by blood sugar it ceases the function properly causing moral inhibitions to either drop to a dangerous low or be wiped out altogether."

If these claims were true, and some of them may even be, these effects are cast entirely in a negative light, the results of a music which should be "eliminated for the betterment of our society, specifically, our young." The pamphlet holds hard rock music accountable for virtually every social ill, including but not limited to "murder, rape, incest, drugs, illicit sex, homosexuality, satanism, suicide, sadomasochism, bestiality and child abuse . . ."

Many young people are turning to, and finding pleasurable, for whatever reason, the (*upbeat*) effects of rock music. Rock music is an effect rather than cause of a profound need in the hearts and minds of young America and other Western cultures, an electric mirror reflecting our collective hopes and most secret yearnings as well as our most horrifying fears and inclinations.

The loss of spiritual union in Western society has left a void that we are trying to fill in the only way we can: with whatever is available. What we want is danger and excitement. Drama. Ecstasy. Failing that we want to satiate our senses; sometimes we try books or classes. But more often we turn to materialism; and most often of all, for the young, for the passionate, music and chemicals and sex.

Guns N' Roses are the raging sound of Dionysus resurfacing—the sound of anger, fear, hope and despair, triumph and madness.... the music of man's animal powers refusing to be denied any longer, gnarling at the oppressive bit, threatening, dancing on the edge of a society collapsing in on itself.

ARRIVAL
BEAST

OF
THE

For every Keith Richards, who could use drugs and create, there are 10,000 unsigned, unsung, deathly pallored, scarf-draped guitarists, replete with skull imagery, who never made it to the recording studio. "I recorded *Exile on Main Street* and beat Jagger in tennis when I was strung out on smack," Richards once boasted. What is seldom pointed out, however, is that he also made *Goat's Head Soup* and turned from "elegantly wasted" to simply ugly in a relatively short period of time.

Izzy Stradlin (a.k.a. Jeff Isabelle) could have easily been one of the 10,000 casualties, as could have Joe Perry of Aerosmith, who almost was one, parlaying his Richards along with Steve Tyler's Jagger and then almost imploding, nearly losing it all, only becoming successful in avoiding death (or a fate worse—solo career hell) by pulling out. Only time has the answer to Izzy's fate but clearly he has already succeeded where hundreds have failed. Whether he succeeds to the

Axl Rose, angel or devil, sporting his signature headdress. *(Courtesy Larry Busacca/Retna Ltd.)*

degree Keith himself or even Joe Perry have remains to be seen. Joseph Campbell biographer Phil Cosineau quotes Campbell saying, "If you don't live the myth, the myth will live you." Or in this case, kill you.

"I don't even remember the first time I got drunk. I was

drunk. Period," Izzy says. All he chooses to remember from his childhood is that he was a rowdy kid who had nothing to do in Lafayette, Indiana. "I don't even like to mention the place—I hated it there; I was thoroughly miserable." Of the band members Izzy is the least talkative and the least forthcoming about his past. The only additional information he'll give up is that he was born in Florida and moved with his mother to Lafeyette after his parents broke up before he was a teenager. Even Slash admits, "Everyone in this band has some kinda quirk—no one had a regular childhood; that's why we fit together so well."

Izzy spent a lot of time alone with a guitar after the split between his parents. He graduated high school in 1979 and at age seventeen hauled ass out of Lafayette to L.A. where he hooked up with another Lafayette native, (William) Bill Bailey, soon to be known as W. Axl Rose. The name "Axel" emerged as a suggested band moniker from a phone conversation with a friend, which Bill Bailey then misspelled. Izzy and Axl were soon living on the streets, protecting each other, trusting only one another, a team hustling to survive, to survive at least long enough to make it in a rock 'n' roll band.

Izzy, who probably knows Axl better and perhaps longer than anyone else, reports Axl "was a serious lunatic when I first met him. He was just really fucking bent on fighting and destroying things. Somebody'd look at him wrong and he'd just, like, start a fight. And you think about Lafayette, man, there's, like, fuck-all to do."

Izzy also recalls his first awareness of Axl: "The first thing I remember about Axl—before I really knew him—is the first day of class, eighth or ninth grade, I'm sitting in class and I hear this noise going on in front, and then I see the fucking books flying past and I hear this yelling, and then there's this scuffle and then I see him, Axl, and this teacher bouncing off a door jamb. And then Axl was gone down the hall with all these teachers running after him ... I'll never forget that."

Steven Adler is the happy-go-lucky, childlike-in-his-simplicity drummer. Born in Cleveland, Ohio, in 1965, Adler couldn't wait to get to Hollywood and partake of the glamour

Duff, Andrew Dice Clay, and Axl backstage at the Diceman's L.A. show. *(Courtesy Steve Granitz/Retna Ltd.)*

and excess that surely awaited his arrival. As it turned out he didn't have to wait long. His family made the move to L.A. and Steven moved from guitar to drums. "The first time I got wasted, I was eight years old. I was in my grandmother's bathroom and I smoked some pot." Drums, getting high, rock 'n' roll, hockey, and motorcycles were all he professed to care about, presumably in that order. "When I drink," Adler reported, "it just makes me normal—like the rest of the guys."

He dropped out of the tenth grade and gigged with a string of anonymous bands in Los Angeles while simultaneously working at assorted day jobs. Since the first flush of national success, Adler is said to have been in and out of Betty Ford's detox program three or four times (one time being when the band performed on the 1989 American Music Awards broadcast with Don Henley handling the drum chores in his absence). The official excuse for Steven's absenteeism was "the flu." Rumors were flying as early as fall 1989 that the already-on-band-probation drummer had stepped out once too often and was officially out for good. The band, at the rehearsal stage of their third release, auditioned replacements only to let go the new drummer after bassist Duff walked out of the session, shaking his head saying, "I can't do this." Adler was promptly reinstalled only to fall off the wagon again. The drummer for the Cult, Matt Sorum, was brought in and rehearsals for the new LP continued apace.

Duff (Rose) McKagan personifies the rock star bassist: tall, blond, lean, tending more toward elegance than any of the others. He wouldn't have seemed out of place in Duran Duran. Duff recalls with fondness and clarity his first indulgence into the chemical realm as a child in suburban Seattle: "My old man gave me some whiskey when I was real little. It was Hawaiian whiskey, and it had this long Hawaiian name. He said, 'Take a swig and pronounce the name.' After about four swigs, I couldn't pronounce the name because I was already too drunk."

Duff, born Michael McKagan, February 5, 1964, is the youngest of eight kids from a good Catholic family. Music took priority over school after playing drums and guitar in a few dozen local Seattle area groups. At the age of nineteen, he moved down to Los Angeles. After the move, he switched to bass guitar for the simple reason there was a greater demand for bassists than guitarists. Duff is the only band member whose chemical indulgence has not reached notorious proportions, although his fondness for alcohol, particularly Stolichnaya vodka, is well documented.

Slash—now here's enigma. Resembling a dark cross between the Mad Hatter and Cousin It, or as Axl once described him: "part man, part beast," Slash defies easy categorization. If the others are unabashed about their chemical (ab)use, Slash seems almost proud of his. "I drink every day—a lot, and I pass out at night, but it doesn't ever get in the way. I get to rehearsal on time. The music is the most important thing; it's our lives." During Guns N' Roses' first European trip in 1987, Slash gladly explained to a journalist what his and the band's drinking habits were while on tour: "When we get up in the afternoon to do a sound check, we drink

Drummer Steven Adler, childlike in his simplicity, only wanted to be a star. But he clearly wanted to do drugs more. Booted from the band because, as Axl said, "Steven couldn't stop using drugs." *(Courtesy Larry Busacca/Retna Ltd.)*

so much that we can't play, because our hands are shaking like windmills. So what happens? We drink! We drink more and more, and then we're fine, and we wake up the next day with some floozie.... You don't know her name.... You've got fucking weird shit on your dick.... Your bed's all wet from pissing in it and you go, 'Listen, will you do me a favor and find me some booze?'"

But where Axl has demonstrated the ability to indulge and then set indulgence aside when it's time to work, Slash, just like Adler and Izzy, seems unable to effect such a balance. Born into what has been called an ultra-liberal family, he is the mulatto son of an American black mother (a clothing designer named Ola) and a white, British, hard-drinking father who designed album covers. Born Saul Hudson, on July 23, 1965, in Stoke-on-Trent, England, Slash's father brought him to live in Los Angeles when still a child. Visitors to the Hudson household remember the child's early and innate talents as an artist and a particular gift for drawing dinosaurs. His parents' marriage has been an on-again, off-again affair ever since Slash was a kid. He never cared much for school and chose music as his escape, pursuit, and interest. When he started playing guitar, as he puts it, "that was the beginning of the end."

As a child Slash experienced in his words "total freedom." He recalls his mom as a "real happy-go-lucky hippie." He grew up on the fringe of the music business, which provided work for both of his creative parents. "It was a time of 'free love' and there was no saying no," Slash recalled.

Is this trusting and supportive? Or is it just old-fashioned permissiveness, as in "Spare the rod/spoil the child"?

Slash has developed an objective yet resigned attitude about his upbringing: "It's one of the things that's made me comfortable with myself as a person." . . . And yet . . . and yet, if he were totally comfortable with himself he wouldn't be sticking drugs into his veins. But let Slash continue: ". . . and at the same time it has probably made me . . . not necessarily the way I should be, in certain areas."

Ultimately cautious about not laying blame, he levels a summary aimed less at his parents than at himself: "My parents were always supportive and I love them for it." Meaning that nothing he did to himself was their fault.

One school of thought regarding substance abuse would say that he's letting them off the hook too easy. "Total freedom" is the same as "lack of responsibility" and a drug addict, or as Slash so delicately put it "not necessarily the way I should be" is not produced by an ideal family situation. Then there is the school of thought that believes no one is responsible for the child/person becoming an addict other than the addict him- or herself. One inculcates himself with the virus and develops it, nurses it on their own, by themselves.

Inordinately fond of both alcohol and junk, it's not standard practice to enjoy alcohol during a heroin high—as William Burroughs has pointed out, the cells that employ smack seem to satiate any desire for alcohol—yet it can be done as Slash has successfully demonstrated. The possibility of overdose, though, is increased a hundredfold, and this type doesn't tend to live very long. Junk alone on a human system isn't that bad—hepatitis and AIDS come from the needle; the life-style can wear you down; an unusually high or pure dose can kill you; but junk itself is relatively benign in purely *physical* terms—it does not disintegrate a body the way booze does. In cold, clinical, objective language, Dr. J. R. Black wrote in *The Cincinnati Lancet* that heroin is "less harmful to healthy life than alcohol because it calms in place of exciting the baser passions." In short, he claimed "the use of heroin in place of alcohol is but a choice of evils and by far the lesser."

The author of *The Heroin Solution* wrote, "Alcohol destroys human organs; heroin does not, whatever its other doleful effects are." However harmful either chemical is, the two combined can be positively fatal. If you're mixing both

Slash, sublime, subdued, submerged in the music. *(Courtesy Anastasia Pantsios/London Features International)*

in large doses, it's not that difficult for them to act together to still the heart from an overdose, not of one or the other, but because of both. This is most likely what killed Jim Morrison—drunk already, being offered or finding his wife's stash of heroin, which in Paris at the time was said to be pretty pure, snorted it up, went to take a bath and never got out. Or, as some insist, got out and never came back, which is pretty unlikely.

Slash seems to resist categorization—even in the areas he chooses to inhabit. What is obvious is that he is the perfect counterpoint to Axl: his dark to Axl's light; his curly black hair to Axl's straight, thin, and wispy. Axl is all up front, pushing his hair behind his ears and back behind his shoulders in concert and on video, striving to make eye contact, staring you down; Slash's eyes are virtually nonexistent, and when the irises of his eyes are seen they are usually cast down, face obscured by hair and hat. Mainly though, what strikes me most in terms of their point- counterpoint relationship is how masculine Slash is to Axl's feminine; one is rough, the other smooth.

A member of the Cult tells a story a tattooist told him about Axl wanting to get some tattoos so he wouldn't look so much like a "fucking chick." In drug terminology cocaine is called "girl" and heroin "boy." Axl's cocaine, to Slash's heroin. Coke is fast tending toward violence—heroin is slow, languid. What both personalities have in common is the potential for vio-lence. You sense the slow dark clouds of hostility lurking within Slash's moody presence. Axl is an original, blending the Morrison-Jagger, shaman-Dionysus archetypes. His ser-pentine dance is reptilian in its splendor, as sensual and evo-cative as Morrison's Indian rain dance, or Jagger's rooster strut. And we musn't forget that the serpent is identified with evil, as in the garden of Eden, and is also a powerful archetype loaded with Freudian symbolism and sexual energy—as in kundalini yoga.

Within Axl there is always the sense of unpredictability, quick to anger or to offend. Slash seems to hide his feelings better than Axl, succeeds in keeping it all in check, held in —which is probably where the drugs come in (or one of the places where drug use for him comes in handy), keeping him calm, helping him cope with the powerful forces moving around on their own agenda within. With Axl, even when he is calm and friendly, his reputation precedes him, and it seems well founded, because somewhere beneath the surface you sense it—the wrong word, the wrong action could set this guy off.

"The first time I got drunk, I was sixteen," Axl remembers. "I know, I was a late bloomer," he admits before confessing. "But, before that I believed in God. Then he let me down." Presumably, Axl commenced to make up for some lost time. He had sung in the church choir, won Bible-reading contests, and taught Sunday school, but he never felt truly in touch with God. Until he got turned on to music. And drugs.

Born February 6, 1962, in the small town of Lafayette, Indiana, he was raised as Bill B. (for Bruce) Bailey, eldest son of L. Stephen and Sharon Bailey. At around the age of sixteen he began letting his bronze hair grow out, started singing in rock 'n' roll bands and engaging in a type of behavior psychologists call "acting out."

Unbeknownst to Axl, Stephen Bailey was in fact his stepfather. His surname at birth was Rose; his natural father left Sharon and him soon after he was born. When at the age of seventeen Bill discovered the deception regarding his birth, he exploded with angst and rage, rechristening himself W. Rose, and intensifying what by then had become serious antisocial behavior. For a time, later, he would request to be called "Babe."

Today, less angry and more wise, Axl regards his stepfather as his "real dad" but he nevertheless officially changed his name to W. Axl Rose not long before Guns N' Roses signed their Geffen contract in March 1986.

No one in the band illustrates as well as Axl the intoxication-as-sublimination-of-God thesis. Achingly, he recalls an almost sublime, yet terrifying, image of his father plugged into the God socket: "I watched my father sing in perfect Japanese— on key, with his eyes closed, driving down the freeway at one hundred miles per hour and not hit a car. And my father doesn't know a word of Japanese. Nothing like that ever happened to me," he recalls. For a while, he was an altar boy, a choir boy. Nothing happened. He felt nothing different. The emptiness and anger remained. "I always thought I was cursed."

The Bailey family was religious, attending a Pentecostal country church. Yet Axl's religious sentiments were clearly not in tune with the rest of his family. "I've seen people healed.... I've seen people with no eyes read. It's very strange. But nothing ever happened to me. I always won all the Bible contests, I taught Sunday school, played piano, and I knew more gospel songs than anybody else I knew. If there's somebody up there, I don't know him. I just don't have a clue about it." What he did know was what he liked: rock 'n' roll and getting high. "When I was in school, there were all these stereotypes. If you liked the Stones you were a faggot because of the time Jagger kissed Keith Richards on *Saturday Night Live*. If you liked the Grateful Dead, you were a hippie. If you liked the Sex Pistols you were a punker. I guess that would make me a faggot hippie punk rocker."

In and out of school, Axl went on a rampage, becoming a serious juvenile delinquent. He reportedly was thrown into jail more than twenty times, once for a summer-long stay, before skipping town and making it to Los Angeles in 1980. One of the first things that had to be done when the band made it was to get a lawyer to clear up Axl's dubious past in Lafayette—a town about which Izzy says, "There's like, fuck-all to do." In fact, beyond a criticism or two, Izzy doesn't even want to talk about the place.

Taken individually, they may appear to be almost cartoon-ish. Even Axl says half-jokingly that "Slash is one of my favorite cartoon characters." But taken collectively the image they impress is nothing less than dangerous, decadent, excessive —wasted and proud of it. That they appear so does not appear to have adversely affected their popularity. Far from it. In an era when the popular sentiment is stridently antidrug, getting "sober" in some circles today is as popular as smoking pot and dropping acid was in another day. Guns N' Roses have made looking fucked-up hip (sort of like a heavy-metal Dean Martin). Again.

Duff at an early gig.   *(Courtesy Michele Matz/Retna Ltd.)*

The solidification of Guns N' Roses as a band commenced within a week after the lineup rose from the ashes of two Hollywood bands, L.A. Guns and Hollywood Rose.

"All of us commuted to L.A. at different times," Slash recalled, "but we were like the only guys who were as hardcore as we were and into doing the same kind of thing. It's weird, how we got together; it just sort of happened." Duff McKagan had found Slash via an ad in *Music Connection*. Slash and Steven knew each other already from a band called Road Crew. Briefly, Duff worked with the two as the lineup then became Hollywood Rose. And, of course, Axl and Izzy had known each other since school days in Lafayette, Indiana. Axl hooked Izzy up with Slash after seeing a caricature of Aerosmith Slash had drawn. Slash was eager to work with Axl from the start but there was a catch, and when the time came for Slash to share responsibilities with another guitar player, he was positively reticient. Slash possessed musical tastes almost as eclectic as Axl's, listening to Cat Stevens one day and Aerosmith or Zeppelin the next. Slash recalls how he felt at the initial stage of his involvement with Izzy.

> When Izzy and I first met, we didn't click at all. Izzy and Axl had a band together and I wanted to get Axl and I didn't want to work with another guitar player because I'd never done it before. Working with other guitar players, I couldn't be in control of what was happening guitar-wise. What I wanted to do was get Axl away from Izzy which was just impossible. At the time I met Axl, we started a band and Izzy naturally was in it, but then he split to join a band called London, which I had just quit. That was cool, so me and Axl had a band going. Then that broke up. Eventually Axl joined L.A. Guns. Then Izzy joined L.A. Guns because everybody just wanted to be in a band and working. That didn't work out and I got this call that said, do you want to come back and play with us. At first, I didn't want to do it because me and Axl had been through some bad times together. I did it and worked with Izzy because that was what was happening. It was the only band I could find that I could relate to.

Slash's last band before Guns N' Roses and after Road Crew was an affair called Black Sheep, and Slash was in the band for three days including one gig at the Country Club in Reseda, California. It was to be his last performance before joining Guns N' Roses. Then drummer Steven Adler showed up and said, "Get rid of your drummer; he's not good enough." Adler was in.

June 6, 1985, marks the official start date, the day all five looked each other over and knew they were a band. Within the week, they played their first gig at a once-famous folk club, the Troubadour, which since the early eighties had been catering almost exclusively to heavy metal and the burgeoning audience it was engendering on the L.A. scene. That show was on a Thursday night.

Four days later, the still unexperienced band left on their previous band's gig commitments and intended to plough through Seattle, Portland, Eugene, Sacramento, and San Francisco. On paper it all looked good. It would take them out of the L.A. scene and out of their squalid living conditions in West Hollywood. If they behaved themselves they might even bring some money home. On the road, however, in Fresno, their plans fell to pieces far too soon. The car they had broke down. Then commenced what Slash likes to recall as "The Treacherous Journey." Guitars in hand and decked out in full rock regalia, with the summer heat steaming down on their black-leather-clad backs, walking through the barren middle of deserted farmland, they stuck their thumbs out into the air and then they waited. And they waited.

This is the unofficial unification of the band. Izzy, like Axl, being from Lafayette, Indiana, and no stranger to open spaces, remembers the day well:

> The moment of the revelation, the moment which began this whole *movement*, the first time. . . . It was when our car broke down one hundred miles into the fuckin' desert in the middle of nowhere when we were drivin' to our first ever gig out of town. Duff, when he joined, had these gigs in Seattle to play. Duff said, "Yo! Seattle, it's right on top of America." We said, "Hey, cool, you know, let's fuckin' *go*." It was a complete disaster. So, we're stranded in the fuckin' desert, right? Ain't no way we're going back to Hollywood. I mean, these are three hundred bucks a night gigs we're talking about here.
>
> So, we hitchhiked. After two fuckin' days in the desert a guy in a semi picked us up. Finally, we made it to Seattle. We played. There were ten, maybe twenty people there. We didn't get paid. It was downhill from there. Somehow we got back to L.A.
>
> And from the day we got back to Hollywood, it's been like, whatever goes down, y'know, we're still united in this conflict against . . . everything. Really, Guns N' Roses' motto from that day on has been *fuck everybody, fuck everybody,*

before they fuck with you. Fuck the whole fuckin' world, y'know. Just let's keep *movin'*.

It was like a test . . . and after that little adventure, L.A. didn't seem so bad, after all.

"We do have a fuck-you attitude," Axl admitted. "But our goal is to break down as many barriers as we can. I mean not just musical, I mean we want to break down the barriers in people's minds, too."

Once back in L.A., hard times continued to plague the band. Members drifted from place to place to crash. Axl remembers he never spent more than two months at any one location in one place and welcomed brief sojourns in abandoned apartments. Slash remembers, "We'd walk up and down Hollywood Boulevard and visit every porno store 'cause they stayed open twenty-four hours." Then at one point, all five moved in together, to cut down on expenses and to focus their vision, and consolidate the energy expended to articulate that vision.

By generous standards, it's been called a combination living quarters and rehearsal space, but in reality the location at Gardner Street in which they grouped was a hovel, measuring a mere twelve feet by twelve feet; it lacked a bathroom, a shower, and a kitchen. "A very uncomfortable prison cell," recalls Slash. "But God, did we sound good in there! We're a really loud band and we don't compromise the volume for anything! We'd bash away with a couple of Marshal amps in this tiny room, and it was cool because all the losers from Sunset Boulevard and all the bands would come over and hang out there."

Axl, remembering those early days, says, "Every weekend, the biggest party in L.A. was down at our place. We'd have five hundred people packed in an alley and someone was selling beers for a buck out of his trunk. It was like a bar and everyone had their whiskey. We could get away with whatever we wanted, except when the cops came. . . . If there was problem with someone, they'd be escorted out. By 'escort' I mean, we'd drag 'em out by their hair down the alley, naked.

"The funny thing is," Axl added nostagically, "we almost miss it . . ."

"God," Slash adds, "did we sound good in there."

During this time, they experimented with their look and they rehearsed, focusing on their sound, each member contributing his uniqueness, fusing the band's overall sound and presence into a vision that aimed high—all or nothing. Clearly they believed in themselves, yet they also possessed the clear-eyed objectivity to know that, if they were to succeed in articulating the vision they shared, hard work was the one thing they could do to help ensure success, which is as fickle as it is elusive. But these guys already had one of the main ingredients of success—luck. They concentrated on coalescing a uniquely powerful style of music resulting from each member's own individuality, ultimately creating a total presentation much greater than its individual parts.

They might have partied hard, and they might have gotten loaded a lot, but they also worked just as hard and just as often. They didn't get discouraged because they saw and heard for themselves—the early results were tangible and encouraging. They started working even harder.

But, while the music was improving, their financial security was nil and their living standards were becoming more substandard by the day. Amps needed fixing, they needed transportation, guitar strings, drum sticks, a drumhead, clothes, and so on. To survive, they depended on the odd gig, but their main proceeds came from girls and drugs . . . uh. . . . We just got by. We managed.

During this time, Steve Adler simply endured a variety of menial jobs including dishwasher, bowling alley janitor, lawn mower, and pizza maker. Izzy was briefly employed in a guitar shop, but is remembered on the L.A. junkie scene as being a consistent face among the customers for the Iranian brown heroin that was flooding in back then. It was shortly after the Shah had been overthrown and forced into exile and the country's subsequent descent into turmoil caused many of Iran's elite to transfer their wealth into something easily hidden and cash—convertible; namely, heroin. Slash began re-

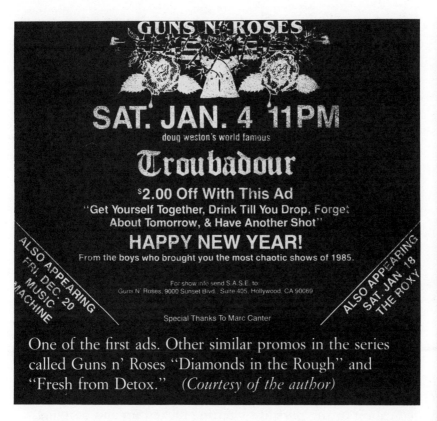

One of the first ads. Other similar promos in the series called Guns n' Roses "Diamonds in the Rough" and "Fresh from Detox." *(Courtesy of the author)*

lationships with heroin and Izzy at about the same time. Slash also supposedly worked in a clock factory while Axl did telephone sales and sat around a while as a night manager at the Tower Video on Sunset Boulevard, behind which he often slept, using the rear staircase as a roof. To help make ends meet Axl and Izzy also volunteered as medical test subjects for UCLA, smoking cigarettes for scientific reasons for $8.00 an hour.

As Slash has pointed out, "You can barely survive here [in L.A.] with just a day job and have any kind of decent living standards. Seriously, it's too expensive. I had a day job and I got fired because I spent all my time on the phone booking gigs and trying to get fliers made. We paid the rent at the studio from the gigs that we played and then for lunch money, we'd scam off chicks—forty-five cents worth of food, I swear to God. Soup at fucking Denny's Coffee Shop."

In an early 1987 press release, Duff reinvoked the reality of the Gardner Street rehearsal room life-style: "We were living in this place where we had one little box of a room. We had no money but we could usually dig up a buck to go down to this liquor store which happened to sell this great wine called Nighttrain that would fuck you up for a buck. Five dollars and we'd all be gone. We lived off this stuff."

Mainly, they scammed. Duff recalled a typical hustle: "You call a girl and you go, 'Look, my bass was just shipped from somewhere and they forgot to loosen the strings, so all the strings broke and I need a new set. Can I have twenty dollars?'" Slash adds, "I used to go to the Whisky and the Rainbow and the Roxy a couple of nights out of the week and panhandle money from everybody. I'd tell them that my rental van got towed and that I lived all the way out in Silverlake and the only way I was gonna get back was please, just give me five bucks, or twenty bucks to help me out. It sounds pretty scummy, I admit, but it gets to that point." Duff obviously agreed: "It's survival."

What is really impressive about this presuccess period is that for all their streetwise bravado and attitude, for all their dedication to the pursuit of getting fucked up and partying, this band was able never to let themselves get irretrievably sidetracked by all the possible diversions that surrounded them. They managed not to get pulled under and sucked up by the vicious yet alluring undertow that swallows whole so many less talented, less dedicated, and yes, less lucky musicians. Music was their number-one priority. If need be, they would kill or die for it—not a unique devotion in the swarming mass of competition in the L.A. scene, which is more intense than other cities because of the proximity of all the major record companies, as well as many of the independent labels. It's not uncommon to see a band live the rock ethic to the hilt in a sort of decadent devotion. What *is* uncommon is for a band, especially one that first begins to make it, to survive the irreverent rituals of intoxication and sex combined with good old-fashioned devil-may-care attitude. It is the type of noble yet warped sacrifice *cum* devotion one finds among kamikaze pilots.

Slash agrees with that.

> If you lose touch with that, then you're not really into it in
> the first place. If you find the bigger priority is to hang out
> and try to get laid and not rehearse and not do what you're
> supposed to do, then you're going to get sucked up. If you
> drive up and down Hollywood Boulevard, you'll see hundreds
> of kids who went that way, who are just standing on the street
> corners in front of the hamburger stands and the video ar-
> cades. That's a really sad scene that happens constantly. They
> come from Wyoming, thinking Los Angeles is an instant thing.
> They all come rushing out here and end up being pulled
> down, the whole scenario.

**Duff seconds the motion here as well. "It goes hand in hand
with people moving here. They get overwhelmed. You gotta
really be focused. You gotta be in the right frame of mind
and probably at the right stage. For me, I can adjust to almost
anything—especially when I have to. I lived here; I had to
adjust."**

**"What we did," Axl points out as a reference to their sur-
vival skills,**

> was we'd fucking yell at each other like crazy, kick the shit
> out of each other if somebody's fucking up, doing drugs.
> "You're blowing it dude! We have no time for this." To the
> point of, like, we'll make contracts, you know, "Here sign
> this; you do drugs, you're fucked." It's like we don't want to
> fuck anybody over in the band, we just want to scare the shit
> out of each other 'cause we don't want to lose what we have.
> And, it's like the thing about the drugs, we talk openly about
> it. We used it, you know. We're all wasted, and we were
> exploring drugs. But then that was just what was happening.
> Not a lot of people knew about it. Then big bands started
> coming around and wanting to score off us and stuff like
> that. And, we needed the money, sure. . . . So it was like it
> became something we found ourselves in the center of. And,
> then it got messy. . . .

**It was ironic, but the band with the worst reputation in
town, the band predicated to go down in flames first, also
happened to be the band with the vision and stamina to go**

the whole nine yards and make it to the next first down, which was the exclusive record contract.

In the midst of trying simply to survive one day and one night at a time, they scuffled their way into the thoroughly competitive dog-eat-dog Hollywood hard rock scene, where thirty times a week another hopeful bus load of starry-eyed musicians arrives in Southern California to take a crack at the big time. The competition among the hard rock bands had become so fierce in L.A. that a new practice had been invoked by the club owners. In order to play on their stage, the band had to pay them—the club owners. That those bands continued to do so illustrates just how desperate and congested the L.A. rock 'n' roll scene had become. And all the boys in the band had one fervent prayer: to Make It Big. It is a high mark for Guns N' Roses that from the start of their performing career interest was rabid. Word on the rock 'n' roll grapevine was hot enough that people paid to see them, thus the clubs had no choice but to hire the new young band. It didn't take a visionary to know they would improve business—a packed house of cash-paying, hard-drinking customers was better business than the few hundred bills they could squeeze out of another band who brought in fifty of their friends.

In the wake of Guns N' Roses' success, an already overflowing, burgeoning hard rock scene exploded, and the number of bands competing for the limited number of club stages increased tremendously.

"You fight for your place," Axl said.

> I remember two years of standing at the Troubadour and talking to no one, everybody thinking they're so cool. Eventually we did our own thing, made new friends, and brought our own new crowd to the Troubadour.
>
> When we first were a club band, we were sort of a sore thumb on the glam scene—in the middle of it, but at the same time not into it at all. We put across kind of a fuck-you attitude, and that gave the band a foundation.

It also gave off an attractive glow—by not pandering to the record industry mentality, they aroused a strong interest among the record labels.

"We just kept playing," Izzy stated, "and we didn't go away and we made so much noise in the city ... that the labels started to come to see us. *They* came to *us*!" He recalled it as if still incredulous that it worked so well. "They would come over to the studio and come in the alley and see drunks ... and the next thing you know we're going to their offices. We made them take us all out for dinner for a week or two and we started eating good! We'd order all this food and drink and say, 'Okay, talk.' " But record companies were wary of this band. As much as they attracted attention and accolades, there was something about them that scared a lot of people away, too. While their musical and performing abilities were already clearly evident, many wondered whether that talent justified working with and investing in five maniacs clearly bent on destroying themselves and intent on taking advantage of anyone within their sphere of influence stupid enough to let them.

At one point, early in their career, the five lived with their equipment at Vicky Hamilton's West Hollywood apartment. Vicky booked their shows, Vicky fed them, Vicky washed their clothes. Vicky believed in them, perhaps the first outside the band to do so completely. Slash once stated in an interview that prior to Vicky's involvement there was no label interest. "She was the only person that way back when we were doin' our first gigs she'd say, 'You guys are *great*; you're gonna make it.' I've gotta tip my hat to her."

After the release of *Appetite*, Axl told a different version about their unofficial ex-manager, explaining that Vicky Hamilton "basically had a monopoly on booking bands at the Roxy and the Whisky and we needed to get those gigs. And we also needed a place to live. Vicky offered us help. She said she'd get us $25,000, money we desperately needed for the proper equipment to start getting close to the sound we wanted. She never managed the band, we—Slash, Izzy, Steven, Duff, me—*we* managed the band."

One thing is certain. It was during their time with Vicky that they all, Izzy and Axl specifically, wrote to Kim Fowley. He was a Hollywood legend-mogul-producer-singer-song-writer-scene-maker, whose six foot five inch, towering presence had been a Hollywood staple since the early Sunset Boulevard days when the Whisky A Go-Go hosted Buffalo Springfield, the Doors, Love, the Byrds, and others. Kim was a survivor, if nothing else and he was a professional of impeccably high standards whose modus operandi in business has offended as many as it has pleased. In the first letter from Guns N' Roses (who then called themselves Guns & Roses), the band displays a sense of purpose, individuality, and image remarkably sophisticated for a band still so young. I've seen the first bio Jim Morrison wrote for the Doors and gave to Elektra Records to be used when their first LP shipped, and it played a crucial role in establishing their image. The legitimacy of that image is important in a world where image is almost half the battle.

Guns N' Roses displayed a similarly articulate and developed sense of themselves. It appears obvious these guys believed in themselves, fought against overwhelming odds, and together formed a vision that their collective faith coalesced into reality.

In the letter, Izzy and Axl make a point of stressing their street-level credibility and their rebellious, untamed attitudes, already aware of the potential value of such ingredients in the public arena. As early as this, they claim authenticity and loyalty to the self as a cherished ideal, along with raw power and a commitment to their collective muse. The formation of the group is credited to the embryonic nucleus of Rose and Stradlin, a partnership founded in youth in Lafayette, Indiana, and carried over to the dog-eat-dog streets of Hollywood. With the addition of the team of Slash and Adler who had also been knocking around together for quite a while, and then the recruitment of Duff McKagan, the rock 'n' roll family was complete.

The immediate primacy and objectivity of the letter demonstrates a perspicaciousness rare and surprising in a band still so fresh. Grandiose on the one hand and endearingly naive on the other, Izzy and Axl focus in on their future and with the energy of faith behind that vision they proceed to make their dreams happen. Their vision of the band is clear and confident; they allow no room for doubt. After confessing the music is composed and performed primarily for selfish reasons, they go on to display the "Us against Them" mentality that they would continue to develop and nurture to such an angry effect on their debut LP. They announce to the world that they are out to please only themselves and anyone that doesn't understand or agree is an outsider and a potential antagonist. You're either with them or against them. The letter they wrote to Fowley displays an incredibly developed sense of objective awareness as they announce that they will not hesitate to be themselves and that they refuse to compromise their values or beliefs for anyone anywhere anytime.

Already we can see the complete commitment and dedication to the band that in later interviews and articles became such an important characteristic of the band members. After announcing his intention of giving everything he has to give, Axl proclaims his variation of Hamlet, to do or die, to sacrifice every last iota of energy and life he can wring out of the meat and muscle and sinew of his body in exchange for the trancendent glory that only rock 'n' roll can offer him. Complete devotion. His destiny is sealed the moment he begins. It's already too late to turn back.

Axl ended the material that would soon form the basis of the first official bio with: "I'll be damned if it isn't everything we can give or there's no point in existing."

After needlessly defending the crudity of the piece, Izzy scrawled in handwriting at the bottom of the page: "Dramatic, eh?"

Yeah, and not only that, *smart* too. In retrospect it can be seen as pure vision. Honestly reflecting their true nature, articulate yet unapologetic, sensational, desperate. Out to please who they can by being who they truly are and infuriate and to hell with the rest.

As the phoenix of Guns & Roses was struggling to rise out of the molten belly of the heavy metal rock scene, history was being made over at Elektra Records by another hard rock band, Mötley Crüe. The Crüe had come on with an image similar to the one Guns N' Roses wore with such an ignoble grace—leather clad, hard living, hard drinking, hard rocking, hard fucking—but the Crüe had one problem: no one took

Percy Bysshe Shelley, opium addict and poet.

them seriously. Actually, more people took them seriously than you might have thought, still the popular consensus in the record business in 1986 was that not only did Mötley Crüe have no songs, but their image was a pose, a stance, a sham intended to create an impression for mere press coverage and had nothing to do with their real lives. Whether they actually lived up to the press or not didn't seem to matter; it still felt like a shuck. Then they started selling records in numbers hard rock hadn't achieved since Grand Funk Railroad or Kiss, the latter with whom they seemed to share a cartoon *cum* fright image.

Meanwhile, the record company representative who had signed the Crüe was having some problems with his boss at Elektra Records and was simultaneously being wooed by several other record labels. The so-called kid was a cherubic young blond man barely twenty-two years old named Tom Zutaut. He had discovered and developed Mötley Crüe as a junior A&R (artist and repertoire, literally; the singing department) person. Known affectionately in the industry as "Zoot," he lived and breathed his rock 'n' roll, the same way the kids who bought the Crüe's records did.

About this time, enter David Geffen, an unlikely suitor when you consider his history and involvement with such laid-back, well-behaved, clean-cut artists as Jackson Browne and Linda Ronstadt. Geffen had some dealings with Elektra as president of Asylum Records, a corporate sister of Elektra. After a decade-long sabattical, David Geffen was now back in the record business with John Lennon and Elton John in tow and was looking for a heavy metal lookout with seasoned ears to get him some good, young, hard rock 'n' roll to round out his fledgling artist roster. Geffen wanted his own Mötley Crüe; who would be better to find them than the twenty-two-year-old kid who had discovered Mötley Crüe? Geffen didn't have a doubt that lightning could strike the same person twice—or if he did, he decided to take the gamble anyway—and he signed Tom Zutaut away from Elektra with specific instructions to get him his own Mötley Crüe. Within a year, Zutaut had them.

To find that band, Zutaut simply walked into Vinyl Fetish, the hip Melrose Avenue record store specializing in the kind of hard rock he loved, and he asked the clerk if he had heard of any great new bands. The answer was "Just one." Yet the industry, and Geffen perhaps, were still skeptical, as they had been when Zutaut had brought Crüe into the fold. He must have been wondering when he was going to get some respect, some trust. Geffen offered him a fledgling development fund to go ahead and bring the young band called Guns N' Roses along. In March 1986 the band signed with Geffen, via Zutaut's efforts, for the sum of $75,000 ($37,500 as a memo deal with the second $37,500 confirming the deal) and an album budget.

The band was happy: they had a home, a record deal, a contract, and they didn't have to hustle quite so hard to survive. Now they could devote more time to writing and rehearsing their songs in order to record the best possible album they were capable of producing.

Geffen was happy: he'd gotten the hottest band in town and had gotten them for a low price even though that price was not without some risk.

Zutaut was happy: he'd gotten the band signed to the company for a pittance, although it was in reality an excellent deal for all parties involved, most particularly Geffen. Geffen had invested no more and no less than he had to, on a band who most people in the industry doubted would even live to go on the road to promote their first album. But Guns N' Roses had something Mötley Crüe didn't have: believability. These guys were clearly fucking nuts, not to be trusted alone in your house, and not be crossed on the street. This was the impression that seeped from their pores to the steel tips of their boots.

Everyone was happy with the new record deal except for Vicky Hamilton. She had been left dangling. Implicit in their record deal was the understanding that the band members would utilize the front money to develop material for their first LP. Vicky Hamilton had other ideas and sued the band for $1 million, part of which she claimed was owed for out-of-pocket expenses and part of which she said she had coming to her. This brouhaha was eventually settled out of court for $30,000, half of which the band paid, the other half of which Geffen paid.

On the street, the word was that while it was true the Gunners were rehearsing material for the album, the boys, having paid back the dealers they owed, were spending most of that seventy-five grand on dope. Everybody in the band was supposedly strung out or drinking heavily. They were living what they were writing and they were writing what they were living and they weren't expected to be living much longer. The reality was somewhat different—of the first $37,500, most went for clothes and equipment. Of the second $37,500 installment, a *lot* went to drugs and drug dealers.

There was something else that was bugging Vicky Hamilton, as she recalled the period just before their acrimonious split: "You're talking about a bunch of street creatures here. They had never had any money before and suddenly it was like, 'Life's a party now.' The day they signed, I was crying because I knew what was lying ahead." Her fears were not without foundation. In an interview held shortly after their Geffen deal was signed, Slash appeared to confirm grounds for worry: "Our attitudes haven't really changed at all—the only real difference is now I can fuck up and get away with it."

True enough. Within two months, the five musicians had spent the $75,000 and were already clamoring for more.

Then just as major record company attention peaked with their Geffen signing, rape charges were filled against Rose and Slash (and subsequently dismissed). Amid legal threats, accusations, rampant drug use, a prevalent sense of impending doom, and a seemingly inexhaustible rumor maelstrom, Guns N' Roses released their first record in December 1986, their self-produced EP, on their own label Uzi-Suicide, entitled *Live?!*@ Like a Suicide*. Without any advertising, with little if any promotion, accomplished solely on word of mouth, the EP sold 10,000 in four weeks, a very respectable number for an EP on an independent label. It was an astute way for the fledgling band to demonstrate the readiness of their potential audience. Geffen eventually bought the rights and released it during the period between the release of *Appetite for Destruction* and the tardy second album.

Kiss member Paul Stanley, who had already proved himself an astute businessman by way of Kiss's longevity and the investments that longevity provided, expressed interest in the band. He met with Axl and Slash about the possibility of coming aboard as their producer. The three listened to the demo they had already done with producer Spencer Proffer, but as Axl put it, "He wanted to rewrite two of our favorite songs so it was over right then and there." Stanley knew the band could be big, but the band didn't believe he understood why.

Slash recalls Paul Stanley attending one of their early shows. "I'm looking at this guy watching what we do. He's a nice guy, but he didn't have a clue as to what we were doing. Everyone gets the basic idea: 'They're a rock 'n' roll band.' But they don't get the formula." Guns N' Roses passed on Stanley.

When Guns N' Roses signed with Geffen, it wasn't the only deal in town, or even the best deal, but as Izzy put it, "They were the coolest: they were hip to what was going on. They knew about rock 'n' roll. There were labels we went to who didn't know who fuckin' Aerosmith was that wanted to sign us. At one label, something came up about Steven Tyler, and this chick said, 'Who's that?' " Then Zutaut came along. "He's the main reason our record happened," Axl admits.

Axl's appreciation would be short-lived, however: Zutaut's editing of the second single—the one that went to the top of the charts, "Sweet Child o' Mine"—from six minutes to three minutes, infuriated Axl. But that was still some time away.

When they started the rehearsing process, Guns N' Roses had by this time acquired enough material from playing around town that they didn't need to do too much actual writing before they started the recording process. What they needed, though, was polishing and honing. Just enough to express their edges with verve yet at the same time not significantly dull their sound.

Then came the matter of finding a suitable manager—one that could take the band to the top, handle the recording process, work with the record company, deal with the booking agency, and keep all five guys standing on their feet and breathing at the same time. In August 1986 Zutaut introduced the band members to Tim Collins, Aerosmith's manager through thick and thin. Collins had ample experience with the maintenance of a successful rock 'n' roll band with temperamental artists with serious drug problems i.e., Tyler and Perry. After the meeting, Guns N' Roses ran a $400 food and drink bill and moved themselves into Collins's room, causing Collins to check into another room in order to get some sleep. In the morning, Collins passed on the dubious honor of managing Guns N' Roses.

"It wasn't an intentionally bratty thing," Duff explained. "It's just what we were used to, it's what we were, but the industry and record company weren't."

"If I remember correctly, they wanted to drop us at one point," says Izzy, "about a year after they signed us."

Slash recalls, "Well, what happened is, we got restless. We get signed, they give us a bunch of money, put us in an apartment, we can't go out and do any gigs—so we got fucking bored and started doing a lot of drugs, drinking a lot, tearing up houses . . ."

Izzy agrees, "We partied pretty hard for a while there . . ."

Slash adds, "And, just about every single manager that we met was scared shitless of us. And it was bad. We couldn't help it. We were bored. So we started to fuck up. But, we finally got it together and gave them what they wanted."

Which was their debut LP for Geffen.

Izzy says, "So, now they all love us."

Zutaut had one more possible candidate in mind: At Elektra Records, his secretary had been married to a young Englishman who managed another struggling L.A. hard rock band called Great White. In a state of near desperation, as Guns N' Roses were ringing up a small fortune in studio costs with little of substantial value yet in the can, they met with Alan Niven up at their new band house in the Hollywood Hills. As Axl recalled, Niven personally delivered Jack Daniels, porno mags, and pizza to the boys and while the band members did not feel immediate affection for the brash manager and were certainly no fans of Great White, they did feel Niven understood them, would be sympathetic to their cause, and would aggressively protect their best interests. GNR legend has a third version with Niven then taking the band to a meeting at a West Hollywood eatery called Barney's Beanery where he proceeded to impress the Gunners with his tolerance for alcohol. Whatever the scenario, he got the job.

Guns N' Roses was now complete. An abrasive manager, a record contract, a reputation, a sound, now all they had to do was *do it*—do the one and only thing any of them had ever wanted to do; what the past ten years had been leading up to. The realization of their dream was upon them.

CHAPTER 4

IMITATING THE GODS

C ulture, as the Greeks observed, gets the leaders it deserves, so it shouldn't come as any surprise that we also get the musical entertainers we deserve. When they mirror us, and we don't like what we see, we try to blame *them*. Confucius knew better: "If one should desire to know whether a kingdom is well governed, if its morals are good or bad, the quality of its music will furnish the answer."

Until Guns N' Roses lead singer Axl Rose appeared, Mick Jagger epitomized what Nietzsche called "nihiline," anti-bourgeois ire. Jagger was all things to all fans and he promised everything to everyone: simultaneously male and female, unencumbered by modesty, beyond the law, moral and political, thumbing his nose at authority and getting away with it. Jagger was, in his time, to entertainment what Napoléon was in his time politically among the French. With Jagger and his Stones (without whom he is impotent) sidelined for much of the eighties and now continuing to fade as a rebel force, along came Axl Rose, making Jagger look tame by comparison—just as Jagger and his band made the Beatles look quaint two decades before, and just as the Beatles rendered tame Frankie Avalon, Ricky Nelson, Pat Boone, and yes, even Elvis Presley. Not since Jagger and Morrison has there been such a Dionysian (including his androgynous aspect) singer as Axl.

The comparison to the Stones is apt, if referring to the young, uncouth, angry, rebellious Stones, rather than the polished professionals they've become. A uniquely American band, Guns N' Roses are exploding everywhere, with both releases on the British and American, as well as Canadian and German bestseller charts. Like America, they do not reflect their components, they absorb them, digest them, and make them influences. They're not the sum of their parts; they are something larger and different and stronger. One part punk in dress and attitude and sound, another part heavy metal in strength and fury, another Stonesian rhythm and blues, another part New York Dolls, Aerosmith, and Sex Pistols . . . They are a product of our times, bringing into sharp focus the conflict of living in the year 2000, in the city, on the edge of Judeo-Christian culture, which is falling apart because it doesn't fulfill our needs anymore. They are the sound of revolt and the dance of death that precedes rebirth, the soundtrack for T. S. Eliot's "Waste Land."

They are without question the best American band since the Doors and the comparison isn't only true, it's appropriate. Axl Rose, is the most purely real and brilliant performer since Jim Morrison, L.A.'s first-generation wild child. Morrison arrived in L.A. after a half-life of navy bases and moves, and then blossomed out of its desert womb fully grown. In lieu of other worthy candidates (Van Halen and Mötley Crüe were only a glimpse of what was coming), L.A. adopted Axl Rose and suckled him as her own. "The West is the best," Morrison sang in his song "The End." "Get here and we'll do the rest." The Eagles of course had their own paen to L.A. in "(Welcome to the) Hotel California." But in "Welcome to the Jungle,"

Axl worshipping at the altar of rock 'n' roll. *(Courtesy Chris Lee Helton/Retna Ltd.)*

Axl snarls, with obvious relish and inhospitality, "You can have anything you want but you better not take it from me."

In fact, no one in L.A. was even tempted to take anything from any one of them. People were afraid of this band precisely because they weren't posers and they didn't appear the slightest bit hesitant to prove it. Which made procuring a producer a difficult proposition. Zutaut's assistant, Teresa Ensenat, recalled, "They were scared shitless—all of 'em got scared off. Mike Clink wasn't anyone's first choice—he was mainly known for being Ron Nevison's engineer." Nevison was known for his production work with Chicago, Europe, Heart, Kiss, Eddie Money, and Ozzy Osbourne, among others.

Produced and engineered by Mike Clink and mixed by Steve Thompson and Michael Barbiero, *Appetite for Destruction* was released in July 1987. It then took ten months just to crack *Billboard* magazine's Top 100. The record and the band needed something, some extra push.

For a while, it looked like that something might be *The Dead Pool*, a Clint Eastwood–Dirty Harry vehicle that would also carry Guns N' Roses into the national eye. Clint's son, Kyle, who had already discovered Guns N' Roses for himself, was the impetus for their involvement. He thought they'd be perfect.

As Slash summarized their role in the film, "Ya see the movie's about this kind of betting thing where people bet on who is going to die, only they start fixing the bets. So, there's this rock star guy who's a junkie.... We're like friends of this dead rock star." The irony wasn't lost on the guitarist: "I guess they picked the perfect band." In the final cut, it wasn't a big break at all, but rather barely ten seconds of screen time.

On the surface, it had looked good. They wanted to employ "Welcome to the Jungle" on the soundtrack and the hope within the Guns N' Roses camp was not unlike that for many other rock 'n' roll film projects: the song would benefit from the exposure, get picked up by the radio, and pave the way for the rest of the album. The marriage of rock songs and film projects had been enjoying an almost unprecedented run of success, both sides profiting immensely from the marriage.

From the film producer's side, the hope was that the song would pull a new crowd of people into the theater. A hit song could benefit the move, and the movie could certainly benefit the song.

Despite a short cameo in *The Dead Pool* by the band, the movie's theme song, "Welcome to the Jungle," benefited from the additional lifespan the movie generated for it. A promotional video clip, already independently filmed for the song, got another chance. That was all that was really required.

"Welcome to the Jungle" resurfaced on radio and in video outlets and it blasted down those avenues like a welcome stampede, bypassing everything in its path. Its strength simply unequaled by anything else competing with it, its message compelling, its visuals providing the first real glimpse of Axl Rose and the band, unrivaled by any of the dozens of heavy metal monsters. It really was threatening; it was primitive yet polished and very compelling—you couldn't help but watch them. It was dangerous, daring, and strangely beautiful, and music rocked like a locomotive. As for dozens of acts before them, the rock video outlet ultimately paved the way. They looked like they sounded and they sounded fucking great.

In retrospect, MTV will claim they broke Guns N' Roses. That boast is not altogether wrong; it's just that they were a little late. Teresa recalls, "It took about six months of consistent lobbying to get anybody at MTV to play that video. Now, they show ads saying, 'You saw 'em here first.' They resisted to the very last inch. It was ridiculous what that channel put us through to get them to play this band."

It wasn't long after they played them, though, that it became clear MTV would need no further encouragement. All hell broke loose and the clip for "Welcome to the Jungle" went from sporadic to heavy rotation, creating an impression that stuck like paste to the young and impressionable who made up the core audience of MTV's 30 million. The network stays in constant touch with this crowd through call-in request numbers and marketing surveys and all the signs were positive—overwhelming, in fact, the kids couldn't get enough of this brash, intense new group.

The song "Welcome to the Jungle" was the perfect introduction to the band—ferocious yet commercial, uncompromising yet accessible, but best of it all, it was real, in the same way the band was real, with its roots in harsh autobiographical truth.

"I slept one night in a schoolyard in Queens with a big fence around it," recounts Axl. Then he hitched around New York and discovered himself the only white kid in the Bronx. Amidst the surrounding burned out and bombed out devastated area, Axl was confronted by somebody trying to warn him of his trespass. "This black guy came up to me and said 'You know where you are? You in the jungle, baby! You gonna die!'"

The song was also Axl's and Slash's first cowriting effort. Axl wrote the words in Seattle. "It's a big city, but at the same time it's a small city compared to L.A. and the things you're gonna learn. . . . I just wrote how L.A. looked to me.

Slash and Axl during a song break. *(Courtesy Chris Lee Helton/Retna Ltd.)*

If someone comes to town and they want to find something, they can find whatever they want. Plus, I had just been to New York ... and it's like, I love L.A. I just know a lot of people there and I know where everything's at."

"Welcome to the Jungle" was their first single release, and it set forth their ethic as quickly and as clearly as possible: you're crazy—I'm fucked up but I got what it takes. They became the kings of the jungle, by divine right and by accomplishment. L.A. is the jungle and the jungle is the metaphor for every major city. The fact was that little Axl Rose wanna-bes, foul-mouthed runaways, filthy yet angelic, teenage he-devils were already arriving in the bus stations across the U.S. every day, every hour. It was Los Angeles that Axl found inhospitable, not altogether inappropriate for his angst and rage, his innocence and his sense of romance, a willing battleground for his own personal war, a turf for his own one-man mission. This wasn't so unique, really. Axl wanted to make it, but on his terms and then at any cost. He heard the call—as certainly as the shaman hears it—of his heart. His perfect occupation awaited him—to sing in a Sunset Strip hard rock band. A dream that is dreamed a thousand times a day in the desert that meets the sea. It was either that stage or a locked psycho ward, or maybe even prison. It was no choice—it was simply the proverbial gutter or the stage —it was life or death, it was all or nothing; it was pure Axl Rose.

Axl made it, he survived, and now he's King of the Jungle, no easy feat. He speaks for all the other runaways or wanna-be runaways who want something more real, more satisfying than what they have in the situations they are caught up in. Axl's been in that place, he's been down that street and he made it off. He not only survived, he did it on his own terms. He is ruler of all he sees—the whole heavy metal village that has sprung up around Guns N' Roses—the scene in L.A. on the Sunset Strip at the Rainbow Bar & Grill, the Cathouse, the Whisky, Gazzari's ... above it all yet still an intrinsic part, Axl's presence is now everywhere on this scene. The band's name and presence is invoked every other minute. It's pervasive. When a member arrives on this scene, it is as if royalty has entered the domain. The L.A. attitude of cool, unimpressed jadedness disappears and the kings hold court.

It must be strange, especially for Axl, someone who dreamed a dream that came true, to be feted by others dreaming the same dream. Does he pinch himself to awaken? Axl enjoys telling the story about how frightened his parents were of him ending up a failure: "My dad's biggest thing is, he loves to go to a restaurant or someplace back home where if he sees people he knows, they go 'Hey, what happened to that son of yours?' 'Ahhh, he went to California to become a rock star,' Dad says. 'Well, what happened?' they ask. 'He became a rock star.' I think he likes that." But does Axl believe it's really true? Has it registered? Or does he know inside he's really just like them? And if so, does it scare or reassure him?

Which isn't to imply he is unexceptional. Not at all. Wayward and rude, maybe. Impulsive, energetic, dangerous, capricious, and unpredictable, yes, too. But Axl is also gleamingly bright, at times self-defeatingly honest, compelling and charismatic and even at times startlingly, movingly, vulnerable and innocent in the old romantic sense. As a writer, a cultural commentator and communicator, he is a hard rock singer and songwriter currently without equal. As a performing front man, no one alive even comes close. A rock 'n' roll Hamlet, he's looked into the city's black heart and gained knowledge and what he's seen nauseates him. The nausea infiltrates any action because as Hamlet knew and Axl knows, his action cannot change a thing. It's not surprising that Axl refuses to take responsibility for being a role model to his flock—he doesn't want to fail. Both Hamlet and Axl Rose feel it is ridiculous that they should be expected to set right a world that is out of joint. Insight into horrible truths outweighs any motivation for action, beyond the stage—for Hamlet and for Axl Rose as well. Nausea begets anger, anger begets rebellion, and rebellion begets rock 'n' roll—the scream of protest, of shock, reborn into a terrible form. In the first video, "Welcome to the Jungle," Axl arrives on the streets hopelessly naive, in bell-bottoms and a baseball cap, carrying a string-wrapped old suitcase, stepping off a public bus. You can even see a blade of straw jutting from his jaw.

Then suddenly he's transformed, through some grotesque shock therapy. You next see him on stage, in leathers, boots, and in control of his audience. The death of innocence. It is tragic and yet strangely triumphant. He dances the dance of survival and celebration, but he also knows terrible secrets . . .

Maybe he does; maybe he doesn't. It really doesn't matter. Maybe it's unconscious, all an accident—but then what a brilliant mistake. What a fine actor he has become. And what if he *is* aware of the power? Then he deserves everything he gets and more. Then he truly is Jim Morrison's psychic little brother, pushing the same bounds of reality in the same direction—always forward and never retreating. It's not surprising he never compromises offstage—he can't, just as Morrison couldn't. He'd have to change his very nature; he'd have to fake it, and like Morrison, he can't or won't do that. I don't think either knew which, because a step backward, a step off the path, and the band would have lost the hard-won progress they both fought for. The opposing force could gather momentum and pitch him off balance and that must always be guarded against. It is his only obligation to his audience, and to himself, to be real, to be ever vigilant, to guard against the fall at all costs, even if it means forever hurling oneself against the tide (which he does), but only because the reward of riding those breakers, those tidal waves of power, strength, and supreme rightness, those precious minutes onstage justifies all. All opposition is vanquished and he's in his element and brings the audience into theirs and together there is nothing they can't do, nothing they can't have, no one to deny them a thing.

Axl dares to speak the truth; emotional honesty and a direct connection to his heart is his genius. In the same way his lyrics can move from dangerous (or arrogant) to innocent (or vulnerable), so too can he be absolutely honest. Truth is all-important; expression and communication are everything. When asked if he does drugs—he tells the truth. Yes, I have. As a result of this honesty in both word and behavior, the sanctimonious accuse the band of being irresponsible by not being positive role models to their fans.

At what point does honesty become glamorization? At what

Axl Rose: the best hard rock voice since Robert Plant. *(Courtesy Larry Busacca/Retna Ltd.)*

point does one pass from being a musician to a role model? By admitting drug use, it appears, they are accused of glamorizing that usage. What's so glamorous or irresponsible about "I used to do a little but a little wouldn't do," as sung in "Mr. Brownstone"? And that a lot got to be a lot more? Building a tolerance to heroin sounds more unattractive than attractive to me.

Is it just that they appear to be so successful and hip and well liked that by admitting they do drugs and abuse alcohol that drugs and alcohol appear in some way part of the package they are selling? When a kid sees Axl Rose onstage, transcendent, and totally out of it, he does not think, "Oh, of course, Nietzsche, ecstatic principle, right, I understand." When he sees a picture of Slash looking wasted on a magazine cover with a bottle of Jack Daniels between his legs, eyes hooded and dark, he doesn't think, "What a painfully sensitive young man," or "What a pose, what an unhip fool." He thinks, "Cool." Where does it say these guys are supposed to feel a moral responsibility because people, kids, identify with them. When did they ever claim to be responsible or moral? Well, I'd rather have my kid looking up to someone who's honest about his abuses than looking up to a liar in denial about his drug use. These five guys might have set out to be rock stars, but it's pretty unlikely they considered the responsibility inherent in that role until after the questions of responsibility arose.

Still, Axl doesn't appear to be recommending his style of living to anyone. "I learn every lesson the hard way. I go all the way or I don't go at all. Things catch up to you—I wouldn't recommend it."

Duff confronted the role model issue head-on when he told a heavy metal monthly magazine, "We never set out to be role models for kids. We're just us. If some kid is dumb enough to try and act like us, we take no responsibility for what might happen. The kind of life we lead is good for us—but we've been lucky. You could end up dead just as easily as having a number-one album." In fact, Duff was understating the situation. You can end up dead sooner, and more often that's the end result, not stardom.

At a time when rehab, recovery, and Just Say No are so in vogue, are Guns N' Roses a good thing? Damn right! They are! And, of course not, no, they're not! I guess it depends on what side you're on. Personally, I don't know whether to spank them for being so stupid and for making such feeble attempts at gaining attraction, or congratulate them for being so brave and honest and for returning to rock 'n' roll its legitimate mantle as the music for misfits by misfits. Maybe rock 'n' roll shouldn't be safe and sanitized. In the way the world views things, Axl Rose and his band are not good boys by any stretch of the imagination. But that makes them not only relevant, but important and maybe even necessary. As old Will Rogers said, a free society needs artistic articulated dissension to keep everyone honest and on their toes. Plato believed that "music and rhythm find their way into the secret places of the soul—musical innovation is full of danger to the state." We need Guns N' Roses, or to be precise, rock needs them as we need rock 'n' roll. By being seen as the worst in the world's eyes, we can see why they are the best in their own and in their audience's. "Nice boys don't play rock 'n' roll" they sing in one of their earliest songs (a cover of Rose Tatoo's), "Nice Boys." They know rock 'n' roll should not be rated and rock 'n' roll should not be safe. So, maybe they're not "good" in the everyday sense of the word. But then again they just might be one of the three or four greatest bands working today.

It's not just the kids and fans that love Guns N' Roses, either. The music industry supports them as well. As early as the summer of 1988, U2 manager Paul McGuiness made the keynote speech at the New Music Seminar, focusing on the then-new band.

> Guns N' Roses is the most exciting new thing to happen in rock 'n' roll for a while. They will go on to break the whole world. And what they've figured out is that fortune belongs to the brave. And in 1988's bleak musical landscape, they stand out to me like a beacon. They're the biggest band in L.A. now. . . . They'll need no help from me, but I wish them nothing but luck. They're so interesting. The fundamental

law of the music business is this: only the fit survive. Second law: the public vote with their feet.

He was right on all counts.

What the critics of Guns N' Roses fail to see, acknowledge, or accept is that great rock 'n' roll should not be safe. Corporate America shouldn't want to sponsor a truly great rock 'n' roll band because rock is the sound of dissension, not sponsorship. And a great rock 'n' roll band gives no inch and takes no quarter. Real rock 'n' roll is the sound of freedom, not commercials—the kind of rock 'n' roll that liberates and changes the lives it touches. The type that instills its listener and follower with the unshakable tenet that anything is possible, everything is permitted, and if you die tomorrow it's all right because you made the very most of today. There is no tomorrow; there is only the eternal now, and you shouldn't wait for tomorrow because it doesn't exist.

Boredom is the enemy. For band and audience.

"No limits," Jim Morrison screamed in concert in Miami, the night the whole house danced upon the fire, "No limits, no laws."

"I drink and drive, everything's in sight," Axl sings. Part confession, part boast.

Barriers don't exist in the minds of the truest rockers; their thoughts are elsewhere, locked into a feeding frenzy. At its high end, rock 'n' roll not only eats its young, it eats everything in sight. The appetite is beyond gluttony, beyond selfishness, beyond caring; it is a banquet nonpareil, oblivious to all consequences. As Tim White in *Rock Lives* writes, "the rapacious rocker believes that all history, whether personal history, rock history, or human history, is redeemed by eternity."

This kind of hero, rock or romantic, Rose or Rimbaud, "dances over the abyss," the abyss of self-destruction created when the self, instead of expanding the limits of the universe toward the infinite, falls back on itself, tortured by its own thwarted desire. Baudelaire was instinctively the poet of ennui, and Dostoyevski's *Notes from the Un-*

derground points out that the choice is "either to be a hero or to grovel in the mud—there is nothing in between." Rocker Iggy Pop says, "I'm bored, I'm the chairman of the bored." Axl sings, in "It's So Easy," "and I'm bored," too. As Jim Morrison told an interviewer, "you could say I'm interested in the extremes . . . anything in between is . . . well, in between." Axl confirmed his place in the pantheon of the impatient and restless when he told *Circus* magazine "I'm always living on the edge and that can be a very dangerous place to be." Exciting too.

For rock and for romanticism the poles of experience are self-denial and self-fulfillment. Boredom must not be repressed, it must be exploded and demolished. "The sunshine bores the daylights out of me/chasing shadows built on mysteries," Jagger sang. "The future's uncertain and the end is always near," as Morrison wrote, is the attitude to adopt and Axl Rose lives this philosophy to the hilt in life and in song: "And I'm ready," he yells, "to crash and burn." Just like Icarus.

In that grace state, anything is within your grasp— drunk with the power the music imbues you with, you've forfeited all your constraints and given yourself over to the music, and by letting yourself get thoroughly out of control, you have discovered the greatest power of all: it is a way out. You can banish not only tomorrow, but death as well. And anyone who has touched Dionysus (or allowed Dionysus touch him) through the intoxicating power of music knows what it feels like to stomp Death into the dance floor—where nothing can touch you, the music becoming as a hurricane, whirling before and around you as you stand in front of its howling tumult. The temptation fills you to possess and rise above this powerful force, to plunge headfirst into the center force and join it, belong to or own it, and finally to ride it. Then you've got *it*. That's when you're *rocking*. The impulse is every bit as instinctual as a child putting his finger in the fan, or walking on top of a high ledge and wanting to jump, or fly. It is terrifying and it is inviting and it is very exciting and it makes you feel incredibly alive.

This was the sort of transformation Antonin Artaud was hopeful for with his theater of cruelty: "The theater like the plague is a crisis which is resolved by death or cure. It releases conflicts, disengages powers, liberates possibilities, and if these possibilities and these powers are dark, it is the fault not of the plague nor of the theater, but of life." He goes on to write: "It invites the mind to share a delirium which exalts its energies: and we can see, that from the human point of view, the action of theater, like that of plague, is beneficial, causes the mask to fall, reveals the lie, the slackness, baseness and hypocrisy of our world. It reveals to men their dark power, their hidden force, it invites them to take, in the face of destiny, a superior attitude" (from *The Theater and Its Double.*)

This is as good a review for a Guns N' Roses concert as I've ever read. Artaud illustrates better than any rock critic why Axl Rose is such a hero to so many kids today and why he's even a hero to me. He's getting away with something where most of us can't anymore. He refuses to compromise, insists on a divine right to be himself. On this, I can't think of a better role model. He's stirring people up—exciting many and angering almost as many.

The look may be new, but the swagger is classic. Rock music is notorious for mirroring the nineteenth-century tradition of Romanticism. The Romantics' veneration of the instinctual blooms fully in the rock idiom—Shelley in the classic arrogant yet wounded artist's voice wrote, "I fall upon the thorns of life; I bleed"—a line from which the Stones made their riposte to the Beatles tepid "Let It Be": *Let It Bleed*. To which Axl adds: 'I'm gonna watch you bleed." The Romantics were considered vulgar to the prevailing sense of refinement of the day in the same way the members of Guns N' Roses offend so many today. The world today no more appeciates Axl Rose's volatile emotionally honest genius, or Jim Morrison's LSD-soaked inspired brilliance, than it appreciated Chatterton's precocious romanticism, Egon Schiele's youths, Baudelaire's correspondence, Rimbaud's attitude and genius, or Van Gogh's trees and crows.

Romanticism and rock also share protocols for heroism in

excess—chemical, sexual, and behavioral. The extrovert, the hedonist, the madman, the criminal, the suicide, rise to heroic stature in rock for the same reason Byron and Rimbaud became Romantic heroes: they both defied the limits imposed by society. The Romantic hero challenged death with excess and the rock artist is entitled to do the same. Death as the ultimate form of excess. "To live life more than forty years is bad manners," Dostoyevski's Underground Man remarks. As much as the black blues artists—up to and including R&B, as well as Chuck Berry and Little Richard—set the elemental sounds of rock 'n' roll, the Romantics established the attitude. Twenty years later, the Decadents revived it, Schopenhauer's pessimism defined it, the doomed surrealists revered it; they all exhibited strong inclinations to debauchery, intensity, and excess—a fascination with death, eroticism, and mysticism. All share a compulsive need to escape from a materialistic society, whether by reveling in it, fleeing from it, or destroying it. Preservation was a bankrupt notion, destruction and creation, the ideal. (Philippe Jullian from *Dreams of Decadence*.) Exaltation takes the place of truth. Experience replaces knowledge. Dance is preferred to thought. Behavior over thought, madness over sanity. They live in and for the moment only because the answer, if there is one, lies there.

Intensity is the constant goal, moderation is beyond useless, yet intensity and duration, as Jack London has written, "are ancient enemies—they are mutually destructive. They cannot and do not co-exist" (from *John Barleycorn Must Die*).

None of these heroes nor Axl Rose are evil or bad. They are, however, somehow compelled to do bad by a sort of nostalgia for an impossibly high ideal, an unrealizable good. These men be they poets or rockers, actors or playwrights, get away with it because they know the truth. They get away with it up to a certain point; if they aren't careful and if they live long enough, society steps in and says "Enough!" Society does not necessarily want the truth known when it differs from their version or concept and especially when it threatens its status quo, which great art does. Society cannot succeed if everyone wants to be a hero. Someone has to go to work. Heroes are dangerous for this reason because they say it's possible. Musical heroes are perhaps the most dangerous of all. Hearing again from Plato in the *Republic*, "When the music changes, the laws of the state change with it." Stop the music makers and stop the change. Plato advocated keeping the status quo, because he knew the powers that rhythm could excite. Aristotle in *Politics* seconded this theory, adding, "Emotions of any kind are produced by music and music, when true, has the power to form character." Not just music, but any true art. And it is high time the world acknowledges what the rock critic has known for years—great rock 'n' roll is art.

That this opposition (society versus the artist) arises is one of the cornerstones of Nietzsche's philosophy involving good and evil. In *Thus Spake Zarathustra*, he writes, "The 'good' are unable to create; they are always the beginning of the end; they crucify him who writes new values on new tablets; they sacrifice the future to themselves and in doing so they sacrifice the future to themselves and in do so they sacrifice all man's future."

So society bans the artists' work, puts them behind bars, and institutionalizes and ridicules them. Society says no to these guys. And if you want to make anything attractive to a healthy teenager, then Just Say No to it. And stick to your guns no matter what. It is the dictum of forbidden fruit: if you can't have something then it *must* be good. No sex; no drugs; no hard rock; no release from insecurity, fear, isolation.

> When the young heart is impossibly heavy, when the crowded mind grows ineffably lonely, when urges seem too dizzying to dare act on—and yet you do act on them because they're a part of you—you're *rocking*. Rock 'n' roll is the darkness that enshrouds secret desires unfulfilled, and the appetite that shoves you forward to disrobe them. And, as Jerry Lee Lewis can tell you, if you want to rock, you do not go gently into that good night.
> —Timothy White, *Rock Lives*

To help codify these raw rituals, Carl Jung coined a term for the personality traits and smoldering drives all men refuse to acknowledge—*the shadow*. Carl Jung might not have heard Jim Morrison sing "When the Music's Over" or Jimi Hendrix perform "Are You Experienced?" or Axl Rose wail "Welcome to the Jungle" but he would have understood and he would have applauded the outlet that produced these works. Jung would also have understood the rock 'n' roll ethic, "nothing is true—everything is permitted."*

> When you confront your own shadow in all its incarnations, you're inside rock 'n' roll. When you do it musically, onstage, in a terrible, wonderful chilling contact with your audience, encouraging them to stir some measure of their shadow into the spiraling maelstrom, then you're a rock star.
> —*Timothy White, Rock Lives*

The same authoritarian society that said no to Vincent Van Gogh, Oscar Wilde, Edgar Allan Poe, Arthur Rimbaud, Antonin Artaud, Vaslaw Nijinsky, William Burroughs, Allen Ginsberg, and Jim Morrison is now saying no to Axl Rose and Guns N' Roses. The greater the noise, the greater the condemnation; the greater that condemnation, the greater the exposure; and the greater the exposure, the bigger and louder the original sound.

"What sort of repression are you talking about?" you may well ask. "They sold fifteen million records!"

True, they did. And on the surface they do not appear to be repressed at all. But take a step back and you will see it is the environment that attacks them, not their audience. The audience, those 15 million are responding to their animal nature, being gratified after a longer hunger. This is the appeal of Guns N' Roses and the threat. They refuse to slip comfortably into the niche hard rock bands have been so content, as of late, to fit themselves into. Yet they don't appear to mind fitting themselves into some of the opposite places.

---

*The term was originally used by Hassan I. Sabbah, a Persian figure of the eleventh century known as the Old Man of the Mountain, a contemporary of Omar Khayyám. Hassan I. Sabbah was a religious agitator who founded a sect called the Ismailis and for thirty-five years he lived on a mountaintop.

The band isn't stupid and they're at least partially aware of their position. Says Slash, "There's always been that slightly dangerous side to rock music, all the way back to the Stones. Kids enjoy things that they know their parents don't like— something that's a little wild and crazy. That's partly what made Guns N' Roses successful. But you've also got to give 'em good songs. Without that, all the outrageous things you do don't really mean a shit."

Most rock 'n' roll is not blatantly suppressed or denied, but it is judged, and in that judgment there is the patriarchal voice of damnation that can't make up its mind whether this music is insignificant or a grave threat to our youth's mental and spiritual well-being, but it knows it's bad. Even for the mildest rhythm, there exists at America's authoritarian heart a flinch, a puritanical knee-jerk reaction, a wish to *stop it*. The harder the beat, the louder the drum, the louder the protest, the stronger the desire to *stop it*. Slash is only too aware of the intense feelings of opposition the band arouses among its opponents. "We don't go out of our way to look for trouble, but the slightest incident takes on unbelievable proportions. We cause some chaos, sure, because we think that's what rock 'n' roll is about. Most groups are happy to do as they're told in order to achieve commercial success, even give up their identity. We never wanted to do that. That's why we're the new public enemy number one, and every sheriff and cop wants just one thing—to nail one of the Guns N' Roses." He's right.

Today, most bands are satisfied with being sponsored by a big corporation for millions of dollars, and organizing a tour around that show, where all sense of spontaneity is either planned out or denied. America has digested and homogenized too much of its musical entertainment, tours are too big and the money too much to take any risks. The entertainment must be served—there can be no room for a misstep, no chance of failure. Look above the heads of those playing, into the colors that light them. Those lights are the result of literally millions of dollars of construction, and they are hooked up to and run from a complex computer preset to react to certain determined cues. The singer is choreographed to stand at this point on this stage at this point in this song so the blue light can come on during that sad lyric in that ballad placed at a certain point in the set. There is no room for improvisation, or if there is, even that is planned, there will be two or three minutes for a solo, but there are still restrictions. The set must be planned and everyone, the mixer, the lighting man, the prop man, the road manager, the stage manager, the guitar roadie, the drum roadie, and every member of the band, must have the same set list, and that list cannot be changed without everyone knowing and agreeing and totally understanding beforehand. But eliminating the possibility of mistakes also ensures the absence of magic.

This snare of restrictions and all it represents is just what Guns N' Roses refuse to cooperate with. They will not become safe, they will not become predictable, and they will not sacrifice spontaneity, because *it wouldn't feel good*. Because they know that rock 'n' roll works best when the chemistry is right between them and the audience—they know the stage has to be set all right, but set in the ideal way for the muse to visit. This is what they live for, this is why they formed the band, this is why Axl answered "the call" to be a rock singer. Rock 'n' roll is the sound of freedom and while it's one thing to be professional and give the audience the value of their dollars spent, it is another thing entirely to sacrifice spirit to achieve predictability. It is worth risking failure as entertainers to potentially succeed as gods. It is this quality Guns N' Roses so recklessly pursue and when they capture it, they capture it with an unprecedented brilliance. It is this quality they will not forsake to become compliant, reliable, professional, or commonplace. Dionysus is the god of action "who comes, who arrives." But he must be invited, there must be a place for him—if every last footstep and lighting cue is preordained, where does he fit in?

"Rock 'n' roll in general has just sucked a big fucking dick since the Pistols," Izzy, the least talkative and least forthcoming of all the Gunners, summarized.

"I hope we've reintroduced the idea of being natural, or being for real and adopting a down-to-earth approach," Slash agreed. "We want to put integrity back into music. What this industry's about these days is pretty obvious—trying to polish everything up. Everything's technopop, even the heavy metal stuff. We go against every standard of this industry."

It doesn't matter if they're playing to an audience of twenty or twenty thousand. "We do whatever we feel like doing."

Whenever, it needn't be added, they feel like doing it.

During an interview with MTV, Axl responded to the interviewer's remark about how Guns N' Roses seemed to be one of the only bands the VJ had seen who possessed an electrifying sense of spontaneity. "You kind of regrouped after a song to determine what you wanted to play next. It made the whole thing seem so . . . alive."

Instantly Axl knew exactly to what she referred. "That's something that's been very hard to maintain," he explained. "Everybody somewhat hated me for that because one reason people don't do that is not because they don't want to be spontaneous, it's because that's hard on your light crew, it's hard on your sound man. They have things pre-programmed on their boards and their cues are taken and it just throws everything off and the show suffers, but I think it's worth it. On the song 'Paradise City' I sang all those parts in the studio, all five parts. We can't do that live and we don't try to because it's not possible without using tapes and I'm not going to use tapes. Also, if you're using tapes and stuff, everything has to be so perfect and tight. And we never know quite how fast or how slow a song is going to be played. It depends. And once tapes are programmed in, you're stuck. It's just not worth it. You know, there are computers running and guys with headsets locked into those and they're ready for you to do 'Paradise City' and what if we decide to do 'Rocket Queen' for whatever reasons, which is a totally different setup the way they're gonna run the lights and run the sound. It's just hard on them. But we've worked with some of these people long enough and they're quick enough and . . . they're kind of excited because it challenges them and they don't get bored. So I understand why bands sacrifice spontaneity, but I won't, I can't. I can't get bored because if I get bored . . . "

Because getting bored is intolerable to Axl and if he gets bored then that means the audience is going to get bored and that's not what they came to see Guns N' Roses for, and it's not what Guns N' Roses came to be seen for either.

"We'll open the show with the same three songs in a row, because that's a good way for me to get warmed up, get the band warmed up and get the groove going. But we'll even change that around. Because, see, we can't fake it."

In a discussion about James Dean, who Axl cites as one of his heroes, Axl admits, "I am very shy and can be very insecure sometimes, but you have to find a way to communicate your feelings every night on stage. You have to try ... it's very challenging ... like an actor on the screen in a way. The only difference is that I'm not playing a part. I'm playing myself."

It's commitment to their true nature that their fans sense and respond to and appreciate and it is this commitment to this spirit that scares their opponents so much. They are not merely entertainment, they are not a mere act, because they dare to be real. Because they're real and true to their spirit, anything can happen. They don't play it safe. And they don't play it safe because, as Axl sang in "Patience," "I can't fake it."

Fifty weeks after its release, *Appetite for Destruction* became the number-one album in the country. Touring and MTV's airing of the video "Welcome to the Jungle" was credited with pulling the album up the charts. Then Geffen released the edited version of "Sweet Child o' Mine," the version that originally upset Axl so much. When it, too, went to number-one on the singles charts and Guns N' Roses had the number-one album and the number-one single in the country, Slash in an interview modestly called "Sweet Child o' Mine" a "fluke," insisting the record company was behind it. Slash tried to see the positive side of the edit and justified the compromised version this way: "If it will make that many people aware of us who normally wouldn't be, cool."

Duff explained the band's lackadaisical attitude about the song: "The thing about 'Sweet Child' is that it was written in five minutes. It was just one of those songs, only three chords. You know that guitar lick Slash does? It was kinda like a joke because we thought, 'What is this song? It's gonna be nothin', it'll be filler on the record.' And except that vocal-wise, it's very sweet and sincere, Slash was fuckin' around when he wrote that lick."

While working on the song, Axl took a trip back to his musical heritage and listened to Lynyrd Skynyrd to make sure he got that "home heartfelt feeling" down. Lyrically, the song was composed for his then-girlfriend, now annulled wife, Erin Everly (daughter of Don Everly). "I had written this poem," Axl recalls,

> reached a dead end with it and put it on the shelf. Then Slash and Izzy got working together on songs and I came in. Izzy hit a riff and all of a sudden this poem popped into my head. It just all came together. A lot of rock bands are too fucking wimpy to have any sentiment or emotion in their stuff unless they're in pain. It's the first positive love song I've ever written, but I never had anything to write anything that positive about before, I guess.

Axl compares his relationship to Erin to that of Jim Morrison and his common-law wife, Pamela. One of those dramatic love-hate affairs; can't live with you, can't live without you. The downs were debilitating but the ups seemed to justify life itself. "They were always fighting," Axl told an interviewer, "but they were soulmates. That's how I feel about Erin."

Encouraged by the public's and the industry's reception to "Sweet Child," band and record company picked the follow-up single, "Paradise City," a song Axl notes is "more about being in the jungle."

If "Welcome to the Jungle" showed off the band's transformation from street kids to kings of the jungle at the nightclub level, and "Sweet Child o' Mine" introduced them to a larger audience utilizing a video that showed the band at its raw, simple best (in rehearsal flexing their collective muscle and appearing every bit as galvanizing in that setting as they were in the live nightclub setting of the previous clip), then the clip for "Paradise City" was the capper. Alternating the footage of the band on the street, backstage, and onstage at Donnington, it is as pulverizing and magnetic a live concert video as any. It arrived at just the right time, too, as the Guns N' Roses audience was just about to burst at its seams. There were millions clamoring for another look-see at the band they had only recently been introduced to via the previous video clips, which showed the band in a club setting ("Welcome to the Jungle") and a rehearsal setting ("Sweet Child o' Mine"). They had the album and they loved what they saw and heard, but they hadn't seen or heard nothing yet. "Paradise City," a song Axl virtually dismisses as a little ditty, "just some more lyrics about the jungle" is a song that perfectly encapsulates the Guns N' Roses duality that their young audience readily related to. The crossfire emotions of young innocence contrasted with the arrogant swagger, filtered through the street smarts and animal survival instincts that "Welcome to the Jungle" defined, and that makes Guns N' Roses the unique unit they are.

"Please take me home," Axl begs in the song. We all want to go home. But there is no going back, there's no turning around. We have to go forward; we have no other choice. Axl has what it takes; he will survive; he will stare down the nausea of the city's black heart. He will scream into the vacuum until he hears the echo he seeks, confirming his existence. "I've seen it all a million times," he snaps at the song's end. Nothing can shock him anymore. The innocent is transformed into a survivor. He is both and because he is not afraid of either side, he can have both and connect us with the aspects of the universal psyche we share. But can he bear the tension of these opposites he expresses so keenly?

The "Paradise City" video did something more; it showed the Guns N' Roses audience to itself. It held up a gigantic mirror into which the millions of fans saw themselves captured in the dance, the dance that Axl instructs and leads—that Guns N' Roses demand. That clip had an electrifying effect on its audience. They saw themselves and they sensed their strength and confirmed their purpose and sense of belonging. Their following swelled.

Axl wearing leather the right way—black and tight. *(Courtesy Joe Bangay/London Features International)*

Into this wildfire gasoline was poured that would provide the combustion sufficient to send Guns N' Roses into an orbit of such stellar proportions and powerful momentum that nothing would be able to stop them.

Remember that little EP of live material the Gunners released on an independent label two years before "Paradise City"? Well, someone at Geffen did. *GNR Lies* (subtitled *The Sex, the Drugs, the Violence, the Shocking Truth*) was released by Geffen Records on November 30, 1988. Containing on one side a reissue of the Uzi-Suicide EP *Live?!* *Like a Suicide* and four newer acoustic numbers on the flip side, *Lies* served the dual purpose of fanning the growing fire and buying the band some time in widening the gap between *Appetite* and their still-to-be-recorded follow-up LP.

"We wanted to put something out between the last tour and the next album," Slash explained at the time. "We also heard that kids were having to pay fifty dollars to one-hundred dollars for the original *Live?!* We wanted to do some new songs that showed another side of us. These are songs we just felt like doing." In defense of the anticipated complaints that the Gunners had gone soft, Slash explained, "Yes, this is a rock 'n' roll band, but there's a lot of different influences within Guns N' Roses. We write a lot of our songs on acoustic guitar. So doing *Lies* seemed a natural thing for us."

The album's artwork was designed to resemble a tabloid magazine cover and presents the band's ironic response to the incessant and ridiculous rumors continually swirling around them. "We've been the center of so much attention and hype and sensationalism," Slash said, "and all of it is bullshit. We've heard that we've all died, in a car crash, that we've done this or that. This was our chance to turn it around and stick it back in their faces." Or to reduce a potentially aggravating situation to absurdity by playing it up with a sense of humor. Fire with fire. Use it to their advantage by turning a negative into a positive.

The first and only single off *Lies* was "Patience," an acoustic song Gram Parsons influenced by way of the Stones circa *Beggar's Banquet*. The song and emerging video clip became another hit for the band and also served the purpose of issuing correspondence from the band to their audience, who would now have to endure a lengthy wait before anything else would be released by the group.

With the release of *Lies*, they showed they had courage in their ability and willingness to change and they demonstrated strength in their determination to continue to create in the face of seemingly insurmountable obstacles. The question is this: will Guns N' Roses, Axl Rose specifically, be able to succeed where so many others have failed? Will they be able not only to survive, but to grow, and through that growth succeed in developing themselves, and by extension their art, and via that art, benefit their audience as well? Or will they burn out, young, tragic, spent?

The road to heaven leads through hell; that's what Blake meant when he wrote, "The path of excess leads to the palace of wisdom," in the first proverb of Hell. To achieve salvation one has to become inoculated with sin. One has to savor all, the large as well as the more trivial sins. The following, lesser-known proverb reads:

> Prudence is a rich ugly old maid courted by Incapacity
> He who desires but acts not, breeds pestilence.

In other words, do not say no.

It's been proposed that the stance of the whole band, especially Axl Rose, is a pose, that they are accomplishing what they are intentionally, intuitively, aggressively, grabbing—the collective subliminated libido of teens and young adults around the world. Maybe some of the image—the tattoos, leather, the scarves, the boots and hair—is a bit self-conscious and planned to achieve desired effect, but the zeitgeist is for real. Their look is surely as pure an expression and representation of how they feel and who they are as is their music. If they did steal some of their look (and there are those in L.A. who say they did), then they have done it with such sureness and flair that they make the look their own at the same time they appropriated it. Their denim, boots, and leather wardrobe in the early days was probably more the result of need than anything else. Initially, they experimented with the "glam" look complete with teased hair and makeup, a phase very quickly abandoned as they grew into a look more representative of their internal world. As Oscar Wilde said in his own defense, "Beggars borrow, geniuses plagiarize." Regardless of who started it, Guns N' Roses were the ones who wore it with enough flair to be imitated. Obviously, they wore it well—from the cowboy boots, to the backwards baseball cap over the gang scarf.

Axl Rose is real, and he makes those who have ears to hear feel real too. You can call it "real" or you can call it "vulgar" (and there are those that have), or "Dionysian" or "natural" (or "primitive" as Jim Morrison preferred when he feared "Dionysian" would sound too pretentious). It is ancient yet always fresh and new. It is power and it is powerful. Natural and strong. It is only rarely possible and we do well to appreciate it rather than to offend and drive away its authors.

In the end, the church, the state, fathers and mothers will continue to damn Guns N' Roses as devils, their fans will proceed to elevate them to gods, and the truth will remain somewhere out of the reach of both and at the same time somewhere in between. Average teenage kids around the Western world are trying to survive the best they can while overwhelmed on all sides, trying to articulate impossible feelings and urges; they are turning to a band and a music that does for them what they can't do for themselves.

Every other day another "Axl is dead" rumor hits the streets and spreads like wildfire into the media throughout the world. It's like Morrison all over again: life cannot contain the monster either guy became. It's like this guy Axl is too big and too bad to get away with what he's getting away with, or to believed, or even possible. But he is getting away with something—something vulgar yet elegant; important yet inconsequential; both good and bad; sacred and profane. Guns N' Roses will not go away; however, they might succeed in doing themselves in. All five have admitted to habitual drug or alcohol use. At one point early in their careers they ran an ad for an upcoming L.A. gig, "Fresh from detox" and another occasion, "Addicted: only the strong survive." The joke around L.A. in early 1990 was that the reason their third release, the long-delayed second LP, had not been started was because none of them were all clean long enough, simultaneously, to go to work. One person would go into detox as another went off the wagon or resumed his addiction. Finally, in a desperate move they drew up contracts to en-

The superstar as shaman, complete with animal skins, scarves, and tattoos. *(Courtesy Larry Busacca/Retna Ltd.)*

sure the others' continued sobriety. When that failed and drummer Adler breached for the umpteenth time, a replacement drummer was brought in for the preliminary rehearsals so the process of making the hotly anticipated LP could commence.

We are all fascinated by the tragic hero who is destroyed by the fate he created for himself. The tragic poet suffers a collapse in his bid for immortality. He dies, conquered by time, to create art that will live forever. The hero and the poet sacrifice their lives to gain immortality.

"To build a new sanctuary the old sanctuary must be first destroyed," wrote Nietzsche. For something to be born, something must die—primitives certainly believed bountiful life could not exist without a sacrifice to the gods. Creativity, be it an idea, a song, a story, or a painting, is certainly a sort of birth. The relationship between self-destruction and artistic creation, real or imagined, exists. But does it exist because it is real, or does it exist because it is convenient?

Rock 'n' roll is the place where music, art, singing, dancing, writing, poetry, drugs, myth, and religion all meet and the rock star can be seen as the creator of magic, a modern-day sorcerer, alchemist—hero. Rock stardom is a present-day equivalent to winning the princess, the proverbial brass ring. Drug addiction and the enormous fight to kick it can be seen as the contemporary equivalent of slaying the dragon—giving credence to the phrase "chasing the dragon," i.e., smoking heroin—fulfilling as it does the human need to confront one's own mortality, to choose clearly between life and death and to have to fight to the possible death for that choice. Freud addressed this topic when he wrote, "Life is impoverished— it loses interest in itself—if the highest stake in the game of life itself, living, cannot be risked." Guns N' Roses are real; they're really risking their necks. Only they could know the real reasons, and perhaps even they don't. What is certain is that their death-defying behavior fascinates and attracts even as it repulses and repels. It makes us sit up and take notice. Its relevancy to life confirms our own existence. Their dare to make us feel alive—"My God, they're willing to die for it," for the rock 'n' roll life-style, for the rock 'n' roll ethic, for their *art*. Guns N' Roses are thrashing it out onstage, on record, in life, loyal only to the holy force of rock 'n' roll.

"I have something I want to do with Guns N' Roses and this is part of me that I want to get out and take as far as I

During the summer of 1990, Axl wasn't drinking alcohol, at least not in public, and appeared clutching a can of Coca-Cola each time he was spotted by the camera. *(Courtesy Steve Granitz/Retna Ltd.)*

can," Axl told the *Los Angeles Times* in July 1986. "That can be a long career or it can be a short explosive career —as long as it gets out and it gets out in a big way." He is serving notice early on—watch me, he says, you will not be bored. Axl has lived up to that promise and more, up to a point.

The fact that drug addiction explodes with particular strength in societies involved in "overly hasty modernization" has been viewed as "an unconscious and desperate attempt on the part of many people to offset the psychic onesideness which this process causes."

Guns N' Roses have articulated this psychic pain, this imbalance, this angst, in song as well as deed, better and stronger than any other band currently recording. Oscar Wilde once suggested that there were only two ways to deal with a consuming appetite for something—either fast or feast.

"The route to personal truth," the Eskimo shaman Igjugarjuk said to the Danish explorer Knud Rasmussen, "can be reached only through suffering. Privation and suffering." Or indulgence, excess. Feast.

So now I would like officially to welcome you to the jungle. Time to eat.

PART 3

DEATH, DRUGS, ROCK 'N' ROLL

AND

THE FOURTH DRIVE

That humanity at large will ever be able to dispense with Artificial Paradise seems very unlikely. Most men and women lead lives at the worst so painful, at the best so monotonous, poor, and limited, that the urge to escape, the longing to transcend themselves if only for a few moments, is and has always been, one of the principal appetites of the soul. Art and religion, carnivals and saturnalia, dancing and music— all these have served, in the H. G. Wells phrase, as Doors in the Walls.

—Aldous Huxley
The Doors of Perception

Is rock 'n' roll predicated on excess? What exactly is the relationship between intoxication and creativity? Is the same thing that makes one great that which makes one turn to narcotics? Why do some survive, some not? Why are some never even tempted? Why is it that so many of the artists that we love the most are the same ones destined to

Visionary, mystic, poet, painter, William Blake wrote in the first proverb of Hell: "The road of excess leads to the palace of wisdom."

live the shortest? In *Twilight of the Idols*, Nietzsche continued to explore this theme, which he had addressed in previous work: "For any art to exist, for any sort of aesthetic activity to exist, a certain physiological precondition is indispensable: intoxication. In this condition one enriches everything out of one's own abundance; what one sees, what one desires, one sees swollen, pressing, strong, overladen with energy." Nietzsche also believed destruction begets creation as surely as death does birth. For something to be born, something must die. It is a natural law. A very, very *old* law.

In reading over two thousand pages of interview conversation with Axl Rose, conducted on five separate occasions, I was struck again and again by how adamant and aware he was of creating something that would stand the test of time. Something that could not be easily labeled, catergorized, and stored on a shelf representing the Past. A creation that would be timely and modern today, classic and timeless tomorrow. Axl speaks of the EP *Lies* as a way to maximize the availability of divergent styles the band possesses. He also refers to a song he has written called "November Rain," slated to appear on their second album, titled *Use Your Illusion*. It is an epic song, along the lines of "Stairway to Heaven" or "The End," that should appeal to both hardcore fans as well as to people who don't ordinarily respond positively to the sort of music Guns N' Roses usually composes and records. Described as a melodic mid-tempo ballad with a gorgeous lead vocal by Axl and an elegiac lead guitar from Slash, "November Rain" is called "our Layla song" by the band members. Axl hoped E.L.O. leader and Traveling Wilbury Jeff Lynne would be available to produce the track.

The band has also chosen to record Paul McCartney's "Live and Let Die" for the same album, an unlikely choice it would appear first. A James Bond theme song written by the same guy who wrote "Silly Love Song"? Yet, lyrically it's custom-made for Guns N' Roses. The innocence of McCartney, the light, balanced by the darkness and drama that Guns N' Roses bring to it—the same darkness Lennon once brought to the same equation—make the song great and different from its original presentation.

The same theory applies to their cover version of another, at first, unlikely song, Bob Dylan's "Knocking on Heaven's Door." But these guys are nothing if not reckless. Their version of the song was recorded during their Japan tour and dedicated to Todd Crew, an old friend of the band who had recently overdosed on heroin, later to be included on the *Days of Thunder* soundtrack album. What the Byrds did with their Dylan folk-rock interpretations in the sixties, Guns N' Roses accomplish to the same successful degree on a hard rock level in the nineties. The song's originally soft and resigned lyrics become transformed into a protest, a wail, a scream of pain and loss, a brilliant and thoroughly valid interpretation.

In addition to the above mentioned, some of the other songs on the forthcoming third release, second LP should be familiar to those who were lucky enough to catch the band on one of their early tours. "Down on the Farm" was performed at Farm Aid Spring 1990. The band has reworked and rearranged a few songs from the early days like "Ain't Goin' Down," and one sure to delight women's groups and feminists, "Back Off Bitch." Slash plays the banjo during the introduction of one track and Izzy picks up the sitar for a few bars. Slash's song contributions tend to be more complex than Izzy's, whose style tends toward simpler, more straightforward structures. There's a song titled "Coma" that's about ten minutes long with "about five hundred chord changes" as Slash described it. Also being considered is a funk-blues styled number called "Bad Apples." And there's a chance a song called "Don't Cry" may also be included in the final song program as well. Over thirty-five songs have been recorded in all and there's a good possibility that what hard metal songs don't make it onto the long-playing work will come out in an extended play version, à la *Lies*, a "punk EP" as Axl called it, to be released, possibly "a year or so after the album."

The versatility comes easily, naturally to the band and they insist on the right to present the music they create—damn the consequences.

When a writer compares Guns N' Roses to Mötley Crüe

and Poison, two other successful L.A. hard rock bands, Axl politely demurs, explaining that he's sure they have their goals, but that Guns N' Roses want to break away from any slot into which they've stylistically been placed. In fact, Poison and Mötley Crüe held on to their glam image well into their careers, while Guns N' Roses discarded early on any vestige of makeup or silk. Instead of pointing this out, though, Axl accentuates the positive, using U2 as an example of a band who stands alone, unique unto themselves. "They've broken into their own role, taken it to a different level," he says, "they're not down there with new wave, or the underground, or heavy metal, or this or that. They ascended into their own class of music. And that's exactly what we want to try to do. And the only way you really are gonna be able to do that is if you really have the music."

Of course, the easy thing for the band to do, and some would argue the smart thing for them to do, is to stay exactly where they were on *Appetite*. Stick to the proven formula, do what they did on the first album again and don't change a thing. If it works, don't fix it. But Axl knows, and the whole band knows, what they did on the first album was *listen to their hearts*. "We just try to be ourselves," Axl shrugs when asked what they hope to accomplish in the future.

"It's weird," Axl admits, "but all I know is it works—as long as I keep trying to follow my heart, I keep reaching the right destination whether I want to or not. And whether I think I should have gone another way, as long as I'm following my heart, I know I'll reach the right destination."

The same standard applies to the art and packaging of their material. For the band, the title summarized the environment in which the album had been recorded. When Warner Brothers Records, which distributes Geffen, Guns N' Roses' label, refused to continue printing the initial album cover artwork, depicting a gruesome rendering of a robot raping a beautiful, nubile, young teen girl, Axl felt compelled to point out that the picture in and of itself wasn't indecent, it's what people chose to see. To him it represented the robot as society, the girl as a metaphor for either the band, or individual humanity as a whole ... in other words, he picked artwork that represented the very same thing that Joseph Campbell has become such a hero for saying—the progress of Western culture has outstripped man's spiritual and emotional ability to deal with it. The band had been drumming their collective fingers in an effort to come up with a suitable title for their debut LP when Axl flipped over the postcard which contained the surreal robot versus girl scenario. At the top of the postcard, in the back, in small capital letters read the following words: APPETITE FOR DESTRUCTION. There was also another, albeit simpler, reason why the band liked the title: it was simply appropriate. This discovery was made during "a very heavy period of drug use for the band," Izzy explained. "A lot of the music reflects that—there's a lot of drugs in Hollywood and we were right in the middle of it then."

Rack jobbers and distributors and outlets would not give in; they were shocked and many refused to stock the LP with the offending cover art the way it was. When Warner requested another cover, the band, surprisingly, delivered it: an iron cross with skull renderings of each member's face at the end of each bar. The previous art work was relegated to an inside sleeve; the title, however, remained.

What made *Appetite for Destruction* so special was not the band's penchant for extreme experience but rather their ability to reflect it in their songs without wallowing in pseudo-romanticism or cheap sentiment. The power of a song like "Mr. Brownstone," which Izzy admits was written in about five minutes, "while I was cooking something up," is in the way it evokes not only the thrill of the fast lane with its Bo Diddleyish rhythm, but also with Axl's wild cadences and its implicit terrors. From the come-hither decadence of "Welcome to the Jungle" to the prayer for deliverance of "Paradise City," the relentless paranoia of "Out ta Get Me" or the wary, fragile hopes expressed in "Sweet Child o' Mine"—the point of view is invariably existential. Nihilistic, too, yes; the songs are as strong as they are heartfelt. The edge of the abyss is skirted, celebrated, and probed with an exhilarating effect. This is where Guns N' Roses reside, precariously perched. In song as in life, always on the brink of disaster or breakthrough.

Professionals in the medical field have long been aware of a phenomenon that takes place on the death bed, a "spontaneous remission" that takes place in certain patients who from every medical viewpoint have been expected to die from an incurable and fatal illness. When for no apparent reason other than spiritual the process reverses itself, sparing the patient who stared death in the face close enough to feel its dank breath, it gives him a new deep and profound appreciation for life. In *The Idiot*, when given one minute to live before being hanged, the hero has a breakthrough experience as he begins to perceive life as it is, in the moment. In jail for alleged subversion in 1849, Dostoyevski knew well of what he wrote. As he faced execution by a firing squad, at the very last moment a retreat was sounded. It had been a mock execution to shock and frighten the prisoners. Facing death so directly had a profound affect on Dostoyevski. After this incident, he wrote a letter from prison to his brother saying, "I have been reborn."

In the more enlightened cases, young artists are hoping for this sort of epiphany, this spontaneous conversion that is achieved via a flirtation with death. Throughout history, the courting of death just to evade the final embrace has directly led to the deaths of scores of literary and musical geniuses. There is something combustibly creative about shoving together the opposite qualities of life and death and the resulting incipient sparks. There is something irresistably alluring in approaching death to be reborn.

Mankind's impulse to take off the metaphorical brakes is true and pretty well documented. Death-defying, life-exciting behavior is not exclusive to the creauive personality, but there we find it most pronounced and celebrated and, as often as not, with tragic results.

One sure way for the artist to thrill to the grim reaper's proximity is via chemicals, of course. Yet, even so, drug use, be it casual or compulsive, simply does not appear dramatically to affect the creative process in any positive way. While there is some fascinating and speculative information available, there is absolutely no concrete evidence that excessive drug use incites or contributes to the act of creation. On the other hand, there has been no material evidence that drug use *does not* excite the creative process. Although, how would we know if drugs do not help—how would we have heard of them? There would be no success with which to gauge the results. By the same reasoning, it's impossible to gauge to what extent the artist's genius was enriched from his use of drugs since we cannot know what he would have done without them.

But, drugs can kill you. You can't write, sing, or perform if you're dead or near-dead.

It's near impossible to refute the evidence that there are dozens of well-known painters, musicians, writers, poets, lyricists, performers, and so on who have been drunk and drugged, and the art they produced was a wonder to behold. To the casual observer this might indicate a constructive relationship between the chemicals and the human being. If it worked for them, then why shouldn't it, or why wouldn't it, work for me just as well?

In the rock pantheon, addicts/alcoholics now or then have, both alive and dead, included Keith Richards, Marc Bolan, Eric Clapton, Ringo Starr, Pete Townsend, John Lennon, Iggy Pop, Janis Joplin, Jimi Hendrix, Jim Morrison, David Crosby, Elvis Presley, Jerry Lee Lewis, Little Richard, Steven Tyler, Joe Perry, Sid Vicious, Duane Allman, Greg Allman, Lowell George, Brian Jones, Dallas Taylor, Ian Curtis, Bon Scott, John Phillips, Brian Wilson, Jim Carroll, Darby Crash, Sly Stone, Ginger Baker, Jerry Garcia, Boy George, Grace Slick, Danny Whitten, Keith Moon, Tim Buckley, Mike Bloomfield, Paul Butterfield, Sid Barrett, and, of course, Slash, Izzy, Axl, Duff, and Steve.

The relationship between drugs and musicians began to flourish during the jazz age. We are all tragically familiar with the many liberal applications of the faulty syllogism: Bird (a.k.a. Charlie Parker) is a genius of jazz; Bird cannot live without heroin; therefore, heroin is essential to jazz genius.

Some of the other jazzers on (or once on) junk, besides Charlie Parker, include Mezz Mezzrow, Art Pepper, Billie Holiday, Miles Davis, Fats Navarro, Archie Schepp, Hampton

Hawes, Stan Getz, Art Blakely, Chet Baker, Buddy Arnold, Ray Charles. Again, it's difficult to think of more than a few passionate muscial artists who haven't taken drugs. It's something we not only accept but in some cases expect, as a sort of "mark of Cain" identifying the truly interesting and talented.

The jazzers sang about drugs, as well. Songs such as "Can't Kick the Habit" in 1941, and "Pipe Dream Blues" released in 1924 extolled the pleasures and pains of opium smoking, and are both good examples of songs extolling the virtues of drugs. As jazz entered the fifties, direct reference to drugs in song became more discreet as the antidrug hysteria began to mount.

The use of drugs by the artist goes back a lot further than that. The Greeks were probably the first to use opium, the mother of morphine and heroin. The word *opium* in fact comes from the Greek word *opion*, meaning "poppy juice." Homer, in *The Odyssey*, is the first on record to mention it: "A new thought came to Zeus-born Helen; into the bowl that their wine was drawn from she threw a drug that dispelled all grief and anger and banished remembrance of every trouble. Once it was mingled in the wine-bowl, any man that drank it down would never on that same day let a tear fall down his cheeks, no, not if his father and mother died, or if his brother or his own son were slain with the sword before his eyes." Helen had obtained the drug from a woman from Egypt, Homer explained; the "bounteous earth yields a huge wealth of drugs, healthful and baneful side by side." Additionally, there are countless references to wondrous drugs appearing frequently in the literature of Egypt as well as Mesopotamia, Chile, Persia, and of many other countries, ancient and modern. (A. S. Trebach from *The Heroin Solution.*)

Helen of Troy wasn't the only one to combine her opium with alcohol (a mixture known later as laudanum). There are reports that the Pilgrims brought laudanum aboard the Mayflower. In 1803 a German pharmacist isolated the chief alkaloid of opium and called it morphine, after Morpheus, the Greek god of dreams. In 1874 a German pharmacologist refined the drug one step further, naming his medicine heroin from the German word *heroisch*, meaning strong, powerful, or heroic. Popular myth has morphine being invented and introduced as a cure for opium addiction and then heroin invented as a cure for that cure. The truth is that people were dying in extremely painful circumstances from pneumonia and tuberculosis and modern medicine at that time was powerless to prevent it. The search was on to find the most powerful drug possible that would at least allay the coughs and pains. If it made the patient feel better in other ways too, well, what was wrong with that?

In 1914 the American government decided there was plenty wrong with it—people were getting sick and other people were getting rich. Enter the Harrison Narcotic Act, the basic thrust of which was to take the sale of narcotics away from grocery stores, mail-order houses, and other commercial peddlers and place it in the hands of capable medical authorities who could provide open and orderly records of all transactions. The future key to the use of all narcotics was to be a physician's prescription. When could a physician, in conforming with the law, issue a prescription? After having registered with the district collector of the Internal Revenue Service and after having paid his registration or license fee. Not long after, there was a massive campaign led by the U.S. Surgeon General, soon to be in the league with Harry Anslinger, the zealous head of the Federal Bureau of Narcotics (and the American representative on the U.S. Commission on Narcotic Drugs) to ban *all* use of heroin. The Harrison Act was repealed and a resolution was passed that heroin was not to be prescribed, manufactured, dispensed, administered, taken, or sold in the United States of America, under penalty of law. Heroin (and cocaine, too) were said to (1) be completely unnecessary in the practice of medicine; (2) destroy all sense of moral responsibility; (3) be used by criminals only; (4) recruit their army from the young and vulnerable.

The Harrison Act was passed as a revenue and record-keeping measure and nothing more. The act was more of a tax law than a control scheme. Yet it sought to control drugs and lost control; it sought to end addiction, and addiction increased.

* * *

Axl   (Courtesy Larry Busacca/Retna Ltd.)

A very early performance.   *(Courtesy Monica Dee/Retna Ltd.)*

Axl decked out in codpiece, chaps, and ratted hair—the vestiges of his glam period. *(Courtesy Geffen Records)*

An early color publicity shot for the *Appetite for Destruction* press kit. From left to right: Steven Adler, Slash, Axl Rose, Duff McKagan, and Izzy Stradlin. *(Courtesy Geffen Records)*

Duff, posed on site of childhood trauma. *(Courtesy Eddie Malluk/ Retna Ltd.)*

Original art for *Appetite for Destruction*, by Robert Williams. It was later replaced by a less offensive, more commercially viable image. *(Courtesy Robert Williams, Far Arden, Inc.)*

Slash, in the light of day. *(Courtesy Geffen Records)*

Slash, with friend Les Paul. *(Courtesy Christopher Helton/Retna Ltd.)*

(Courtesy Eddie Malluk/Retna Ltd.)

Axl, resplendent, transcendent. *(Courtesy Geffen Records)*

A subdued Axl with an
early hero and influence, the
reformed and unrepentant
Steve Tyler, front man for
Aerosmith. *(Courtesy Steve
Granitz/Retna Ltd.)*

Axl Rose remains an ardent Alice Cooper fan and recorded "Under My
Wheels" with Coop for "The Decline of Western Civilization: The Metal
Years" soundtrack. *(Courtesy Dave Lastik/London Features International)*

Axl *(Courtesy
Larry Busacca/
Retna Ltd.)*

Kali, the Hindu goddess of death, known for her powers of creation and destruction.

Lipstick, blush, and Budweiser: a 1988 publicity shot. *(Courtesy Ross Marino/Retna Ltd.)*

Axl and Mick Jagger:
American rock 'n' roll hero,
and the British royalty, in
the summer of 1989.
(J. Bellissimo/LGI)

Slash and Les.   *(Courtesy
Geffen Records)*

"If you are an artist," John Cheever wrote, "self-destruction is quite expected of you. The thrill of staring into the abyss is exciting until it becomes contemptible."

According to author Leslie Fiedler, every age requires its geniuses to have a fatal "charismatic" flaw: blindness in the Homeric age, incest in Byron's time, in twentieth-century literary America, drunkenness; and in late twentieth-century America rock 'n' roll, drug addiction.

Unlike Jack London and F. Scott Fitzgerald, who eventually found they could write only when they were drinking, Faulkner drank when he wrote right from the start, an ability he shared with Eugene O'Neill and Hart Crane. He drank just enough, it appeared, to instill in himself the mood or the way of looking at things that he believed he needed to produce creatively. In time, this ability to write and drink concurrently and productively left Faulkner, too; alcohol became the necessary fuel to get the creative engine going.

What many of these writers believed was that alcohol made arrival of the muse possible. Some sober artists get disturbed about the role of chemicals in the creative process, arguing that the use of chemicals while writing produces fuzzy thinking and a distorted view of the world. For some, an altered state of consciousness is sought to permit a freedom some artists don't believe they possess in sobriety. The fact that this freedom might be illusory is beside the point; many artists have convinced themselves that they obtain it in no other way.

As much as drink has been associated with the literary shining lights, even more so are drugs at one with the rock star. Alcohol and writing. Drugs and music. Destruction and creation. The formula seems almost too simple to be true, yet this is exactly what Dionysus represented. Creativity is not rational—it is impulsive. To stir the embers of creativity, an ingredient may be added to ensure the results. The lesson we have learned at the expense of literally dozens of burntout lives is that this ingredient must be honored, respected, and not abused—yet these same lessons show us how impossible that restraint is to practice.

Faulkner believed he needed alcohol to write, partly as a

result of his love for Baudelaire, Swinburne, and Verlaine, all of whom affirmed the liberating effects of alcohol on them. All three were alcoholic. Faulkner, O'Neill, London, Fitzgerald, and Hemingway set the standard for American writers: to drink might not be to write; but to write was not possible without drink.

Alcohol wasn't the only source of inspiration.

Certainly the lives of many poets and artists bear out the theory of drug use as spiritual displacement. English poet Francis Thompson (1859–1907) became addicted to opium shortly after failing to achieve his goal of joining the priesthood. After being taken away to a country monastery for a cure, Thompson returned to London and city life and opium. It was to prove to be a pattern in his destined to be short life—when he wasn't in the monastery, he was on opium. In a poem rich in the narcotic fancy, "The Poppy," he writes with a precognition of his fate—the poppy signifies both the instrument of his release and his destruction.

About the same time, poet William Crabbe, too, partook of the two consolations, opium and religion; the only difference being that he grabbed the white collar of deaconhood, but unfulfilled, he went on to use opium without apparent ill effect for forty-two years until the day he died.

John Keats (1795–1821) wrote his best-known poem, "Ode to a Nightingale," in a single burst of opiated insight, à la Coleridge with his "Kubla Khan," and was sufficiently strungout on the drug that by the time he was a young man of twenty-two he was already praying for deliverance. As a youth, his family believed strongly in religion and impressed the young Keats with the serene opiate-like allure of God intoxication.

Baudelaire believed he would benefit from the use of opium as did his hero and favorite writer Edgar Allan Poe. Baudelaire was not the only one concerned with the relationship between opium and writing. The issue was passionately discussed in the salon at the Hotel Lauzun in Paris, better known as the Club Des Haschischins. Included among its members were Balzac, Théophile Gautier, along with Baudelaire. Where De Quincey and Coleridge deceived themselves and hoped to deceive others about the motivation of their opium use, claiming it was the result of specific pains, Baudelaire had no such misgivings: he acknowledged that curiosity was his motive.

Baudelaire (who had translated Poe's macabre works) was so impressed by and identified so passionately with De Quincey's *Confessions of an Opium Eater*, he considered his adaptation of it into French along with his own *Les Paradis artificiels* as one work. Both writers confronted the reality of opium—its charms as well as its horrors.

Baudelaire gave up hashish in favor of opium and believed that drugs do, to some extent and in some ways, affect the literary imagination; but they give only to those who already have much; they give less than they seem; and they take away the power to make use of what they give. "Drugs reveal to a man nothing but himself," Baudelaire wrote.

> It is true that the memory impressions will remain when the debauch is over, and those who hope to make use of drugs do not seem at first to be altogether unreasonable in their hope. Also this hope is a vicious circle; even if we admit for a moment that hashish or opium could confer genius or at least increase it, it must not be forgotten that it is the nature of the drugs to weaken the will, and so to give with one hand what it takes away with the other, that is, to bestow imagination without the power to make use of it. (Althea Hayter from *Opium and the Romantic Imagination*)

Of opium, Baudelaire would one day summarize the tantilizing yet horrifying dilemma, thusly, calling the drug, "an old and terrible friend, and like all women, rich, alas! in caresses and betrayals."

Baudelaire's importance and influence cannot be underestimated and, therefore, Poe's gothic-soaked influence on Baudelaire cannot be underestimated either. The two seemed to share a mutual admiration. Baudelaire loved Poe so much he virtually demanded the privilege of translating his work. Poe was quite taken with Baudelaire as well. It was, and is, hard to tell where the influences of one begins and the other ends. These men set the style and the action of the creative life for many years and many people to come.

Alcoholic poet, drug addict, and inventor of gothic fiction, Edgar Allan Poe was as brilliant as he was self-destructive. Poe's influence is felt from Baudelaire and Rimbaud to Jim Morrison and Axl Rose.

Baudelaire eulogized Edgar Allan Poe, as if for his own tombstone and appropriate for the entire pantheon of the fatal destinies we speak of in this chapter: "All you who have ardently sought to discover the laws that govern your being, who have aspired to the infinite, and whose emotions have had to seek a terrible relief in the wine of debauchery, pray for him. Now his bodily being, purified, floats amid the beings whose existence he glimpsed."

Poe is important for his effect on Baudelaire and Baudelaire is important in his own right as both an influence and ex-ample, but also for his immense impression on the young

Rimbaud, whose style, behavior, and work, along with that of Baudelaire and the Romantics, eventually affected profoundly a rock 'n' roll generation. "Baudelaire is the first seer," Rimbaud wrote, "king of poets, *a real god*."

It is a near certainty that Rimbaud based his concept of becoming a *voyant* and his systematic "derangement of the senses" from the texts left behind by the members of the Club des Haschischins. A young and impressionable Rimbaud read Baudelaire with an uncritical eye, blinded and too impressed by his own reflection in his predecessor's writings. Rimbaud, leading a miserable life in the country when he wanted to be in Paris at the center of it all, craved escape and the experiences of Baudelaire. "An unhealthy thirst," he wrote, "darkens my veins." His associates offered Rimbaud not only an easily available escape route, but the promise of untold delights, insights, and visions—an irresistible glimpse into the unknown.

"One must make oneself a seer," he wrote. "Why? To be a poet." How? "By a long, gigantic, and rational derangement of the senses. All forms of love, of suffering and madness."

Rimbaud put forth the proposition that being a poet, an artist, is not so much an act of will as an act of reception and the trick is to do whatever is necessary to increase one's power of perception.

Rimbaud wrote in a letter that "the poet is truly the thief of fire." What a truly diabolic idea! Prometheus, risking his life to travel to Olympus to bring fire back to benefit mankind. The poet risking his neck to travel to the unknown to benefit the consciousness of fellow man. To risk death in order to achieve immortality. The ultimate gamble. All or nothing. Rimbaud writes:

"Let him die as he leaps through unheard of and unnameable things. . . . At least he has seen as he reaches the unknown."

One of the few verifiable, documented accounts we have of the leaps and sprints Rimbaud might have made in that direction is his experiences with hashish as reported by Delahaye, an old friend, who arrived one Paris morning (after the young poet moved into the city) to find Rimbaud sleeping off the effects of an evening spent smoking hashish. The only visions it induced, the poet reported were "some white moons, some black moons, that were chasing each other." This is unlike the hallucinations of opium, a classic description of which includes space—vistas of boundless oceans, exotic landscapes, even faery seas forlorn—coupled with "brilliant colors like cascading jewels, brightly illuminated scenes with elaborate buildings ornately decorated and the like." (*Opium and the Romantic Imagination*)

Picasso's interpretation of Arthur Rimbaud. Rimbaud advocated "derangement of all the senses, all forms of love, suffering, and madness." One of France's greatest poets, he was published at fifteen, had quit writing at nineteen, and was dead at thirty-seven.

Hashish was rather an expensive indulgence at the time and Verlaine and Rimbaud could only afford it infrequently. By contrast, absinthe could be had for fifteen to twenty cents a shot in the sort of cafes Rimbaud frequented. It was *the* fashionable drink of the decade and it remained popular until its manufacture was declared illegal in 1915. "Long live the academy of absinthe," Rimbaud wrote in a letter regarding his drink of favor, "the most delicate, the most tremulous of garments—this drunkenness induced by virtue of that sage of the glaciers, absinthe." Even young Rimbaud though was only too aware of the cost such a blissful encounter would extract: "In order to recline in shit afterwards." Rimbaud and Verlaine weren't the only artists of the time affected by the liquor. Manet made an etching of the solitary brooding figure with an empty bottle at his feet in 1862. Degas' painting of a seedy couple drinking absinthe in a cafe dated from 1876. Picasso painted absinthe drinkers several times; he painted the poet Cornuty drinking absinthe, and a set of six absinthe glasses from 1914.

Picasso told writer-designer-artist-filmmaker Jean Cocteau, an addict to opiates, "I think opium is the least stupid smell in the world." Cocteau, in one of his diaries writes, "Except for the wheel what else has man discovered? It's only a shame we cannot make use of it as freely." (From *Diary of an Unknown*.)

Initially a drink for the lower classes, by the 1860s, absinthe became a favorite of the writing and drinking class. There was only one problem, the liquor was making people, literally, insane. Actually, the problem lay not with the alcohol content (as high as 80 percent) but with the wormwood. Regarding one of the most influential elements on writing of all time, it has been written, "When given in moderate doses, it promotes the appetite and digestion, quickens the circulation, and imparts to the whole system a strengthening influence." (W. Beard from *The Family Physician*.)

The writer goes on to tell us that wormwood has a long tradition of being used medicinally, successfully, as a stimulant with tonic properties. And then he cuts to the chase:

You seem to lose your feet and you mount a boundless realm without horizon. You probably imagine that you are going in the direction of the infinite, whereas you are simply drifting into the incoherent. Absinthe affects the brain uniquely, unlike any other stimulant; it produces neither the heavy drunkenness of beer, the furious inebriation of brandy, nor the exhilirating intoxication of wine. It is an ignoble poison, destroying life not until it has more or less brutalized its votaries, and made driveling idiots of them.

Despite such widespread knowledge, absinthe continued to enjoy immense popularity. Writers, artists, and musicians in particular believed that "the liquor renewed and increased activity to the brain, developed new worlds of ideas, expanded consciousness and therapy inspired noble works of the imagination in literature and art." And, it might be interesting to note, to top the tonic's public relations value quite nicely, absinthe was also believed to possess aphrodisiacal properties. (Enid Starkey from *Baudelaire: A Biography.*)

There is no doubt that Rimbaud and Verlaine were frequent, if not habitual, imbibers. Nearly every account of their time spent together describes them as drinking night after night, until they staggered home intoxicated.

But Rimbaud was fascinated with the idea of intoxication even before he moved to Paris and met Verlaine. His most blatant comments to be found on his alcoholic life are to be found in *Illuminations*. At one point, he bursts forth, almost as though in song:

> Terrible fanfare of music where I never lose step! Magical rack! . . . This poison will still be in my veins even when the fanfare dies away . . . [I]t ended with a riot of perfumes. . . . Brief night of intoxication, holy night! Even if it was only for the mask you bequeathed to us . . . I believed in that poison. I can give you all of my existence each day. Behold the time of the ASSASSINS.

Already Rimbaud is acquainted with both the pleasure and the horrors of intoxication. That *assassins* is derived from *haschischins* was most likely known to both Rimbaud and

Baudelaire and most probably both were also familiar with Hassan I. Sabbah (a.k.a. The Old Man of the Mountain) and the maxim he coined: "Nothing is true/Everything is permitted."

Besides Rimbaud and Baudelaire, the story of this "Old Man of the Mountain" has captured the imagination of almost everybody who has heard it, most notably Patti Smith, Jim Carroll, and William Burroughs. Not only does the story speak directly to the rock 'n' roll mentality, but it also offers a powerful undercurrent appealing to our subconscious fascinations and our archetypal needs concerning drugs, initiation, violence, and charismatic negative heroes.

As Marco Polo told the tale, Hassan Sabbah, a very powerful man, notorious as the Old Man of the Mountain, had at his mountaintop fortress the most beautiful gardens in the world. There were crystal streams that flowed with milk, honey, and wine and the most beautiful young women one could imagine danced and sang in the fragrant meadows surrounding the grounds. They granted, with innocence and devotion, their favors to the lucky few who gained entrance to the palace. The sound of harps filled the air—all was enchantment and magical pleasure. Every now and then, the Old Man of the Mountain would instruct one of his minions to go out and find a certain young boy among the neighboring villages to whom would be given a mysterious alcoholic drink containing opium and hashish. When the lad would lose his senses, he would be carried into the gardens. When he would awaken, he would be convinced that he had ended up in paradise, where the only law was "Nothing is true—everything is permitted." He was encouraged to partake of the joys. From time to time, the old man would have someone from his court give the boy the liquid again, but this time he would have him taken into the palace. Upon awaking in the court, the young victim would be ordered to kill someone for the old man. The killer was assured that if he succeeded he would be brought back to the garden paradise where he could perpetually enjoy the delight he had tasted. If he was killed in the attempt, he would obtain more or less the same results, according to the Koran. So intense was the desire to be readmitted into this garden (of Allah) the executions were carried out most readily and efficiently.

Those who belonged to this sect were called Hashshashin, a term which in Arabic means "hashish people" and is transliterated as "assassins."

Writing on the aesthetics of Rimbaud's intoxication, Enid Rhodes Peschel tells us, "After the paradise comes the fall. The beauty of his brilliant but evanescent visions is based on the continual conflict between warring contraries; strength and weakness, sanctification and damnation, hope and despair, pride and shame, self-glorification and condemnation. The intoxication and intoxicating quest for beauty necessarily implies love, power, and poetry as well as the antithetical grandeur of madness and defeat." And like Lucifer, and so many of the other addicted artists, his fall was of his own devising. (E.R. Peschel from *Flux and Reflux: Ambivalence in the Poems of Arthur Rimbaud*.)

Baudelaire ends "La Chambre Double" with the warning, "He who makes use of a poison in order to think may soon not be able to think without the poison. Think of the frightful state of a man whose paralyzed imagination can no longer work without the help of hashish or opium." On the one hand it gives the illusion of freedom and contentment, and on the other hand it enslaves and traps.

He could have been describing Samuel Taylor Coleridge, who for years denied his reliance on opium. Even when he finally acknowledged it, he still insisted the drug was used only medicinally.

At the age of thirty-four, Coleridge sought medical assistance in breaking his habit. His once-pleasant opium reveries, which were credited with inspiring his most famous work of verse, "The Rime of the Ancient Mariner," and which was believed to influence dozens of other poems as well, had turned sour. Once comforting and idyllic, he noted with great agitation, the visions were now becoming increasingly difficult to manage: again and again they veered toward images which, instead of giving pleasure, brought distress. Distress meant an opium jag; opium meant further neglect of work and more domestic fighting; this brought anxiety and guilt;

anxiety and guilt in turn brought more opium; more opium spelled illness; and so the "tragic carousel revolved and, in time, evolved into a spiral of overwhelming and complete disaster." In his notebook, he confides, "I dare not stop for I cannot stop; I cannot, for I dare not."

Another Coleridge poem "Kubla Khan" evokes the dreamy qualities, music and magic, fantasy and dream, as enchanting a creation ever to have surfaced on the opiate-induced sea of veritable reverie: "In Xanadu did Kubla Khan/A stately pleasure-dome decree/Where Alph, the sacred river, ran/Through caverns measureless to man/Down to a sunless sea ...."

But where "Kubla Khan" evokes an image of the tranquil fantastic, another, less well-known poem, was delivered at the same time to the same publisher: "The Pains of Sleep." It is almost a clinical description of what happens to the junkie when the "honeymoon turns sour and horror takes the place of delight": (Molly Lefebure from *Samuel Taylor Coleridge/ Bondage to Opium*)

> ... yester-night I prayed aloud
> In anguish and in agony,
> Up-starting from the fiendish crowd
> Of shapes and thoughts that tortured me:
> A lyric light, a trampling throng,
> Sense of intolerable wrong ...
> Desire with loathing strongly mixed
> On wild and hateful objects fixed.
> Fantastic passions! Maddening brawl!
> And shame and terror overall!
>
> (from *The Portable Coleridge* edited by A. A. Richards)

Guns N' Roses' honeymoon with chemicals was already in progress when the band signed with Geffen in March 1986. It continued through the recording of *Appetite* and into their first few tours. By May 1988, Axl was beginning to manifest physical signs that his honeymoon with drugs and alcohol was nearing its end. He was plagued with throat problems due to polyps in his throat, presumably caused by his drinking and drugging. When cocaine and alcohol are mixed, the throat and vocal cords are numbed, making it easy to abuse and overuse them. Axl was sent off to recover because, as Slash put it, "We didn't want to fuck up the Aerosmith tour."

Slash, meanwhile, had already begun demonstrating signs that his creative use of drugs was turning against him. During the previous tour with Mötley Crüe, the band's unruly behavior prompted second thoughts from headliner and promoter alike. There was an incident at the Doubletree Hotel in Dallas where Slash "got really drunk and destroyed a room. They had the cops after us." Because of some fast talking by the group's tough and capable yet even-tempered and shrewd road manager, Doug Goldstein, serious consequences were avoided. For the time being, "Our attitude epitomizes what rock 'n' roll is all about," says Slash. "At least, what *I* think rock 'n' roll is all about, which is all that matters. You know how some bands go out and the whole thing is completely wrong but they can put on a good show anyway? We're not like that."

In Atlanta, Axl jumped from the stage to grab a security guard who had manhandled a friend of his without provocation. The police restrained Axl backstage while the band played "Communication Breakdown," and "Honky Tonk Woman" with a roadie singing lead. To avoid a trial, Axl pleaded guilty to assaulting the police and paid a fine.

In Philadelphia, just minutes before a concert was scheduled to begin, Axl got into a fight with a parking lot attendant who, according to Axl, shoved Stuart (a.k.a. S.C. Bailey), Axl's younger half-brother and personal assistant. Once again, Doug Goldstein used enough charm to persuade the cops to release Axl in time for the show and before a riot began.

In Saratoga Springs, New York, a local paper printed "Police and security guards are calling it a night they won't soon forget." "There was nearly a riot," Izzy says, "I get off on that, where everything's just about ready to crack. When there's twenty-five thousand people and they have, like, three unprepared security guards. It's intense. It was just on that fucking edge." When fans began springing onstage, the band bailed out. Then three nights later, in Weedsport, New York, the guys topped that with a show Axl describes as "just, like, psycho." This from a guy who's idea of normal is seventy-five degrees left of center. In Hamburg, Germany, Izzy and Duff beat up the drummer in Faster Pussycat, Mark Michaels, bound him with duct tape, and tossed him in an elevator.

In Chicago, the band members got hassled when they tried to check into their hotel early. A fight was narrowly averted. Later that same night in the hotel bar, Axl punched a businessman who hassled his friend and called the singer a "Bon Jovi look-alike," an insult that apparently, and some might say justifiably, set off Axl. Dozens of cops were called in to break up the brawl, and Axl and Steven went to jail. Afterward, Goldstein found Slash drunk in the bar, threw the guitarist over his shoulder and carried him back to his hotel room. To show his thanks, Slash peed on his shoulder.

One of the more popular stories in Guns N' Roses abuse lore is how Rick Nielsen of Cheap Trick extended an invitation to the Gunners to meet up at his house after which he promptly challenged the hard-drinking Slash to a drinking contest. Incentive duly issued, Slash rose to the occasion as Nielsen fell down. The story ends with Rick drunkenly assaulting the whole band and Izzy kicking Nielsen in the balls.

An unrepentent Izzy shrugged "I didn't kick him hard."

For the record, Nielsen only agrees to the part about inviting them up to his pad but denies he fought with Izzy, insisting it was Slash with whom he fought, further asserting that he (Nielsen) didn't get hurt but Slash did. Then again, maybe he was too drunk to remember.

The repercussions were now getting serious and couldn't be avoided. As the rumor mill was busily predicting an imminent early demise of the still-young band attributable to a rather amazing array of drug- and alcohol-oriented misfortunes, Guns N' Roses were abruptly informed that they were dropped from the upcoming David Lee Roth tour, in the wake of an aborted show that resulted from a misunderstanding between Axl and the rest of the band in Phoenix, Arizona, when an angry Axl had bluffed that he wasn't going to appear at that evening's concert. Taking him at his word, the band didn't show and a surprised Axl showed up to sing with no one else around. Assuming Guns N' Roses were undependable and maybe not even together any longer, Roth's organization began looking for a replacement band.

Still without substantial airplay on either radio or MTV, a tour cancellation was the worst sort of news. Then a proposed AC/DC tour also fell through when AC/DC, despite a mutual fondness between them and the Gunners, were incapable of offering adequate financial incentive. It appeared the band was as charmed as it was disaster-prone.

"The press really jumped on the tour stories," Slash said, "but the fact is that each time we lost a tour, we ended up with a better one. We were able to tour with bands like Mötley Crüe and Aerosmith and Alice Cooper which was a dream come true for us."

Although the band finally landed a slot with Alice Cooper, their problems were far from over. In fact, Axl didn't even make it to the first date. A management associate of Cooper's remembers being distinctly impressed with the amount of drugs and alcohol all the band members consumed. What impressed this person the most, however, was that no matter how wasted they became no member ever missed a show after that first Santa Barbara gig. Other than that, and one or two minor hassles by comparison, the tour went surprisingly smoothly. So smoothly in fact that Alice and Guns N' Roses collaborated on the Cooper classic "Under My Wheels" for the soundtrack to Penelope Spheeris' *The Decline of Western Civilization: The Metal Years*. "They behaved like complete professionals," the associate says today. "Not one trashed hotel room."

Today, Slash remembers, "After the Mötley Crüe tour was over, we went out with Alice Cooper 'cause we didn't want to go home. Then Steven broke his hand." The break was the result of an incident when an angry Steve, punched out a streetlight. While his hand healed, Cinderella drummer Fred Coury completed Steve's tour obligations. It was only the first of several occasions where chemical abuse would be directly responsible for removing Steve Adler from active duty—despite his declaration that nothing meant more than the band to him, presumably including drugs, specifically, cocaine and alcohol. But addiction is nothing if not cunning and Steve continued his indulgence apace, in spite of the repercussions. His indulgences ultimately took him out of the band for good.

On the subsequent Iron Maiden tour, Guns N' Roses further managed to enhance their reputation for unpredictable behavior when Duff left the tour. Reportedly he couldn't dampen an irresistible urge to get hitched to his girlfriend, Mandy Brixx, a Japanese restaurant hostess and singer for the L.A. band, the Lame Flames.

Actually, this just serves to further underscore how an image once consciously cultivated by the band of bad boys has by now taken on a disturbing life of its own. The assumption was Duff had been drunk and irresponsible when in reality Mandy had been planning the ceremony for quite a few weeks and Duff was well aware of the date. When the band's tour routing couldn't be booked around the wedding, the band worked around Duff employing former Zodiac Mindwarp and ex-Cult bassist Haggis as a one-gig replacement.

Even their dream tour with the newly clean 'n' sober Aerosmith, personal heroes to the Gunners, was not without its problems. Aerosmith wasn't about to take any unnecessary chances. Having spent millions of dollars to put members of that band through detox twice, three, sometimes four times, Aerosmith management added a rider to the contract: Guns N' Roses had to confine their drinking to their dressing room.

But, at the tour's end, the two bands would jam triumphantly on Aerosmith's "Ma Ma Kin," which would soon appear in a different form on Guns N' Roses' forthcoming EP. At the beginning of the Aerosmith tour, Guns N' Roses agreed to leave the arena soon after their sets so they wouldn't tempt Aerosmith. Members of the two bands had met some years before on somewhat more equal terms: "Our guys were selling drugs to their guys," Slash reminds us.

At the end of their Fall 1988 tour, Rose told *Rolling Stone* writer Rob Tannenbaum: "Our drug use is not in the past. We scare the shit out of each other."

Then the boys in the band were free to go to their new homes and enjoy independence for the first time in their lives via their new-found fame and wealth, and that's when the real trouble started. Suffice it to say, the end of touring did not mean an end to their chemically induced destructive behavior. As Keith Richards once offered in defense of his then-continuing engagment with heroin, when the intensive, exhilarating high of performing live for six months at a time comes to an abrupt halt, then the boredom is unbearable. It is a lesson Izzy learned quickly. "Touring is more addicting than any drug I could imagine. It's fucking terrible coming off the road. You come down real hard. It's like the world stops moving." After the tour, Areosmith manager Tim Collins was prompted to comment that "Guns N' Roses need to do about another two million dollars' worth of drugs before they're ready to clean up." Speaking from experience, Collins saw only too clearly exactly where this young band was at —only the end of the honeymoon period. There was still a long way down for the band to go before hitting bottom, which needs to be hit before a sojourn back up into health and sanity can begin. Before one can become well, there still is one more obstacle to overcome: the abyss, the trapdoor at the bottom, the one that leads all the way down, to the pit, to Dante's inferno. What would save the band, except for one member, was their music, which meant more to them than drugs—albeit just barely.

Hypersensitive and easily bored to begin with, Slash felt the displacement from road to stationary life acutely:

"Being on the road, doing that every day and having no other life. . . . And then there is a pace to that, which is kind of exciting. Then all of a sudden, BAM! That life comes to a screaming halt. You don't have your crew guys, the maid doesn't come in, you're laying in bed waiting for the gig to happen, for *something* to happen . . . and it's not going to happen."

"But there was no other life for us to come back to. We'd never had any other life. And now we're all separated—we have our own little places that we never had before. I remember a point where I was just sitting in bed bored and uninterested in anything. You hear one of the guys in your band on the answering machine and you don't even pick up the phone."

Sitting around his unfamiliar new house with no distractions, worse, a self-proclaimed workaholic with no work to do, was not an ideal setting.

"As pathetic as this may sound," Slash confessed, "my personal life and existence has nothing to do with anything beyond the band and being a player. I'm very single-minded. All I do is music, or else I do something—entirely different." In a word, drugs.

Slash eloquently put Steven's worsening condition into perspective when he told *Rolling Stone*, "All he lived for was sex, drugs, and rock 'n' roll. In that order. Then it was drugs, sex, and rock 'n' roll. Then it was drugs and rock 'n' roll. Then it was just drugs."

F. Scott Fitzgerald coined the famous quote, "in the life of American writers there are no second acts." And as an alcoholic and a writer, he knew well of what he spoke. Alcoholism nor drug addiction is capable of sustaining creativity. In the end, it saps the creative reservoir dry, rendering any second acts impossible.

Eugene O'Neill stands alone among the American writers: he was able to stop his addictive habit, endure the ensuing "dark night of the soul," and crank his experiences into an artistic mea culpa: *The Iceman Cometh* and *Long Day's Journey into Night*. A few rockers have attempted this, such as John Hiatt, but no one of Guns N' Roses' stature or standing has yet to pull it off with any authority, poise, or insight.

The use of drugs (which may not heal but can anesthetize) sometimes serves as an alternative to suicide. The tortured artist; the wounded soul; the sensitive poet who feels life too intensely to bear living it. The one with his skin on inside out. The pantheon is extensive. The romantic hero as a butterfly soon broken on the wheel of life. Chatterton is beautiful in suicide, Shelley erotic in untimely death. Romanticism and rock share protocols for heroism of excess. Jim Morrison, Janis Joplin, Brian Jones, Jimi Hendrix, and now Axl Rose we have claimed for our own mythic heroes. Their emotions and behavior have broken out of the so-called prescribed limits and in doing so indicated our own potential. With their profound sensitivity we identify to the point of sympathy. They make *us* feel alive. Their hypervulnerability is both a blessing and a curse, enabling them to express insights and feelings that the outside world is otherwise too busy or insensitive to experience. Yet, this same (dis)ability also makes them overly, uncomfortably sensitive to pain. Through osmosis, these types pick up other peoples' unconscious garbage, in addition to amplifying their own. When the load becomes too heavy, they escape into chemicals. Perhaps drug use among the creative is not notable for its inspirational qualities, but simply its painkilling properties, which then enable the person to more clearly see what is truly there. When one is in pain, after all, relief is as great as pleasure is to one who was not in pain to begin with.

"You see," Truman Capote once said, "I was so different from everyone, so much more intelligent and sensitive and perceptive. I was having fifty perceptions a minute to everyone else's five. I always felt that nobody was going to understand me, going to understand what I felt about things. I guess that is why I started writing."

Kafka supports this point of view as well: "In fact the poet is always much smaller and weaker than the social average. Therefore, he feels the burden of earthly existence much more intensely and strongly than other men. For him personally, his song is only a scream. Art for the artist is only suffering, through which he releases himself for further suffering." (Gustav Janouch from *Conversations with Kafka*)

Early in his career, Carl Jung believed that behind the free will of the poet-artist type there lay a higher force that was capable of producing psychic complications of dramatic proportions. In fact, he believed that the creative urge is so "imperious that it battens on their humanity and yokes everything to the service of the work, even at the cost of health and ordinary human happiness." The unborn work in the psyche of the artist was, Jung concluded, a force of nature that achieved its desired end either with tyrannical might or subtle cunning, "quite regardless of the personal fate of the man who is its vehicle."

Accordingly, when the conscious desire of the poet is at

Axl, with grace and power, breaking out of the prescribed limits. *(Courtesy Larry Busacca/Retna Ltd.)*

odds with this power, the impending psychic fracture can be disastrous, a process unto itself that in the end will only serve to further the wants of the creative daimon. Playing host to such potentially inhospitable and conflicting powers can prove to be a most unpleasant experience.

Dr. Alfred Ribi, in his book *The Demons of the Inner World*, addresses the creative power, ambivalent in terms of good and evil: "The compulsion or urge to create is the fate-fraught *daimon* of some creative people. It can entirely determine the life of its bearer—and destroy it. Many creative people die young, as though their demon had burned them out ... many ... are torn apart by it when they are not able to follow it's urgings."

The *daimon* is that power that drives a man on in his actions and, thus, entangles him with his destiny.

There are certain psychiatric clinical traits a majority of these addict/alcoholic artists all share: most are thought today to have been manic-depressive, or at least prone to depression more than the ordinary person. Most if not all could be described as having "oral" personalities. Many suffered from insomnia, more complained of hypersensitivity—the same gift that enabled them to create made them painfully vulnerable to the world. Almost all, at one time or another, have explained their indulgent behavior as not excessive, but rather as required self-medication. Something wrong is being righted. Not the other way around.

The ancient Greeks believed that creativity and insanity were related. As early as 1913, *The Pennsylvania Medical Journal* published a piece written by a doctor with ample experience with addicts and noted several distinct categories. The first type could easily describe any of the members of Guns N' Roses. "His nerve endowment is not quite sufficient to enable him to live from day to day comfortably and effectively. He will, therefore, desperately grasp at whatever seems to aid his own inadequate efforts. When drugs come his way, with their seeming power to increase energy, or to bring peace and order to his turbulent, chaotic, harassed existence, it is inevitable that he shall anchor himself by their use."

In addition to these individuals, there is still another type. (Neither of these, it should be pointed out, is necessarily inclined to criminal acts or to irresponsible morality.) This type includes individuals much like Axl Rose who seem especially prone to narcotic abuse. This class of person, known as cyclothymic, possesses a peculiar emotional instability which manifests itself in periods of depression alternating with periods of elation. To the casual observer they may appear difficult, erratic, but if we look deeper we find people of immense and exceptional talent—borderline cases showing manic-depressive characteristics.

The Israeli psychologist and author, Erich Neumann, one of Jung's most gifted students, delves deeply into the characteristics inherent in the creative personality. It is important to consider this type in depth here because Axl Rose, as songwriter and vision head for Guns N' Roses, personifies this type, a classically diagnosed manic-depressive who veers from the lowest lows of depression to the highest peaks of joy in a matter of minutes with little time spent on an even emotional keel.

A heightened emotional reaction is one of the most marked, clearly evident characteristics of the creative type. It is this sensitivity which burdens the neurotic, becomes suppressed and finds a bastardized outlet; whereas in the artist temperament, it is experienced and then expressed back outward into art, where other, less sensitive types may be united with their own sensitive nature as a result, achieving what Erich Neumann goes on to call "The Great Experience"—that place where art, artist, and audience meet.

"The great experience of art can lift us beyond the limitations of our egos into that freedom of the self," Neumann asserts, next quoting Kafka's testimony about the world of the Trial: "It receives you when you come and it relinquishes you when you go." Through the art produced in a heightened state of sensitivity, the viewer connects with his own peculiarly human vulnerability and, voilà! is immediately connected with the rest of the humanity and the universal condition.

Yet side by side with this numinous magnificence, there also exists a dimension of uncanniness and sheer horror, which treads the world beneath its feet with the deadly momentum of the dancing Shiva:

> The realm of the daemonic, of malicious sorcery and enchantment, of the morbidly grotesque, the perverse and the bizzare, lives out its spectral life cheek by jowl with the windows and gates of the dwelling place of our consciousness, it is the primordial serpent at the bottom of the sea that girdles our world, creeps up the sky as the dark moon, and brings with it unrest and despair, torment and hopelessness, mental aberration and madness. In the hell of Hieronymus Bosch, the instruments that in Paradise resounded with songs of praise are transformed by a frightful inversion, into instruments of torment. [Erich Neumann from *The Place of Creation*]

The artist avails himself to this darkness as well as the light, and the brave artist swims in the same water the personality of the psychotic drowns. Axl Rose seems to acknowledge this wisdom. If reports and my own eyewitness accounts can be trusted, Axl Rose has been relatively drug-free for almost a year now, as the band begins recording its third release. When he was still drinking and using, he spoke to an on-the-road reporter who asked him, "Are you a manic-depressive?"

"Yes," Axl answered.

> I took a test in Chicago and the doctors prescribed me lithium. Lithium hasn't done one damn thing for me except it's made people think that Axl's trying to do something to help himself, so this must be a good thing. In other words, if I trash my hotel room it's accepted more as long as I'm taking lithium. If I wasn't taking my lithium and I do the same damage 'cause I'm pissed about the same thing, it would be said, "He's not taking his lithium, that's why it's happening." Then I'm fucking up. It pays off for everybody to think Axl's doing good and taking his fucking lithium. I don't feel anything with or without it. I can say though, "Look, I'm taking my Lithium" and it makes things easier.

Axl with friendly advice. *(Courtesy Kevin Mazur/London Features International)*

It's tempting to think for a moment here that Axl isn't what he's been diagnosed, specifically the manic-depressive, creative type. It's not unusual for someone taking lithium to believe that nothing is happening, to report feeling no results from the medication. This is especially true of one who isn't taking it regularly. To be effective, lithium must be maintained at a prescribed level in the bloodstream. When it is combined with other drugs, such as cocaine or alcohol, the effects will not be perhaps as noticeable as without added chemicals. Manic-depression can cause people to swing from being impulsive, reckless, and argumentative to being severely depressed, even suicidal.

Axl eliminates any doubt about the manic-depressive tag when he adds: "I get more serious about things . . . I can be happier than anybody I know, too. I can get so happy, I'll cry. I can get completely opposite, upset-wise. I like to be upset, in a way, because it lets me know I can feel. I think sometimes too much, not all the time. I'm pretty good at controlling it. When I'm bored, that when I get depressed."

A *Rolling Stone* reporter wrote, "Axl is so sensitive and so erratic that even the other members of the band are awed by—and maybe tired of—his mood swings. He travels on a separate tour bus, not only because he stays up at night and sleeps during the day, but also to reduce friction with the other band members."

"Axl's a real temperamental guy," Slash says, adding with characteristic understatement, "he's been known to be difficult to get along with."

If Axl isn't getting loaded these days, which appears to be the case, then it must be frighteningly difficult for him to be at the mercy of the seizurelike mood swings without medicating himself.

"I don't care what hell I have to go through," Axl once said, "if I can get a song out of it, then it's worth it." More recently Axl has taken it to a higher level of awareness when he said: "There's a time and a place to feel your pain and own it and there's a time to let it go. Postponing or suppressing it will only bring you down. The question becomes how far down do you want to go."

Axl mentioned the movie *Frances* and the habit psychiatry has of mistaking passion for imbalance. "Did you ever see that movie, *Frances*? I think about that *a lot.* I wonder if one of these days someone is gonna slide the knife underneath my eye and give me the lobotomy?" It is revealing that Axl invokes the Frances Farmer legend at all. That he apparently identifies with it is obvious, though, and not really all that surprising. *Frances* was based on the life of screen legend Frances Farmer, as revealed in her heartbreaking autobiography, *Will There Really Be a Morning?*, which in an achingly forthright manner chronicles her descent from a vivacious, intelligent, and sensual presence, too sensitive and stubborn for her own good, into a defiant, tortured victim of both the impersonal Hollywood star-making machinery and the harsh consequences of an impervious legal system that recognizes alcoholism and its behavioral consequences as not a disease but rather as a crime punishable by law.

With a terrifying force of forward momentum, Frances Farmer inexorably slid from arrest to unemployment to ostracism into jail and on to the sanitarium, under the custody of a selfish celebrity-hungry mother who, if she couldn't persuade Frances to return to the scene, would rather see her daughter in a snake pit of an insane asylum, which ultimately and tragically resulted in a lobotomy.

The way the story unfolds, through Frances's eyes, is perfectly sympathetic to the subject, whose motives are both understandable and right, as defined and dictated by her own moral turns of heart. In trying desperately to be true to her highly sensitive (yet volatile) nature, she confronts a system, and in doing so sets in motion a series of events that seem to increase in their oppressive nature, according to the force with which she resists.

The story epitomizes the Hollywood tragedy, but it also is a frighteningly real prolonged glimpse of a "third alternative." This is what can happen if you don't die young and you don't dramatically change your ways. It's not surprising that Axl would be both drawn to and mortified by the story. Axl's sympathy with the story provides a valuable insight into how he sees himself in relation to the outside world.

He reflects on one of his teenage encounters with a therapist: "When I was in Indiana, one of the things I had to do was go to see a psychiatrist. I had to go see this lady a few times because as a juvenile delinquent they just automatically put you in this program. I had always gotten lousy grades in school, but then this lady makes the discovery that I'm at the top three percent of my class."

He seems to be thinking, how do I know whether I'm okay, not okay, too smart for my own good, or just basically cracked? Axl continues talking, identifying himself as a class-one underachiever. "After going to her for a couple of months she called me a 'Type B' person, meaning I function best if I have anywhere from eight to fourteen hours' sleep, and my most creative hours are between one and three in the morning, which I already knew." The psychiatrist while noting his high IQ concluded that his difficult behavior was surely indicative of manic-depression.

Yet as capable of unpredictable outbursts of anger and violence as he is, he is also capable of being soft-spoken, disarmingly sincere, even angelic. The same Axl Rose that likes Metallica and Faith No More also spends hours listening to Joni Mitchell, Elton John, and Philip Glass. His bandmates readily acknowledge his split nature. "He does a lot of weird shit no one understands," Slash has said, "but I love the guy. I mean he's also a real sweetheart."

"Yeah," Izzy agrees, "he can be a total tyrant and then turn around and be the nicest guy in the world."

Even Vicky Hamilton, after the unfriendly split, said of Axl, "There's times when he's the sweetest boy in the world, but when he gets mad, he's off like a spinning top—he's not consistently evil," she said, laughing, "and he's not consistently nice either. It's like two separate and distinct personalities.... That's what's so scary."

DRUGS
MUSIC

AND

Drugs first became inextricably linked with music
during America's jazz era in the 1920s: grass,
cocaine—but mainly heroin was tailor-made for inducing a
sense of emotional distance, which is a central tenet of the
hipster ethic. Heroin is the most effective physical painkiller
ever developed, stronger than morphine by ten times and a
hundred times more potent than Demerol. The feelings are
not euphoric or high in the usual sense, but contentment,
cool and detached; many users liken its effect to being
wrapped in a large ball of cotton.

If heroin symbolized for black musicians the flight from
white society, for white musicians it symbolized the flight
toward black society. White musicians wanted to belong,
wanted to become black as black, black as night, or in Norman
Mailer's terminology, "white negroes." Their self-conscious
aim was to "live with death as an immediate danger, to divorce oneself from society, to exist without roots, to set out

on that uncharted journey into the rebellious imperatives of the self." Which, as Harry Shapiro points out in his book *Waiting for the Man*, is as fair a description of the heroin experience as you're likely to get and imparts part of the reason why many white musicians took up heroin—as the ultimate expression of being hip.

Musicians, even in the jazz days, had a myriad of problems, personal and professional. Traveling on the road put unbearable strain on relationships. There were managers, promoters, agents, and record companies of questionable integrity to deal with; hostile or inattentive audiences; ego clashes within the band; uncertainty regarding future work; fluctuations in popularity; bad reviews; the glare of the spotlight. For those musicians who found all this too much to handle, heroin provided a reasonable solution. Rather than having to deal with several problems, one problem—maintaining the habit—took over. As one jazz musician put it, heroin just seemed to help in a bad time.

The idea of heroin as a means of collapsing several problems into one became an active chimera. It didn't get in the way of work, either, unless a musician was out searching for a fix. No musician could play blind drunk, but plenty played while stoned on heroin. For every Charlie Parker wanna-be, who believed that to have a habit would enable him to play like the sax master, there were hundreds who fell resoundingly into failure. What they failed to comprehend was the Bird played well on heroin because he was dependent on it, that was the only time he felt well enough to play normally—i.e., better than anyone else. He wasn't playing better because of heroin; he was playing normally because he didn't feel sick.

Nobody on heroin ever gets the flu, coughs, or colds—the nasal membranes are dried out. That's why you get codeine in cough suppressants. Many musicians eventually discovered they had a heroin habit instead of the flu. In addition, heroin was the perfect solution among those indulging in compulsive behavior—instant gratification. Heroin solved the anxieties of being, or not being enough in the public eye. Some musicians went for the instant gratification of the needle when they realized they were not going to be superstars overnight. Fear of failure was made bearable; the opposite dilemma, fear of success among the well-to-do, was also made tolerable. The superstar doesn't know how he got from where he was to where he is; and he certainly, therefore, doesn't think he can stay there; and usually doesn't think he deserves his success in any event.

What heroin was to the jazz age, acid and grass were to the sixties' musical and cultural explosion. The sixties were more than just a party though; they were also a tumultuous time for self-exploration and discovery, an era marked forever by its sense of celebration and experimentation as reflected not by merely its music but by the chemicals it indulged in as well. The seventies boiled down to two things: work time and bedtime, money and effective escape. It was only fitting then that one of the primary drugs of choice was Quaalude, which is basically a sleeping pill. The music of the seventies appealed to the cultural palate and was just as much a downer. Using drugs wasn't merely recreational anymore, or exploratory; it was mandatory. There was nothing else *to* do. The seventies were a bore. You slept through them or you went to work, which is how and when cocaine became the other preferable drug of use. People didn't want their consciousness expanded; they wanted their consciousness constricted.

In the eighties, an interesting rupture occurred within the musical community, splintering the drug phenomenon—it suddenly became bad news to do drugs. People either stopped doing drugs altogether or else, just as often, they simply hid their habits and went underground. That is until Guns N' Roses came along. Van Halen and Mötley Crüe may have hyped the hedonistic image, but no one really takes them seriously. Guns N' Roses celebrated the live fast, die young edict, and plainly lived it.

When Axl raged at his band in front of that Coliseum audience of 80,000 in October 1989, he was taking a stand that cut to the core of what was not only his band's problem, but the music scene that spawned them. Everyone in the music industry flinched, and those that didn't were still shocked.

After all, Mick Jagger had never confronted Keith Richards onstage about his heroin habit.

Axl's remark just indicated the tip of the iceberg. *Spin* magazine was interested to the extent of sending a New York writer out to L.A. to cover the smack scene from which Guns N' Roses emerged and, it was becoming clear, were only the most visible exponents. Even if not all members were actual users, there were others, hundreds of others, who wanted to be just like them and who really believed the best and easiest way to do so was to do some heroin. Keith Richards may have finally gotten clean but Izzy and Slash clearly were not. Or at least no one wanted to believe they were.

What these other guys want to be are stars. What they invariably get is a habit. Heroin is a hard drug to do only a little of, as Slash and Izzy themselves soon came to attest. It tends to be an all-or-nothing deal, and eventually most week-end joy-poppers end up either strung out or completely off. The number of people willing to bet against the odds is truly astounding, as the writer from *Spin* discovered. Those in the Los Angeles scene already know 99 percent of the people who take that chance end up closer to the homeless scene than the Guns N' Roses glitter. But they still buy and fix as if in mute defiance of the odds.

No one seems to know or want to admit which came first, the prodigious junk scene among the hard rock musical elite that produced Guns N' Roses (which is not to imply that all the band members were using smack), or Guns N' Roses themselves with the cattlelike parade of imitators following them. The answer probably lies in between. Heroin was gaining in popularity on the L.A. scene ever since the punk explosion back in the early eighties. Smack had been appealing to the decadent antihero image since long before that and the punks tried it. Despite their dedication to trash and level anything older and more established, the punks found they liked it. One of the first punks, Darby Crash of the Germs, died from a heroin OD. Instead of becoming less popular, heroin increased in popularity. It was still gaining when the members of Guns N' Roses coalesced into a band in L.A.

"Heroin was big in L.A. with the punks, in the early eighties;

then it went away for a while, right?" Axl asked one writer. "And then all of a sudden with heavy metal, it was real big again? Well, Izzy brought it back!" Axl laughs, only half-joking.

After they hit the scene, the knowledge that four of them were strung out made the junk ID even more attractive, in a negative sort of way, of course. From the very first, the fans who weren't busy imitating their heros' habits were already

A drunken Slash gives his own special thanks to the attendees of the American Music Awards. "It was a very fine wine," said someone acquainted with the band's predilection for a certain spirit. *(Courtesy Ron Wolfson/ London Features International)*

predicting which member of Guns N' Roses would be the first to die. Hundreds of competing musicians steeped themselves in smack, hoping to achieve the same sort of alchemical transformation from starving unknown to superstar. A few musicians even succeeded, but most only found themselves locked in a cell to which they held no escape key. They wanted to be bad boys, they wanted to be outcasts of society, they wanted to be real in a real street way, they wanted to be boys that good girls wouldn't want to bring home to meet their parents. For all the talk of freedom, an alarming number of music lovers were finding themselves enslaved to the very thing they had once used to deify.

It is easy to get panicked during the sudden avalanche of success, craving stardom while being afraid of it, afraid of being seen as a talentless fraud. It is a dilemma inherent to the music business and has been since the beginning. Fear of failure is the most obvious source of uncertainty and angst and drugs are often used as a sort of self-fulfilling doom prophecy. If the obstacle is overcome, there is still another hurdle. Fear of success is more than matched by fear of declining popularity. However hard it may be to make it to the top, it seems even more impossible to stay there.

Drugs obliterate this conflict. In stopping the pain by concentrating it on the addiction, drugs also eventually stop the flow of the creative juices. This is why you can see the artist using drugs to help him to create, and the drugs working, then using drugs to help deal with the flush of success (or failure) and using drugs to deal with such an instable life, and finally using drugs because it is simply easier to deal with the drug problem than with all the others. Guns N' Roses have stated repeatedly the difficulty they have had handling all the fame and its attendant conflicts.

In the summer of 1990, just before an ill-fated band rendezvous in Chicago, where the band was to be rehearsing songs for their already-late upcoming album, Axl gave an interview. When asked at one point about the still-to-be-recorded album, Axl made a reference to it going okay, then it being hard, then it being okay again, then added, "providing we don't kill each other first."

Minutes later he added, "It took us a long time to get over *Appetite for Destruction*." Later he indicated he still might not quite be over it: "I hope this album's more successful because I just want to bury *Appetite*. I like the album, but I'm sick of it. I don't want to live my life through that one album—I have to bury it."

Then he gave us an idea of what's really going on. "I think we were more unprepared for this gigantic success. The next record's gonna be about trying to deal with everything and stay alive . . ." It seemed as if Axl was saying that success, or a lot of the things that he had to deal with now, were a lot harder than he ever dreamed. Axl continued,

> It can eat you alive. I mean we've, you know, never been able, we've never known about dealing with money or anything like that. Our families didn't have it. We're totally inexperienced with it and now we have to be on top of it. You have to learn the business and there's always someone who's real quick, when you least expect it, with a new plan on how to get your money. So we've been doing business instead of working on songs to try and survive and not lose what we've got, what we've achieved.

In Paris in the spring of 1990, months after the scheduled start date for work on the next album, Izzy was cornered by an English writer and asked, "How are the other members of Guns N' Roses right now?"

Izzy the most press shy band member stammered, "Well, uh . . . Axl is probably the most, uh, physically together of us right now. Slash? I hear he's doing better, ya know. Haven't seen him in three or four weeks, but I hear he's doing better. . . . He seems to realize now that with this new album to be made there's like a . . . uh, time period he has to sustain himself in, right. Which he couldn't do before because of the way he's livin' his life."

The journalist gets more specific: "Hasn't your drummer, Stevie, been in and out of detox clinics in the last year like a proverbial yo-yo?"

Izzy appeared to be unprepared for the directness of the question. "Uh . . . Who? . . . Stevie? Uh . . . when somebody in the band just gets too fucked up, sometimes the manager will just . . . No. No, I mean, yeah, well, Stevie has probably been on several of those missions, yeah."

The interviewer continued his aggressive line of questioning. "Are you currently addicted to drugs?"

Izzy waffles, surprised, then serious, confused, "Uh . . . addiction . . . That's a very heavy word. That depends . . . [long pause]. Do you mean physically or mentally?" Does it matter? Does Izzy know he's just answered the question by avoiding a direct response? The interviewer appears familiar with the cunning junkie mentality and continues the grilling, giving Izzy the question he all but asked for.

"Are you physically addicted to hard drugs?"

Izzy clearly doesn't know how to answer this. He can't say no because that would be a lie, something Izzy, to his credit, is clearly uncomfortable doing, and a negative response would also contradict the very same image the Gunners have worked so hard to establish.

"Listen I can't even . . . I don't . . . I'm okay, y'know. Everyone in the group is okay. I mean everyone's talking about this shit all the time. I mean I never said nothin' about drugs. Everyone has to know their own limits. That's all I wanna say." This last sentence is precisely what Keith Richards used to say when people confronted him about his drug problem.

Izzy goes on in an effort to explain himself and his band at this particular stage of their career: "It's just such a twisted and demented effort for all of us."

When the "undignified" way the press claims they've been handling success is mentioned, Izzy responds, "Fuck them! What do they know? . . . Fuck man, it's not success that's hard to deal with it's . . . uh . . . the other thing." Other thing? What other thing? Presumably the drug problem, which he first appears to blame on success and its problematic nature. Now he denies success is a problem at all, and goes on to tell us that, in fact, neither is "the other thing."

"But, we've got it licked," he continues without ever admitting guilt. "We'll just make this record and then just keep movin', y'know."

For Axl, it was either jail or the psychiatric ward. Or the stage. *(Courtesy Chris Lee Helton/Retna Ltd.)*

In a later interview, Slash would be confronted with the question about what happened in Chicago when the band was supposed to begin the laborious process of working toward the next album. Work did not progress well; in fact, it went miserably. Slash and Duff began drinking heavily from the start and Steve and Izzy turned to their respective drugs of choice. Axl was the only one at the time that didn't seek chemical consolation to cope with the disappointment of failing to come up with any new material. The band fell apart, eventually returning to L.A. to estimate the damage.

At least for one member, the damage continued en route to L.A. via Indiana and during his return flight, a drunken Izzy was arrested for urinating in the plane's kitchen deck, making headlines around the world. Having a first-class ticket, Izzy was first wait-listed and ultimately got bumped back to coach. Apparently to the airline personnel, he looked more like a slovenly undesirable than a rock superstar. Then once airborne, Izzy, drunk and needing to relieve himself, tried to enter the first-class toilet. Airline personnel, however, directed him back to the end of the plane, where a line of people were already waiting in line. With no place to go and a dangerous need to empty his bladder, Izzy looked around and proceeded to pee in the next most private place the plane provided—the kitchen. Later, Izzy admitted that he vaguely remembered saying to himself "uh-oh I think I fucked up," as he deplaned.

Slash would not condemn or judge either his fellow guitarist or singer. Indeed, he really can't. He's not in a position to. He's admittedly pissed in a few unsuitable places as well.

"I don't want to point my finger at Izzy because that's not fair. I had my problems, too. I was drinking way too much. I drank up to a half gallon of vodka a day, easy. I got to the point where I was drinking so much. I would have the shakes so bad the next morning, I would have to drink a fairly tall, stiff vodka and cranberry" just to function.

Recalling the period just before *Appetite* took off Slash had said, "We thought we'd made a record that might do as well as Motorhead. As far as we were concerned, it was totally uncommercial. No one wanted to know about it. Really." Slash comments how weird it is for one day to be living out of duffel bags and then getting off the road, "and the record went through the roof, I mean, that was a major change for everybody, and everybody has their own way of dealing with it. For me, it was to fall into doing a lot of drugs and drinking and just clouding the whole thing over . . ."

Referring to the tour Guns N' Roses did with Alice Cooper after the album was first released, Slash seems to be indicating that he wasn't doing a lot of drugging or drinking on the road, which is not the case. Several members of Alice's entourage reported back that Guns N' Roses were hell-bent on self-destruction through the tried and true way of drugs and alcohol. Alice himself, once an alcoholic and not long off freebase when the tour started, was heard to express his impression that he wouldn't be surprised if any one of these guys finished the tour in a coffin.

Slash continued, "I would spend all my time playing my guitar and getting stoned. For Steven, it was sort of the same, but he likes to party and hang out and have fun more than me. Izzy's sort of similar to me. Axl would find these fantastical situations that only Axl would find. Only Duff's remained rooted to a married, domestic kind of life-style." (Not for long. On April 1, 1990, Duff filed for divorce. On May 1, 1990, Axl was married. On May 15, 1990, Axl filed for divorce. On June 1, 1990, Axl recalled divorce proceedings. In January 1991, the rocky marriage was officially annulled.)

Now we cut to Duff and Slash, who are onstage at the live television broadcast of the American Music Awards in 1990, drunk and swearing. The funny thing is that there was no bar at the Music Awards. When confronted with this bit of information, one of them commented something to the effect, "It's only a little bit of wine," to which the other chimed in, "But it's a very fine wine!"

Initially, Slash tried to kick heroin on his manager's couch. It's no secret that Slash has been in and out of an undisclosed detoxification center in Hawaii to clean up on more than a few occasions. The latest and most lasting detoxification attempt involved self-administered injections of a nonaddictive synthetic painkiller called Buprinex. About a decade ago, there was a minor flurry of press coverage hailing the drug as a heroin detox breakthrough. Then there was nothing. The problem? Some junkies discovered they like the Buprinex as much as heroin.

During the American Music Awards, Slash said "fuck" on

the air—Dick Clark, the host, was upset. So was ABC. Also perturbed was a radio station, which yanked their records off the air for a week, which prompted Kurt Loder of MTV news to comment, "Which goes to show, they can get away with saying words like *faggot* and *nigger* but a common four-letter word is the trick that gets them actually banned from the airwaves." In one of his first cover-story interviews, Axl was given the chance to clear up his reputation as a "heavy drug user." Unlike Izzy who denies and refuses to clarify, only to give himself away inadvertently, or Slash, who, while not ashamed, now prefers to put his problems behind him, Axl shoots straight from the hip.

"I have a different physical constitution and different mind set about drugs than anybody I've known in Hollywood because I don't abstain from doing drugs, but I won't allow myself to have a fucking habit either. I won't allow it." Presumably he's referring to the prevailing wisdom of AA and other twelve-step recovery programs that state one is powerless over drugs and alcohol and as such cannot *ever do anything*, no drug, no drink, no chemical in any amount— "nothing that affects you from the neck up," to be precise. "I'll have done blow for three days and my mind will go 'Fuck no.' I'll have the physical feeling of knowing my body needs it and I just refuse to do coke that day."

"I'm not going to do it, because if I was going to do it, I know I won't be able to hit my goals with what I want to do with this band." Which isn't only honest; it's downright perceptive and self-disciplined to the extreme. "I can't let myself get into coke as much as I'm into the band. The same thing with heroin. I did it for three weeks straight and had one of the greatest times in my life." Again, Axl's honesty— I don't know whether it's bravery or ignorance, but it sure is effective. "I was with this beautiful girl I wanted to be with, in this beautiful apartment, and we just sat there listening to Led Zepplin, doing drugs and fucking. It was great, 'cause at that time I had nothing to do but sit on my ass and make a few phone calls a day. I stopped on Saturday, because I had serious business to attend to on Monday. I felt like shit, sweated, shook, but on Monday, I was able to function."

Toward the end of 1990, Axl is clear-eyed, soft-spoken, and courteous and always professional, whether it's onstage in front of four hundred people at the Whisky performing with former Hanoi Rocks front man Michael Monroe, or in front of a live audience of 17,000 and televised audience of 20 million onstage with the Rolling Stones in Atlantic City. The only thing I ever saw Axl drink was Coca-Cola.

Slash, a rock 'n' roll hybrid of the Mad Hatter and Cousin It. Or maybe just a Marc Bolan clone? *(Courtesy Joe Bangay/London Features International)*

When Axl was in New York in the fall of 1989 with his songwriter buddy, Wes Arken, Axl was there obstensibly to write songs. He wasn't writing songs; however, he may have been gathering material as he was seen partying in the open, hard and late, one night jamming with members of the Cult, another night hitting the clubs—everybody seemed to have an "Axl Rose is fucked up" story from that time. Axl had once heard of Truman Capote's theory that in New York a man could conceivably have six seperate existences without them touching and now Axl decided to see if the East Coast literary lion was right. He managed it for three or four weeks until he had to be in six different places at once with six different people and then he decided he couldn't take it anymore and bailed out of New York.

Overheard in the hallway of the Mayflower hotel where Axl was staying the following dialogue took place:

Young Taiwanese-looking teenage girl: "How come you only fuck me once?"

As the elevator doors closed a member of Axl's party was heard to mutter: "Cause he's already fucked five others today."

When asked about the band's ability to deal with success, Axl said, "All of a sudden you're dealing with major record executives and business people and MTV and everybody else. You start becoming one of those people you thought you were against. You have to work with them. They're there for you and kicking ass, so you have to produce. Just saying 'fuck off' for the sake of saying 'fuck off' is cutting your own throat."

With regard to the relationship between success and their band's drug and alcohol use, he explains,

> It's hard to go out and have a thrashing time all the time when you have to deal with these types of responsibilities. Guns N' Roses has had to deal with them since the day we were signed. Slash probably wouldn't drink so much if it wasn't for the fact that that's the way he's able to deal with all these people. He's able to quietly drink his bottle and talk. Me, if I'm drunk, I'll tell everybody to get the fuck outta my house. I can't get wasted because I react differently. As soon

as I'm drunk, I realize, *Ya know, this past week of doing business has been a real drag.* I want to fucking kill something. Another reason is Guns N' Roses might be totally straight for a while doing everything according to the norm, and then all of a sudden go, "Fuck it, I'm not gonna take shit anymore," and go off. We're always walking the edge. Since we're on this edge, that scares people—they freak out and so on.

According to Axl, that is how all those "Axl is dead" rumors got started. "They think maybe what they heard did happen, or they talk themselves into believing we're dead. Then they tell their friends."

About his own drug use, Axl concludes with a response that shows at least a partial awareness of the exhortations leveled at him to be more responsible, and as if making amends for what he had previously said, he ends with, "My advice is don't get a habit, don't use anybody else's needle, and don't let drugs become a prerequisite to having a good time. Do things in moderation and just be careful."

Which should not go far in placating those who want him to be more aware of his role-model position. What his detractors fail to grasp is that one of the reasons he has become somewhat of a spokesperson for his audience is because he is honest—because he can't be bought, won't compromise, because he does call it as he sees it.

And, it could easily be argued on their behalf, that not all people use drugs because they're insensitive cretins—it's often just the opposite.

They do junk because they are hypersensitive and I would suggest beneath all that hair that Slash hides behind is a sensitive soul who feels too much too often and needs a shield to deflect it, a gauze through which to view the outside. Heroin serves an interesting dual purpose for the artist, particularly the rock star of today. Using heroin is a way to deaden the registration of pain on a system too fragile and sensitive to bear up to it. What appears to the outsider, the onlooker, as an act of bravado and cool daring is more attractive than the reality of vulnerability. That vulnerable image might be okay for a folk artist or even a middle-of-the-road singer-songwriter, but in today's hard rock scene, where swagger and attitude count and the hero in exile is revered, it doesn't cut it.

Recent evidence shows that the pleasure of heroin is almost nonexistent for the person who isn't abnormally troubled. For every fifty people who try the drug, only one or two will like it and they will love it. Most will get sick, nauseated, and depressed. Now we know why—endorphins are the body's own opiate, a thousand times stronger than morphine. People with a normal level of endorphin production do not require additional helpings of opiates; however, there is now a school of thought that suggests that the people who have a positive reaction to heroin are those who have an abnormally low endorphin production rate. This discovery also explains the withdrawal mystery. When one consistently supplements one's internal opiate table with external opiates, gradually, the body's need to produce endorphin is diminished to the point of eventual shutdown. When the outside supply of opiates is curtailed, withdrawal results, until the body picks up the production again—a process that for most people then takes about three days to get back within pre-addiction level. Opiates are not "inherently attractive" as one study in England concluded; and even earlier, in 1925, another study was published showing that "the intensity of pleasure produced by opiates is in direct proportion to the degree of psychopathy of the person who becomes an addict." (Robert Anton Wilson from *Sex and Drugs.*)

Heroin seems to affect the normal individual in the approximate way a tranquilizer does, but it produces a definite pleasurable high for the seriously disturbed. The only theory that can account for this conclusion is that heroin is a painkiller and produces no pleasure; the pleasure experienced by the troubled user is equivalent to that felt by normal people most of the time; it appears as a lighting bolt of joy to the user because his ordinary state is one of acute discomfort and misery. The latter is most likely the truest. Heroin acts

From left to right: Steve, Izzy, Duff, Axl, Slash, and a keg of Bud. *(Courtesy Geffen Records)*

as a psychological painkiller to those who are potential addicts. It makes life bearable.

There is even some evidence, summarized in a book called simply *Drugs*, that heroin addicts are people who were, before addiction, well on the way to becoming schizophrenic. Their addiction has in some cellular chemical fashion staved off the psychosis. "It's even possible," the author ironically comments, "that the incipient psychotic who chooses drugs is in a better position than one who tries to cope alone." Addicts are simply medicating themselves, diagnosing and treating a problem no one else has yet articulated. (Peter Laurie from *Drugs*.)

One of the most persuasive arguments attesting to heroin's power to soothe the emotionally disturbed was made by celebrated British psychiatrist, R. D. Laing, who argued in his book, *The Divided Self*, that many disturbed people who turned to heroin, and even became addicted, were making a fairly sensible decision. For them the choice may well have been between suffering from an acute psychosis, on the one hand, and using heroin, on the other. "For some people," Laing wrote, "heroin seems to enable them to step from the whirling periphery of the gyroscope, as it were, nearer to the still center within themselves. In the ethereal world of the mind and the emotions, the choice of heroin versus psychosis seems an easy one."

In 1972, a consultant psychiatrist in Cambridge, England, Dr. A. Mitchell, also voiced support for the theory. "I believe that taking drugs may protect certain predisposed young people from breakdown into serious mental illness. It is as though working at being an addict provides an identity without which the young person could slide into a psychosis. . . . Here the choice lies between taking drugs for a number of years with all the known dangers, or having to go into a psychiatric hospital with the risk of becoming a long-term psychiatric patient."

As any junkie can tell you, heroin is not a drug that will make you crazy. As the good doctors indicate, it may even, to the contrary, keep you sane. If you don't get it when you need it, you may behave crazy, and sick, too. For crazy, for full-throttle-howling-at-the-moon lunacy as in can't-get-back-to-reality, nothing, *nothing* can compete with cocaine. Everyone seems pretty much in agreement on this one. Rich junkies have something over poor junkies here. That is, when a poor junkie's tolerance to heroin rises above the point where he cannot afford it anymore, he tries to go cold turkey and get his habit back down to a manageable level. Not faced with such economic factors, a wealthy junkie, like Slash say, will simply start throwing a little cocaine in the spoon along with the heroin, to give it a "little lift." The problem with cocaine is, of course, that there's no such thing as "a little." But let Slash tell it.

In the fall of 1990, a good half year after the death of his grandmother and the Rolling Stones L.A. appearances, Slash finally confessed: "Before and after the gigs, I'd have my dealer meet me. I'd built a place in the hotel room to hide my shit. Axl was tripping out on the whole thing, but as far as I was concerned, I was fine—at least the gig was happening."

What was he doing, specifically? Speedballs. Heroin and cocaine. Junkies say if god invented anything better, he saved it for Himself.

And remember that passionate little antidrug rap Axl gave from the stage that night?

"I almost walked off the fucking stage," Slash recalled with more than a trace of rancor. "Being in that frame of mind, it was like, fuck you, you dick! But he was also a little intimidated by the gig, I think. Axl always pulls that kind of avoidance." Still, hadn't Slash promised to clean up?

He headed to a resort in Arizona that had recently and successfully detoxed Ringo Starr and his wife from alcohol and had a good track record of keeping their celebrity patients out of the tip sheets. Assuming the patients get there to check in, that is.

"Of course," Slash related, "I took ten grams of cocaine with me. I'd be telling the limo driver to stop at a restaurant to get me a set of silverware and he'd come with a knife and a fork. I'd be like, 'No, the *complete* set . . .'" as in with *spoon*.

The quantity of cocaine Slash was doing had begun to incite hallucinations, and one day in a hotel room he imagined a knock on the door and men with guns—a familiar scenario to any cocaine binger who smokes or shoots the stuff.

"I flipped out," Slash says simply. He destroyed the glass in the shower stall, terrified a maid, and dashed outside bloodied and naked and yelling holy hell had come down inside his head. Fortunately for the rock star some of his friends intervened and Slash avoided jail. Or the state psychiatric hospital. Or the morgue.

"I really should be dead by now," he rather reasonably points out. "That's how bad it was."

"I guess I always felt I was indestructible," he admitted. "And that if I died, I didn't care about that either. I'd OD'd

Shiva, the Hindu god of creation, destruction, dance and sexuality. Shiva also often appears as Krishna who "satisfies all maiden's desires" in Indian literature.

lots of times, would wake up and go, 'What happened?' But finally, the people close to me made me realize . . ."

. . . That it was getting worse, not better. Confronted with the true picture, Slash commenced a cure that would have him clean in time for the reconvened start date for the new album. In touch with himself for the first time in literally months, undrugged and sensitivity consequently sharper and more intense than normal, the creative juices flowed and Slash was able to crank what could have been a very uncomfortable rehabilitation process into an artistic triumph. Axl rose, delighted, to the occasion.

It could be argued that if one is true to oneself from the start, or could get in touch with that omnipresence of who "I" is, then one wouldn't need to use drugs in the first place. That person wouldn't need them to open the doors of creativity or perception, and he wouldn't need them to deal with the repressed urges and neurosis and, in short, wouldn't need drugs to live a relevant creative life—which most don't, regardless of intention. The real effect of drugs sooner or later in a creative person's life is most often an extinguishing of the fire—no more, no less.

Creation is more often than not the result of pain rather than of pleasure. Some insist narcotizing the pain hinders, not helps, in the act of creation, however pressing the need to get rid of that pain may seem. Yet when one is on fire, the scream may be arresting and something to behold, but the man on fire doesn't care about that. He wants the fire out, posthaste, at any cost.

In *The Birth of a Tragedy*, Nietzsche identified as Dionysian the basic drive of life to break through all dogma, morality, and imposed definition; he regarded as Apollonian the tendency to articulate feelings and perceptions into individually defined artistic forms; and he saw as Socratic the impulse to dominate the world through abstract reasoning. He identified himself as Dionysian and called upon the Germany of his time to rejuvenate itself by reaffirming the Dionysian traditions. In particular, he championed the creation of new myths and heroes and, as mentioned earlier, praised the bombastic mu-

Bacchus, the god of exultant drunkenness and pandemonium.

sic of Richard Wagner as embodying the spirit of Dionysus come again.

Nietzsche may not have lived to see Elvis or the Stones or Guns N' Roses, but he would have understood the language they spoke, he would have intuited the meaning of their dances, and he would not have been surprised to see the inflammatory effect of those moves on their audiences.

TECHNI-CIANS SACRED

PART 4

OF THE

BACK

GARDEN

TO
THE

An intoxicated god, a mad god! A god, part of whose nature is to be insane! He who begets something which is alive must dive down into the primeval depths in which the forces of life dwell. And when he rises to the surface, there is a gleam of madness in his eyes because in those depths death lives cheek by jowl with life. Not the medical definition of madness, but that state in which man's vital powers are enhanced to the utmost . . . [Walter F. Otto from *Dionysus: Myth and Cult.*]

The worship of body, sex, and rhythm, the pleasure of intoxication via both rhythm and/or ingested substances, and the appeal of androgynous shamans and priests were established long before white rock 'n' roll institutionalized these elements in the mid- to late twentieth-century and cleared the way for rock to reconcile body and mind, in direct opposition to the dictates issued over centuries of white European and Christian culture.

In a strikingly original book, *Dionysus and Shiva*, by Alain

Danielou, the similarities between the Indian god Shiva and Dionysus are impressively laid out—not only in relationship to the concept of the god himself, but also in the nature of his rites and followers, and in the historical context of his first appearance and subsequent repression.

Like Dionysus, Shiva was associated with the form of a bull, was worshiped in a religious tradition that knew of music as means of transcendence, and was revered as the giver of intoxicants (especially his drink, Soma) and as the lord of the dance. (They also share common epithets such as Bromios [Greek for "The Raving One"] and Bhairava [Sanskrit for "The Terrible One"]; Eriboas and Rudra [both meaning "The Howler"]; and Kouros ["Young Male"] and Kumara ["The Adolescent"].)

As was the case with Dionysus, all forms of sexuality were considered to represent the god's power and were enjoyed in honor of the god, not for procreation, but for their own sake. And also like Dionysus, Shiva is frequently depicted as effeminate, but nonetheless powerful.

"The hermaphrodite, the homosexual and the transvestite have a symbolic value and are considered privileged beings, images of the completeness of God, i.e., both male and female. In this connection, this personality plays a special part in the magical and Tantric rites as they do also in shamanism." (Alain Danielou from *Dionysus and Shiva*.)

As the principle of life, Shiva is the god of youth, erotic activity, and renewal. His festivities take place at the beginning of spring and the same succession of apparent death and renewal that is found in Dionysus, as the god of nature and vegetation, is also found with Shiva—their festivals are the winter solstice and spring equinox. Vegetation deities were supposed to spend a part of the year underground, in the kingdom of the dead, and such is the case with Dionysus and Osiris and Shiva, too, as the lord of life and death.

One of the myths surrounding the cult of Shiva goes back to 1500 B.C. and makes the claim that as the god of sex and intoxication, Shiva blessed his followers with cannabis. Another version of the same myth says Shiva is actually incarnate in the Indian hemp plant. To this day, Shivites use marijuana and hashish in their religious worship and other sects believe it is useful as a spiritual preparation for reading holy writings or entering sacred places. (Akron Durual from *History of Secret Societies*.)

During the spring festival, as the participants sing erotic songs and dance, Shiva is preceded by an intoxicated rowdy crowd wearing wooden phallic emblems. The carrying of the phallic symbols and the excitement of the god possessed the bacchants and announced the triumphant entry of the spirit of the new year. Eroticism, transvestism, and bisexuality all have symbolic roles.

It doesn't take much imagination to associate the guitars of today with the phallic emblems of then, the suspension of values inherent then in the anarchy of the songs of today (like "Welcome to the Jungle"). In short, many of the symbols contained in today's rock concert are strangely and strongly reminiscent of the symbols so effective in the Dionysian festivals (or Shiva's celebration) of 2,500 years ago.

People have always had the need to dance and make music and seek altered forms of consciousness—in a word, ecstasy (derived from the Latin word *exstasis*, meaning, literally, "to stand outside oneself"). Some cultures have made a comfortable place for this behavior, like the Greeks in their festivals honoring Dionysus in the spring and fall. Jim Morrison saw rock as a religious force complete with sacraments and ritual celebrations and called it as he saw it. "In its origin," Jim once said,

> the Greek theater was a band of worshipers, dancing and singing on a threshing floor at the crucial agricultural seasons. Then, one day, a possessed person leaped out of the crowd and started imitating a god. At first, it was pure song and movement. As cities developed, more people became dedicated to making money, but they had to keep contact with nature somehow. So they had actors do it for them. I think rock serves the same function and may become a kind of theater.

From 1200 B.C. to the final fall of Rome, around A.D. 500, the god Dionysus spoke for his followers, despite the official ban enacted by the Roman senate in A.D. 200. Even as late as

A.D. 1700, broken-down strains of the old religion, surviving in scattered pockets of Europe, continued to echo Dionysian themes until they were finally annihilated by the onslaught of monotheistic industrialism. After Christianity became the dominant religion of Europe, the values and practices that the Church forbade continued to live on, but underground, usually in the countryside—outside of the area of strict Church surveillance. After the great persecution of heretics and witches in the Middle Ages and Renaissance, even this underground disappeared. (Arthur Evans from *Dionysus: The God of Ecstasy*.)

Some of the first and most striking departures the Christians made from the Dionysian tradition involved separating themselves from sexual practices, drug use, and religious rites. Sex, drugs, and dancing had the taint of the devil and would no longer be allowed in acts of worship or celebration. These historical ramifications proved to be tremendous, and at a certain point in the culture's movement toward church, hierarchy and class domination, a quantum leap in values occurred, after which patriarchal attitudes became accepted and codified into an established set of values. (Jeffery Russell from *The Devil: Perceptions of Evil from Antiquity to Christianity*.)

Ecstatic, transcendent states have always been considered an exceptional and highly desirable condition and have played an active role in many religions throughout the world down through the ages.

Jungian psychiatrist Dr. Alfred Ribi devoted several years to researching and understanding the relationship between man and his seemingly unconscious, innate need for altered, non-ordinary states of consciousness.

While at the Jung Institute in Zurich, Switzerland, he wrote on such practices:

> "The oracles of the Phythia in Delphi or the soothsaying Germanic seeresses should be seen in this light. The maenads in the retinue of Dionysus were filled with the god . . . A long thread connects the Roman Saturnalia and the Carnival festival in German-speaking countries, which was celebrated in

Axl: "He's not consistently evil, but he's not consistently nice, either." But he's never boring. *(Courtesy Anastasia Pantsios/London Features International)*

the church until the eleventh century. It is obviously of importance for our psychological equilibrium to be able to step out of the everyday ego into a greater world. The techniques for reaching such a state are many and varied—from chemical drugs to monotonous rhythms."

The practice of shamanism strongly resembles the Dionysian ritual; the use of drug, song, and dance. But a crucial element is added: the drum. These are the elements used to achieve the trance state desired by a tribe's holy man or shaman. The drum is the vehicle that carries the shaman on his course to the other world. The drum's cover, its animal skin, is significant not only for its inducement of animal powers via its rhythmic abilities, but symbolic as a mode of transport that the shaman uses to ride into the upper and lower worlds. It's not uncommon either for the drum to have a symbolic link with the center of the world, or the World Tree, the wood of which the drum is constructed from and represents.

Recent research among the Salish Indians found that rhythmic shamanic drumming produced a drumbeat frequency in the theta-wave EEG frequency, a brainwave range associated with dreams, hypnotic imagery, and trance.

With the drum representing the earth and transport, it is through songs and chants that the shaman expresses himself and unites his tribe. Songs are regarded as the sounds of the gods and spirits. The Australian aborigines believe that the songs they sing today are those sung by their ancestors in the Dreamtime and the most special songs are sung where the gods are thought to inhabit. The Senoi Indians, who believe the dream life is as real as the waking, are encouraged when they are children to bring something back from this state; a picture, a poem, but preferably a song or dance.

Long ago Cicero said, "No one dances soberly unless he has lost his senses." And, not much has changed since then. As the author of *Sacred and Profane Beauty: The Holy in Art* agreed, "That is a terrible formulation of an indisputable truth. Intoxication and the dance belong together."

Drugs, music, and sex have been together for thousands of years. Shamanism existed among native Indian cultures, which depended on drugs for contact with their spiritual ancestors' world, although it should be noted that among some tribes, drugs were regarded as only a substitute for "pure" shamanic trance. Particularly among some Siberian peoples, the use of intoxicants (alcohol, hemp, mushroom, opium) is a recent innovation and points to a decadence in technique.

Hemp was widely utilized by the ancient Iranians as a means of intoxication when presenting their hymns to divinities. In fact, the religious value of intoxication, dance, and music for achieving ecstasy dates back to the beginning of recorded time and still exists in isolated pockets throughout the world—from Antarctica to Southeast Asia, even in the heart of America. White America chose, however, not to hear, see, or be affected by the dance and song of the American Indian. But the time was nearing when the American white man would be confronted by a music of such force and primacy that he could no longer ignore it for it contained the potential to turn his culture upside-down.

That music emerged from Africa—Joseph Conrad's "heart of darkness," the original, real jungle, the Congo. When the natives were transported to America as slaves, they brought with them their rhythms, dances, and drums, and their rituals, which provided them with a spiritual nourishment that they desperately needed to help them endure the dark, dark night their people were facing. In their new land, they conducted ecstatic drum-induced explosions that spooked their owners and neighbors, who saw their strange behavior as nothing short of blasphemy. And to appease their white God by "doing right," these guilt-crippled puritans did what they have always done when they saw something they didn't understand— they tried to stop it. First by dismissing it as mere "entertainment," then by trying to outlaw and ban those entertainments outright.

At first, these entertainments were held at night, usually just off the property of the plantations, away from the eyes of their masters. But the sound of those drums in the still of hot Southern nights was too much for the nearby gentlemen and ladies. So using their influence, the city council called a session and informed the blacks they shouldn't have to have their fun out in the middle of nowhere in the middle of the night—why didn't they come into town and utilize the new square for their entertainments? What those white Southern gents really wanted to do, of course, was remove the threat by lifting the veil of night and bring it all out into the light of day. They didn't just politely invite them over, either— the New Orleans Municipal Council passed a law in 1817 that forbade slaves to congregate for any reason, including dancing, except in designated places on Sunday afternoon. In New Orleans in the late 1700s, the only place slaves were allowed to gather for their so-called entertainments was an area called Congo Square.

What the white people were trying to stop, though no one was willing to come right out and say it, was voodoo. And as Michael Ventura points out in his essay, "Hear That Long Black Snake Moan," "It was Voodoo that is the true mother of rock 'n' roll." Ventura notes,

> "Rock 'n' roll" was a term from the juke joints in the South, long in use by the forties, when a music started being heard that had no name, wasn't jazz and wasn't simply blues and wasn't Cajun, but had all these elements and could not be ignored. In those juke joints, rock 'n' roll hadn't meant the name of a music, it meant to fuck. "Rock" by itself, had pretty much meant that in those circles since the twenties and at last when finally in the mid-fifties, the songs started being played by white people and aired on the radio . . . the meaning hadn't changed.

The term *rock 'n' roll* also derives from another spiritual mainstay of nineteenth-century black life. In the black churches, as well as in the slaves' voodoo-derived ceremonies, the feverish high-pitched devotions, the singing and bellowing, the hand-clapping, the foot-stamping, testifying, fainting, speaking in tongues, was called "rockin' the church." As Ventura so eloquently put it,

Upon *that* rock, they built their Church more than on any stone of Peter. The screams of that rock go right through you—high pitched screams that aren't joy and aren't angry but sound like both together . . . screams that yet are beautiful in their raw and naked and utterly committed flight out of the throat; the screams of Little Richard and Janis Joplin and Aretha Franklin and James Brown and Bruce Springsteen—those screams come straight out of those churches.

And like many of them, Axl also sang in church.

Indeed, those screams go back even farther, back past those churches, back into voodoo, back into Africa, back to the people of the Congo. What the southern plantation owners tried to isolate and suppress was the idea of religious worship as a physical celebration—which was also prevalent in pre-Christian Europe. The body, soul, and mind divisions that so conflicted Western man never entered into the African picture. To these people, communication with the gods was synonymous with drums and dance—to dance was to pray, to drum ecstatically was to meditate.

In this African way of worship, the body can become the conduit for a deity, a deity not necessarily the same sex as the worshiper, and drums are the catalyst for the whole process. The trance of the rhythm then begets the hysteria, which begets what Westerners simplistically call "possession." Ideally, body and mind become one (as they could, at least in theory, at a rock show), mirroring and fostering the unity of the human and the divine.

Predictably, European-Christian-trained minds were not fond of this link of mind and body, of the divine and of what they considered the profane. All forms of spirit possession become demonic in their way of looking at it, and the majority responded with suspicion and wrath. African deities may speak through the possessed worshiper, but to the white male ruling class in the south during the nineteenth century, only the devil could be responsible for such possession.

Alfred Metraux wrote in his book, *Voodoo in Haiti*,

> The degree of the African's attachment to his gods may be measured by the amount of energy he spent in honoring

them—and this at the risk of the terrible punishment meted out to those who took part in pagan ceremonies in which the colonist saw nothing but sorcery ... the over-exertion was so crushing that the life of a negro sold to a plantation in Saint Dominique was reckoned at never more than ten years. We can but admire the devotion of those slaves who sacrificed their rest and their sleep to resurrect the religions of their tribes—this under the very eyes of the whites and in the most precarious conditions. Think what energy and courage it took to enable the songs and rites due each god to be handed down across the generations!

But the African traditions were as strong as the rhythms. They survived the long horror of slavery, and in their direct descendant, rock 'n' roll, they would have an extraordinary revenge.

All the influences that created voodoo would have their day. To an alarmingly direct degree, jazz, R&B and rock 'n' roll evolved from the voodoo rituals of Congo Square, New Orleans, carrying within them the metaphysical antidote that proved to be the perfect remedy for so many uptight twentieth-century Westerners. The day was soon approaching when the twentieth-century Western world would dance, as no other white, European-based society had, and through that dance and the music that prompted it, ancient secrets would be passed—secrets that were implied in the liberating movement of the body and passed on to people almost entirely ignorant of the roots. It started in Africa and it followed the black man over to the American South. Congo Square, New Orleans, was the sole place in North America where nineteenth-century blacks, free and slave alike, were permitted to congregate to practice their ancient rituals, dances, and rites of possession. The rituals of Congo Square, permitted by whites in order to discourage voodoo rituals on the area plantations, led directly to jazz taking root in the city, and kept the rhythms alive to be remembered and revived as pure entertainment in the twentieth-century.

The cultural mix of the port city, free and slave black, Spanish, French, Haitian, and Creole, made it a phenomenal breeding ground for Christian-flavored voodoo, and most

Congo Square habitués considered themselves good Christians. This celebration of the physical and spiritual thrived for much of the century.

In fact, the festivities in Congo Square became a major part of the local lore and color, and were written about frequently. This account, written by Henry Edward Durell in 1853, captures the flavor of the weekly event:

> The African population [is] tricked out with every variety of show costume, joyous, wild, and in the full exercise of a real saturnalian. . . .
>
> Upon entering the square the visitor finds the multitude packed in groups of close, narrow circles, of a central area of only a few feet; and there in the center of each circle sits the musician, astride a barrel, strong headed, which he beats with two sticks, to a strange measure incessantly, like mad, for hours together, while the perspiration literally rolls in streams and wets the ground; and there, too, labor the dancers male and female, under an inspiration of possession, which takes from their limbs all sense of weariness, and gives to them a rapidity and a duration of motion that will hardly be found elsewhere outside of mere machinery. The head rests upon the breast, or it is thrown back upon the shoulders, the eyes closed, or glaring, while the arms, amid cries, and shouts, and sharp ejaculations, float upon the air, or keep time, with the hands patting upon the thighs to a music which is seemingly eternal.

The dances began in 1817 when the local city council, annoyed and frightened by these rituals of possession, forbade slaves to congregate in public, except on Sundays in Congo Square. But by attempting to mute the threat of blacks congregating for the purpose of practicing voodoo, by trying to reduce it to the level of light entertainment or freak show, the city fathers inadvertently achieved their worst fear—not only did they provide the means to keep certain traditions, perhaps on the path to extinction, alive, but they also exposed the rituals—with all their physical power and mystical seductive charm—to a white audience. You want to make something attractive, say no to it. But it was more than mere attraction. As Ventura writes,

Here was the metaphysics of Africa set loose from the forms of Africa. In the ceremonies of Voodoo there is no audience. Some may dance and some may watch, but all are participants. What was happening in Congo Square was most likely the first time blacks became subsumed in the music. A secret within the music, instead of the object of the music. A possibility embodied by the music, instead of the music existing strictly as this metaphysics' technique.

Once blacks were allowed their own churches in the 1840s—the rituals of voodoo came into the church, leading directly to the hellfire preachers, whose delivery was to be such an influence on the pioneer rock 'n' rollers a century later. The trappings of Southern fundamentalism, white as well as black, clearly have antecedents in the joyous music and unrestrained abandon of African religious services.

The fundamentalists chose to ignore the contradictions inherent in their style—physical denial preached through physical hysteria and fervor. And praise be for this contradiction, because it's no accident that most of the pioneers of rock shamanism—Little Richard, Elvis Presley, Jerry Lee Lewis, Chuck Berry, Janis Joplin, and Jim Morrison—come from the South. African passion for rhythm and oneness of body and mind had been brutally suppressed, co-opted and evidenced in the churches of its very suppressors, and passed on to a generation of young rebels who borrowed both from the second-generation African furor of their churches, and the second-generation voodoo furors of the juke joints that they patronized illicitly. And these rebels flaunted their unification of body and mind on stages, radio airwaves, and television shows throughout America, spreading their rhythm gospel—a gospel where you moved the loins, as you did in African music, and not just the feet and head, as you did in European music—far beyond the South. It is from this lineage that Axl Rose emerges and to this standard he aspires. The object of the voodoo ceremony, as well as the fundamentalist Pentecostal service, is possession by the god—as it is in the concerts at which Guns N' Roses perform. They will not sacrifice spontaneity, and this exact devotion to their muse put them above and beyond the more programmed Rolling

Stones in 1990; not because they were better, but rather because they *dared* to invite down the gods that would have them.

Congo Square was the first time the white man heard and saw and felt the rhythms of the drum being performed in his hometown. It wasn't only the white man, either, who heard that drum. White women, those who were there felt it too, and it moved them.

Now it doesn't take a whole lot of imagination to picture the puritanical white man's dismay when he saw his white young virginal daughters barely able to resist the relentless rhythms, squirming, gyrating, and wiggling their hips to the music made by these big, strong, sweaty black men—this jungle bunny music getting their respectable women folk all worked up. Their reaction was panic—the same panic the god of music, Pan, personified. The same panic that affected the kings and parents, whose daughters ran off with Dionysus—a panic so deep and so strong that it manifested in hatred. That hatred, in turn, begat repression and you already know what repression of Dionysus brings.

And the Christian church at large was no different. "The desires of the flesh are against the Spirit," wrote St. Paul, "and the desires of the Spirit are against the flesh." Which pretty much sums up that point of view.

The Christians, never too happy about having bodies to begin with, although they had resigned themselves to living in them, were determined not to enjoy themselves, and they were equally resolved not to let anyone else enjoy themselves either. So they did what people of authority and influence have always done in this particular situation—they tried to stop it.

But the music was too strong, too powerful, and too ir-resistible to be ignored or suppressed. Once young Americans, black as well as white, heard the music and danced the dances it inspired, it could not be stopped or denied. It had come too far, for too long, and now it was almost home. It seemed to have a will of its own. Every time someone or some group tried to stop it, it flashed out somewhere else, like fire, like Dionysus.

Beginning in 1942 with Arthur "Big Boy" Cruddup, the electric guitar was introduced in the backwoods blues and voodoo-derived rhythms of sensual jazz. Before long, Sonny Boy Williamson, John Lee Hooker, Willie Dixon, Big Joe Turner, Muddy Waters, and Professor Longhair could be seen performing throughout the South with the basic guitar, bass, drums, sax, harp, and piano lineup that would remain essentially unchanged in rock 'n' roll for the rest of the century.

At the turn of the decade, God-fearing white southern teenagers like Elvis Presley, Jerry Lee Lewis, and Carl Perkins were sneaking out to hear these men, to take in what they couldn't hear on the radio, and what was ironically implied in church—music that moved, moved the body, music that was both by and about the libido.

These rock pioneers were told that attraction to or indulgence in this music was a sin, and they might have even believed that—but it still didn't stop them from being galvanized by these rhythms. Even the threat of eternal hell didn't deter these boys from seeking out this magical, enlivening new sound.

Today, it is difficult to imagine how courageous it was for these white youths literally to step across the Hades and to the back of the bus to absorb a physical culture missing in their own Euro-Christian tradition. But lest we have too many illusions, these young white rebels of Memphis did not abandon repression simply because of their attraction to Beale Street. It was tempting, too. They honestly thought they were flirting with the devil and possibly entering damnation because of their attraction to the rhythms that melded both mind and spirit.

Ventura quotes Texas singer-songwriter Butch Hancock's comment on Elvis Presley's history-making Ed Sullivan appearance: "Yeah, that was the dance that everybody tried to forget. It was because the dance was so strong that it took an entire civilization to forget it. And ten seconds on the Ed Sullivan show to remember it."

The possession by rhythm and the drum-fueled takeover of the soul by a deity now became key elements of rock 'n' roll performance. The metaphysics of voodoo were passed on to the new world of music. Elvis Presley, Jerry Lee Lewis, Little Richard, James Brown, Tina Turner, Janis Joplin, Jim Morrison, Prince, and Axl Rose brought the demons onstage and into their bodies with the drums and the music providing the catalyst for this performance and transformation, much as it did in the days of Congo Square. Now, however, it was a commercial enterprise, with adults far removed from the state of possession endorsing the checks, so the behavior was tolerated as never before (albeit warily) in Western society. Even an American parent could understand the profit motive.

What Michael Ventura said was true and right: "The moment this black music attracted these white men was one of the most important moments in the cultural history of America. It was this music, reflective of both a lifestyle and an integrity of emotion, that would rock America and the world on its ear."

It is no accident or mere coincidence that these singers are all from America's heartland, all fair-skinned, long-haired, more androgynous than not, and all joined at the hip spiritually with Dionysus—Little Richard, Jim Morrison, Jerry Lee Lewis, Elvis Presley, and Axl Rose. They all dance the dance. They are no mere act. They follow no formula. They feel something old and powerful and they respond to it. They are the conduits for their audience who in turn feel this power as it passes through these singers. Dionysus is pleased and ecstasy is passed, or he is displeased and erupts from ecstasy into madness. Either can be delivered. That is the ecstatic risk that is taken and will be taken again—because this is the force, and just as it attracted and fulfilled for centuries under a variety of titles, it will continue to attract. The dance will be danced, but we will always need someone like Axl to show us how. And when he is damned or suppressed, it is not Axl Rose who is being suppressed. It is voodoo. It is spirit. It is Dionysus. It is the dance.

There once was a time when religion and art were so intertwined that it was hard to separate the two. Song was prayer, dance was ecstatic and drama divine.

Among the Greeks, disapproval of the dance was considered blasphemy. Then there were the mystery cults that

An early club date. *(Courtesy Monica Dee/Retna Ltd.)*

could not take place without the dance and the man who disclosed the secret rites was said to "dance them out."

The Indian god Krishna dances for the shepherd girls, fascinating and arousing them. He plays the flute and they come running. Indra, god of war and delight, dances to the poetic rhythm of the Hindu Veda teachings. In ancient Egypt there's the dance macabre where even the dead dance. And remember the animals who liked to get stoned? Animals like to dance, too. Innumerable dances throughout the world are imitations of animal dances: the crane and bear dances in Greece and China, the moor hen dances, the ram and monkey dances in Greece, the Buffalo dances of the North American Indians, the fox dances, and the peacock dances. And, for thousands of years, man has imitated the animals' dances. By dancing the movements of the animals, "man becomes master of the animal rhythm. He subjects himself to the order of the animals and he adds the power of the animals to his own." (Gerardus Van der Leeuw from *Sacred and Profane Beauty*.)

Noted anthropologist Jane Harrison wrote, "Throughout the whole world, the primitive man in the magico/religious stage danced where we would pray or worship." Rhythm is all-powerful; it rules the whole man, the whole world. It gives expressions to the ineffable, loosing all forces and compelling them outward, inward, onward.

Throughout history, man has believed that the negation of the self has brought him closer to a higher life. "Whoever loses himself makes room for God," the German author Gerardus Van der Leeuw concluded about the spiritual significance of dance. Because the universe dances.

This is the body and soul of voodoo. This is what quantum physics is just discovering, what the whirling dervishes believed, what the Hindu gurus have known, what Africa has known, what the shaman has known, what Egypt, India, and ancient Greece all once knew, for thousands of years: that the holy and earthly, the physical and spiritual are supposed to meet; and to split the mind from the body is to do evil.

Dance is a compulsion that assumes control of the man (who willingly relinquishes his will), a madness sweeping him along. The man is danced. The ecstatic dance is nothing less than a kind of taking possession. The original Greek unity was poetry, song, and dance. When the dance was dropped, surrender and ecstasy vanished.

The intoxication is contagious. It is transmitted from one man to another until finally the whole temple, the whole world, is swept along.

"Rhythm gives strength to life. One can rise from the trivial to the most exalted by dancing. It is the spirit of god, the pulse of animal life, the heartbeat of spiritual life as it was and as it is, the movement of the world and the course of the gods. The cosmic meaning of the dance has existed from the beginning." (Van der Leeuw)

It takes us outside ourselves and into another dimension. Dimensions we otherwise have no access through. In the bible, Lucian wrote: "Whoever does not dance, does not know."

The dance overpowers whatever it finds in its path. Everything spins, circles, and leaps to the rhythm of the universe. "The Hebrew poet sees how the floods clap their hands, the mountains rejoice and spring like goats, the hills skip like lambs. Every movement of the world is rhythmically ordered. The same principle reigns in the dance as in the cosmos." (Van der Leeuw)

The rhythm of the dance reaches out to all of us—it cuts across time and nations like nothing else. Yet, just as it embraces life and expresses life, as it is sacred in its ecstasy, so is the dance capable of discarding life. "By its very nature, it makes man beside himself, lifts him above life and the world, and lets his whole earthly existence perish in the maelstrom." (*Sacred and Profane Beauty*)

All feelings find their expression in the dance. "The religious is not a particular sensation alongside other sensations, but the summation of them all."

An old inhabitant of Halmahera, who did not want simply to give up feasts for his dead people, said in his defense to the insistent, insensitive missionary, "My dancing, drinking, and singing weave me the mat on which my soul will sleep in the world of the spirits." Dance is the holy power that frees him.

The Gnostic heretics regarded life as a dance, whose animal powers were to be savored, whose divine levitations were to be relished. St. Gregory Nazianzen and St. Basil also knew the mystery of the dance. Dante saw the dance of the blessed in *Paradise*.

Now today it seems we have lost almost completely the

ecstatic dance as a cultural or religious element. However, it has been saved in music.

And so in music it remains. Music is the sound of dance and dance is music incarnate. It doesn't matter if it's Nijinsky's indescribable grace and precision, the inspired expression of Stravinsky's *Afternoon of a Faun*, or Axl's serpentine, sensuous, sliding, rhythmic swims; we are connected with *it*. And then something really magical happens. *It* dances us.

An excess of leather, of tattoos, fascist symbols, biker garb and S&M regalia. *(Courtesy Jennifer Rose/Retna Ltd.)*

This is another crucial reason why Guns N' Roses are so massively popular, despite all logic and against all the odds: they make us want to throw off all restraints and dance. Not with drum machines and programmed keyboards, not with synthetic voices or computer-programmed tape loops; but with their hearts and souls and bodies.

The question then remains, will Guns N' Roses, or more specifically, Axl Rose, survive? Will he survive not merely the attacks of his oppressors and critics, but the ravenous hunger that produced this jewel to begin with? Will the tension, the friction of the life force against the forces of death be so much that he snuffs himself out? Will his own appetites for destruction consume him? Better and smarter men than Axl Rose have gone down in flames before. The number of sur- vivors is precariously low. What makes Axl Rose so different? And, what exempts him from the lineage of the doomed with whom he identifies so passionately? Are we witnessing Icarus on his way up or on his way down?

In early 1989, Axl tackled this very issue regarding his own mortality head-on. For some months, the members of Guns N' Roses had been backpeddling on the issue of their drug use, indicating to the press that the drug problem was getting better, not worse.

"The only thing that worries me about death," Axl once said, "is I have this new album to make and I'll really be pissed off if I die before I make it. After that, I won't give a shit. That's when it's going to get dangerous."

A dangerous threat for him to make, a tantalizing promise for the rest of us to behold.

In January of 1990, Axl joined the procession of fans from around the world making the pilgrimage to Jim Morrison's burial site. Before Guns N' Roses began their meteoric rise to the stratosphere of success, Axl had read and strongly identified with the Morrison biography I had coauthored, *No One Here Gets Out Alive.*

Not long after he read the Morrison bio, Axl was inspired to write a poem in his journal dedicated to Morrison titled "Artistic Death." Written not long after the book was released, before the crowd came clamoring for more Doors, Axl's re-

Axl's tattoo reads "Victory or Death." *(Courtesy Chris Lee Helton/Retna Ltd.)*

sponse to Jim was on time, pure and true. Dated December 6, 1980, two days before what would have been Jim's thirty-sixth birthday, Axl struggles with how an intelligent "rational mind" can do the things Jim does, knowing the things he does, wondering how either of them can keep their purity in a world so corrupt. The poem strives to achieve a consciousness that can accept if not justify Jim's behavior, a style of living which Axl clearly identified with and was in fact living to the hilt at the time he wrote the poem, comparing "spiritual exile" to "peace giving suicide."

Early on in GNR's career, Axl told a writer: "I must have read *No One Here Gets Out Alive* seven times and I think everybody in my band's read it about three or four times. I sent a copy to my parents 'cause I figure they're trying to be nice and get along with me in the world I live in. So I sent them the book because it gets down to the real points and exposes a lot of things about my life."

When the inevitable comparisons began to be made between the two singers, Axl was at first both flattered and frustrated. The more successful the band became, the more the ambivalence intensified. Until he found himself in Paris, depressed and angry, "sitting in a hotel room, writing poetry, waiting to die," as he recently put it. He had not anticipated on making it past the dreaded 27 year old mark, the age when Brian Jones, Jimi Hendrix, Janis Joplin, and Morrison all died. Axl believed he'd either grab the golden ring of success and then die to fulfill the prophesy of the myth, or he would die trying. The trek to Morrison's grave site at the Père La Chaise cemetery in Paris was his attempt to sort his feelings out and hopefully arrive at some conclusion. He was 27 years old at the time.

Many artists, singers, and musicians, as well as fans, have made the same trek, all for reasons of their own, but mainly to pay homage to the man who stood as the premiere symbol for the hedonistic, sybaritic "live fast, die young" maxim. For those with the eyes to see and the ears to understand, Morrison also stood for individuality and devotion to one's own unique nature and the divine right to fulfill that nature.

Joseph Campbell made the following observations about such icon devotion:

> Whenever a hero has been born or passed back into the void, the place is marked and sanctified. A temple is erected there to signify and inspire the miracle of perfect centeredness; for this is the place of the breakthrough. Someone at this point discovered eternity. The site can serve, therefore, as a support for fruitful meditation ... the shrine or alter at the center

being symbolical of the Inexhaustible Point. The one who enters the temple and proceeds to the sanctuary is imitating the deeds of the original hero. [Joseph Campbell from *The Hero with a Thousand Faces*.]

Patti Smith, Iggy Pop, Jim Carroll, Blue Oyster Cult, Bono, Ian Astbury of the Cult, Billy Idol, Echo & the Bunnymen, and The Lords of the New Church are only a few among thousands who have visited the plot and meditated on the nature of their relationship to Jim Morrison. Axl Rose wasn't all that much different from any of them. Except Axl knew he was on the same path that Morrison had taken and, regardless of what the writers said about the two singers, he knew damn well that he had something in common with Jim. He saw before his eyes that the road to excess did not lead straight to the palace of wisdom. In reality, the road of excess leads to a dirt plot in a foreign land, on which people pour booze and put out cigarettes.

Is that what Axl wanted? To pack fifty years of living into as short a span of time as possible and make a big impact with that life so that after he says good-bye he is remembered forever? To sublimate the light and the energy that animates physical life into the immortality of art? To burn in that spotlight until death? Wasn't that what Axl had already willed? It was; he saw that, and in identifying it, he was allowing himself a choice. It meant trusting what had brought him to this point would be there for him in the future.

When Axl stared at the Morrison grave he saw one thing: death. That was Axl Rose's moment of clarity: "I decided to live for myself, not die for rock 'n' roll," he said. "I refuse to martyr myself on the altar of rock 'n' roll." It was at this moment that *Axl decided to live for what Morrison stood for— personal freedom—not die from what he died from—chemical excess*. In realizing that, Axl, as Carl Jung would say, separated himself from the self-destructive death archetype and in doing so liberated himself from its destructive powers. Consciously, he chose life not death. He wouldn't fulfill the audience's destructive expectations—he refused at that point to immolate himself on the altar of rock 'n' roll. He will endure whatever is necessary. He will survive and he will pass on what he finds, he'll confront—not run toward or away from—the abyss. And it won't be easy. For that is the hero's journey. To travel through the dark night of the soul and bring back the findings. St. John of the Cross writes that Western civilization as a whole is experiencing this dark night of the soul. This is what the postcard titled "Appetite for Destruction" stood for and which Axl intuitively understood. If anyone believes in omens, this is the place to start. Indeed, this is where it did start. That was his omen. His sign, a talisman and totem. Technological production is threatening our very spirit—our Apollonian abilities have outstripped our Dionysian needs.

Heidegger describes the world's night:

> This day is the shortest day. It threatens a single endless winter.... Unless there are still some mortals capable of seeing the threat and they would have to see the danger. This danger *is* the danger. It conceals itself in the abyss that underlies all. To see this danger and point it out, there must be mortals who reach sooner into the abyss.

This is the path for the true artist to travel. This is where the mystics, the poets all eventually have to go; where the poet Orpheus went and returned from, where Prometheus went and returned from. This is the death and rebirth of Dionysus or Osiris, the legendary phoenix rising from flames. In describing the creative process, Nietzsche says it is in this abyss where "creative potentialities come into being. To be lost in the chaos throws us into fertile disorder and it is there where we must begin." The creative process demands a descent into darkness. Drugs can get you there, but they will not get you out. This is where we find the strange, the terrifying, the world of "dreams, night-time fears, and the dark recesses of the human mind." (William James from *The Varieties of Religious Experience*). This is Dante's hell, the "pit." Sartre's *No Exit.*

It's Christ in the desert. Purgatory. Purgatory is in the desert, so spacious it overwhelms. A freedom so complete and so vast it terrifies. Purgatory—the need to endure temptation, the freedom to choose, power, or satisfy hunger.

Inching up to the abyss compelled Rimbaud to write: "I have felt the wing of madness pass over me." Baudelaire fought the chilling and terrible winds eminating from the same place, commenting: "The wind of Fear has made my blood run cold."

In a poem titled simply *The Abyss*, Baudelaire attempts to describe the wordless horror, the indifferent void:

> Each way I turn, above me and below,
> tempting and terrible too the silence, the space
> By night God traces with a knowing hand
> unending nightmares on unending dark . . .

It is our own consciousness, Nietzsche wrote, "which performs the psychic alchemy necessary to transform nihilism into the 'arrow of longing' which posits meaning and value." (Phillis Kenevan from *Man and World*.) But what's that actually mean?

It is the conflicts, the polarity, the isolation, the paradox of tensions that must be endured. Dionysus and Apollo must not only meet; they must learn to work together. Without the raw impulse of Dionysus, Apollo has nothing to work with, and without the discipline of Apollo the mad inspiration of the world comes to naught. Erich Neumann wrote, "Creative people are distinguished by the fact that they can live with anxiety, even though a high price may be paid in terms of insecurity, sensitivity and defenselessness for the gift of 'divine madness.' They do not run away from non-being, but by encountering and wrestling with it, force it to produce being." (Erich Neumann from *The Place of Creation*.) They knock on silence for an answering music; they pursue meaninglessness until they can force it to mean.

As the European desire for dominance and forced submission grew to include South America, crushing the fragile yet ageless and timeless cultures already there, a new folk hero emerged from the rain forests. In primitive Amazonian culture, a mythical sort of misfit existed in one of two critically important zones: huddled on the steps of the cathedral (in the main square) or, like this story about an idiot, splayed out on top of the mounting putrid garbage dump. When the antihero, the idiot, strikes by accident a high-ranking government official, he is forced to flee as if pursued by the hounds of hell, in this mythical case by prehistoric, oversized, bloodthirsty buzzards, attacking him, ripping his clothes, tearing away at his shoulders, piercing his lips, moving in for the kill. In a final and desperate attempt to escape, the idiot* frees himself by falling backwards, deeper into the garbage.

In a fascinating, high-voltage, and hallucinatory account about shamanism and colonialism at the turn of the century, the author summarizes the emerging myths: ". . . stories about transformation; through the experience of coming close to death, there well may be a more vivid sense of life; through fear there can come not only a growth in self-consciousness, but also a lessening of conformation to external authority."

In Dante's *Divine Comedy*, through harmonies into catharsis, through evil into good, lost in the dark woods, journeying through the fearful underworld with his pagan guide, Dante achieves, in the end, paradise. But only after he has reached the lowermost point of evil, and only then after mounting the shaggy back of a long-haired wildman representative of our primitive animalistic nature.

Nietzsche refers to creative geniuses, such as Beethoven or Goethe, as "virtuosos through and through, with uncanny access to everything that seduces, allures, compels, overthrows; born enemies of logic and straight lives, lusting after the foreign, the exotic, the tremendous, the crooked, the self-contradictory." This sounds like the near-perfect description of the creative/addict personality, but there's a crucial difference. In the end the addict succumbs to the temptation to escape the tension of multiplicities by reducing himself to the one thing to which he is addicted, losing all creative

---

*Derived from the Greek word "IDIOTAE," meaning, literally, "Self-Gods" and originally implying "one who will not be governed." That is, one who believed the Divine dwelt within and, it followed, obeyed no higher law for the simple reason that there was none.

"Part man, part beast, and he calls himself Slash."—Axl Rose. *(Courtesy Steve Granitz/Retna Ltd.)*

openness and withdrawing from life. In contrast, the true artist embraces all aspects of life *and* death, not one at the exclusion of the other.

Desolation, despair, aloneness, and fear must be confronted and experienced prior to being overcome. Drug use is more an escape from than a confrontation of these elements. Ultimately drug use leads us to the inevitability of despair. Sooner or later, we must confront the void and if we are to survive, we must at some time, conquer (the fear of) death. The conscious artist knows this and chooses to face death continually as he creates, reaffirming life in the process. Once you accept death, then you are free; no other danger compares, nothing can frighten you anymore. Nothing's more unacceptable than death. "Accept the unacceptable," the mystic told the young disciple, "then you are free." The addictive personality is forced to face death through his addiction and in this way is brought to the very edge of creativity all the sooner. The artist who knows this is the trailblazer. Hopefully this is the destiny of Axl Rose. There is no doubt that he is not only in an ideal position to be that sort of leader, but that he also has what it takes to express what he discovers and learns. Guns N' Roses just may be the vehicle to get him, and us, out alive. So we can all get out of the jungle, through the desert and back to the garden—where we belong. And he knows it.

"You can find it all inside," Axl assures on a new track from the *Use Your Illusion* LP suggestively called "The Garden."

Iggy Pop, himself no stranger to the labyrinth and life on the edge, for one wishes Axl and the band all the best:

"A part of me is really pulling for those guys to come through because, goddamit, right now rock n' roll desperately needs at least one reasonably young, genuinely charismatic band with real talent, a real sense of what's going on around them and how to express it right, real guts—and who look good. A band who can move the reality of rock n' roll beyond this MTV-era obsession with ritualized, codified bullshit and bring it all back home and make it genuinely exciting again."

INITIATION RITES

Of course, it's only rock n' roll and Axl Rose is only a rock singer. Isn't this all a bit much, all this emphasis on art and religion, when we're dealing with a subject that is essentially a game, merely one small aspect of a business we call entertainment? And, of course, it wasn't all that long ago rock that rock 'n' roll was being dismissed as just a fad—"It won't last." First it bloomed into a subculture. Then it was a counterculture. If you think real rock 'n' roll is, or has ever been, anything less than a religious movement, think again. Just like the pagans of latter-day Europe, rock 'n' roll finds its brotherhood with the disenfranchised, those for whom contemporary religion offers no viable alternative. Rock 'n' roll for them is *something* to hold on to, something to get them through the night, something to believe in. The ones who don't belong anywhere else; the ones who seek to know truth at any cost even though it means going out of the circumscribed limits set for good and evil;

Iggy Pop, one of rock's original madman, whose solicitous luck carried him through to survival. Duff and Slash lent a hand on his album *Brick by Brick*.   *(Courtesy Greg Allen/Retna Ltd.)*

the ones whose spiritual energy cannot be contained; the misfits who simply either don't belong or don't fit in any place else, because they can't, find their salvation in the sound of this music.

When the establishment of yesterday's generation believed it wouldn't last, they *had* to believe it, because it threatened the very fabric into which their lives were woven and, in fact, it still does. If rock 'n' roll could have spoken in a single coherent voice, could have articulated a point of view reflecting its independent and truthful nature, it probably would have come back at the patriarchy with, "It's you and your authority that won't last!" Meaning rock 'n' roll was just beginning. It hadn't even begun to explore its potential. As a religion, rock 'n' roll was not only fully equipped with all the proper ingredients, it was right on time too! The time was right for the fall of the old guard and the rise of a new guard. Joseph Campbell liked to make the point that Judeo-Christian theology has outlasted its relevancy. No other religion has endured so many dramatic upheavals, so many sociological shifts and unexpected occurances of mankind. No other religion has ever had to undergo such a surge of progress and change and be expected to fulfill the spiritual needs those changes inevitably produced. Two thousand years! Never has so large and pervasive a belief system sustained itself for so long through so many changes as the Judeo-Christian belief system in the Western world.

Why do you think so many people made such a big deal when Lennon said, "The Beatles are more popular than Christ?" He didn't say they were *better* than Christ, or theologically more reliable than Christ—I can understand someone getting upset about that; the key word was *popular*. I can even understand why they got so upset over him saying what he did—because, at that moment, it was true. More people probably bought Beatles albums than Bibles that year. God knows they were getting more publicity. Moreover, the Beatles made headway into almost as many countries that those ever-eager Christian missionaries had ever conquered. On an international level, Lennon was not only right; he was being modest. The Beatles were being treated as gods. And, when John held up a mirror reflecting our own idolatrous passion, rather than see his point, he was chastised for commiting blasphemy.

The truth is the Beatles couldn't touch Christ in terms of followers, although both clearly inspired intense devotion. Popularity is a fickle state and has a very short shelf life, whereas Christianity has demonstrated an impressively endurable longevity—and yet the Beatles haven't done too badly themselves. The point is, was Lennon chastised for being wrong or for committing blasphemy?

People genuinely adored the Beatles and the joyful noise they made. It was a mania, but not in the sense that it was a sacrifice demanded by the gods that afflicted these people. It was the opposite; it was ecstasy. When you look at photographs today of Beatlemania that's exactly what you see—ecstasy, transcendence, *rocking*, which for our purposes may be described as "participating in the worship of rock 'n' roll."

To some it's amazing that Christianity continues to draft as many young as it does, considering the attractive nature and the instant gratification offered by its competition. Alan Watts, the sixties hip American Buddhist, was fond of pointing out that people are much more interested in hell than they are in heaven. "All the tortures have been specified, and the imagery very worked out in fine detail. But of heaven we just say, 'oh, it'll be great. We'll have streets paved with gold harps to play,' and children get disgusted right away. So you mean after we're dead, we're gonna have to be in church forever?" (Alan Watts from *Western Mythology*)

After working with Ian Astbury and the Cult, Axl reverted to a rougher looking biker scarf.   *(Courtesy Jennifer Rose/Retna Ltd.)*

This same mentality is reflected perhaps in Jan van Eyck's *The Last Judgment*. Above there is heaven with a solid mass of people sitting in pews, a row of heads like cobblestones on the street; they're looking very demure and just sitting there. Below—holy shit!—there are squirming masses of writhing bodies all naked and erotic being eaten up by serpents, and being presided over by a batwinged skull. Hell, Watts pointed out, is at least something to look at.

Mark Twain also had a great time ridiculing the Christian concept of heaven and hell. In his previously banned work *Letters from the Earth*, a series of letters from Satan on earth to his brother and sister angels back home, he observes that most men do not sing, cannot sing, and will not stay where others are singing if it continues more than two hours. More go to church than want to. Of all the men in a church on a Sunday, 75 percent are tired before it is finished. The gladdest moment for all of them is when the preachers end the ceremony. He goes on to elucidate that all nations look down upon other nations. All men look down upon other men, all sane people detest noise, and all people like to have variety in their life. Then Twain summarizes man's idea of heaven, where he will spend an eternity:

> In man's heaven, everybody sings! It goes on, all day long, and every day, and everybody stays, nobody leaves. Meantime, every person is playing on a harp! Millions and millions! Whereas, not more than twenty in the thousand of them could play a harp on the earth, or ever wanted to.

In other words, what Twain was making fun of is the fact that everything we hated on earth is in heaven. And everything we love on earth is in hell. No wonder the threat of hell isn't enough to deter us, nor heaven to enchant us to motivation.

Nietzsche believed in the most extravagant yes possible to life, and attacked Christianity—indeed, the whole concept of God—and belonging to a church or any organization that "denies the will" and "negates life."

The concepts "beyond," "Last Judgment," "immortality of the soul," and "soul itself are instruments of torture, systems of cruelties."

Erich Neumann devoted much time to writing about the need for, and the process of, creation, regarding the artist as a more contemporary answer to the today's problems than the Church is capable of providing. "The actual experience of modern man," Neumann wrote, "is one of meaninglessness and despair, of isolation and loneliness. The transpersonal as something that confers meaning has disappeared. The religions no longer have any hold. . . ."

Neumann tells us that the Western religions no longer measure up to modern man and his particular despair, because man's image of God has not kept changing along with the development of man himself. The great peaks of intellectual and spiritual orientation seem to be sinking under their own weight. "Christianity, Buddhism, Islam, Judaism, all seem to be dissolving and desperate clinging to these sinking systems only drags one deeper into destruction." (Erich Neumann from *The Place of Creation*.)

In lieu of any other attractive movement, rock music became the popular religious movement for the young throughout the sixties, seventies, and eighties. Then the teenage generation, finding nothing of current merit on the radio or on the shelves, save the Sex Pistols or the rare Elvis Costello, those who were simply not interested in Christianity, turned to rock's recent past and uncovered a plethora of wealth. Ironically, the music that they turned to for salvation was what we refer to as "oldies"—or classic rock. It is the same coming-of-age music the previous generation had grown up on—the Doors, Led Zeppelin, the Beatles, the Rolling Stones. Lazy perhaps, but there was no alternative.

Inevitably, things did change. The music industry did improve its standing, and the rock movement proceeded to get bigger, stronger, and more profitable than anyone imagined, bigger than anyone ever dared dream. People not only wanted it as entertainment—they needed it as religion. Just as that belief system had become big business, so did rock 'n' roll.

One of the truly marvelous aspects of rock as religion is the versatility of its effectiveness. It doesn't matter whether your body's genetic code of receptivity is geared toward Elton John or the Ramones—whatever the nature of your response system, there is a stylistic key to fit it. For the young at heart, the rebellious of spirit, the perpetual outsider, the *misfit*, nothing can touch the spirit evoked by Guns N' Roses.

Jung believed that myths were to cultures what dreams were to individuals. It naturally follows that you can know about a particular culture by looking at its mythology, and mythology serves positive, life-affirming ends. Art, arising from the same collective unconscious, serves the same purpose. All myths, Freud felt, are the adolescent wish-fulfillment fantasies of the species, a sort of fairy tale to childlike ignorants of an uninformed age. Science pretty much agreed and effectively rendered all myths improbable and therefore ir-

Pub shot less than a year before *Appetite for Destruction* and *GNR Lies*, both occupied simultaneous spots on Billboard's Top Five list. *(Courtesy Geffen Records)*

relevant. Campbell links the beginning of the end for mythology to the end of the fifteenth century—primarily to the discoveries of Galileo and the voyage of Columbus. Science and reason triumph. Instinct and magic limped away and Dionysus hid, biding his time.

Psychologists tell us we must not do without dreams. Dream-deprived human beings become restless, bored, impatient, distractible—the very picture, in fact, of modern man. So if what Jung said was true, and if as a culture we haven't dreamed in hundreds of years and, in fact, have forgotten how to dream collectively at all, then the obvious conclusion is that due to this deprivation we, as individuals, are adrift, confused, alienated.

In this vacuum, rock music has begun to fulfill the young adult's needs for gods and goddesses, for idols and idolizing. The musicians and singers as the gods or priests; the concert as the ritual; the records as the medium; to dance, to be yourself, to be free, and to love, the message. Dope as the sacrament, the audience as a brotherhood. Our needs, ancient and unchanging, primitive needs, are met. The dance will be danced.

Rock music is the trick our society, or era, has played on itself on its way to the space age. By utilizing our wonderful Apollonian brains and knowledge of technology to entertain ourselves, we have stumbled onto the oldest form of spiritual expression known to man—the song.

The shaman was the original "long hair," the first rock star draped in leather, dancing possessed to a rhythm banged out on a drum. The original androgyny, the original madman, poet, dancer, the original healer, doing for his tribe exactly what Jim Morrison did and Mick Jagger did and Axl Rose does for their hormone-crazed, energized adolescent, adrenalized crowds—connecting, making whole—in a word, healing—bringing them home—to the source.

The shaman took psychedelic drugs 30,000 years ago and danced to the drum and took his audience (tribe) on what can only be described as "trips."

The earliest human communities seem to have required the services of a mediator that fell somewhere between the bright supernatural world of myth and ordinary reality. The shaman fills this role. He is the prototype of the artist, the priest, the dramatist, the physician, all rolled into one.

The shaman was the closest approximation to a rock star that these people had. It's no accident that in the absence of a currently functional, relevant mythology and a dearth of practicing shamans, the rock star is simultaneously one of the most revered, yet looked-down-upon, individuals in our culture. Rock 'n' roll superstars have become a new breed of royalty by financial definition and by a type of devotional decree. Ask any kid who he'd rather be, George Bush or Mick Jagger. Ask any movie star what he'd most like to be—you don't even have to ask—just look at the albums by Eddie Murphy, Don Johnson, Bruce Willis (*look*, don't listen). Because it is not mere fame that is desired, it is more, a power, the kind of religious significance that a great rock star like Jagger or Elvis or Morrison or Axl Rose possesses and inspires.

The shaman's role is very different from that of a priest. No one asks his forgiveness; he asks no one to report or confess. More important, unlike the shaman, the priest does not personally, ecstatically, enter the supernatural dimension. His function is rather to celebrate an encounter with the sacred or a revelation of the divine that happened in the distant past and his listeners are asked to take him at his word. No evidence, no direct encounter with the numinous is available. The priest cannot go there and he cannot take us there either. The shaman maintains that the sacred and ecstatic are right here, available right now.

> As societies became more organized, so did religions. Their objective was no longer merely to establish contact with the supernatural, but simultaneously to support the structure of the human community. There was a fusion of religion and politics, church and state. In almost all orderly stable societies there has been a preference for the priestly ways. The shaman is a much too dangerous character to have around. He is often a solitary, half mad creature through whom a god—or a demon—may begin speaking unexpectedly. Or he may suddenly keel over into a trance, leaving his body lifeless and glassy eyed, only to return from the invisible realm of myth

with some outrageous demand, not at all in keeping with orderly social processes. [Stephan Larson from *The Shaman's Doorway*]

Does any of this sound familiar?

We, as a society, orginally chose the priest over the shaman. Now we are beginning to see a clear-cut need to do the opposite. When religious traditions grow stale and worn out, psychological unease, dissatisfaction, criticism, and alienation, result. During the last major insurrection in Western civilization (approximately two thousand years ago), there was an almost insane proliferation of messiahs, movements, and cults.

The New Age hoopla of today strongly resembles Rome two thousand years ago, when charismatic and absurd figures leaped onto the stage, occult traditions bloomed, fortune tellers and diviners did a thriving business, and psychics were consulted by the kings.

The shaman becomes himself by divine appointment (i.e., by hearing the call). The shaman who has been elected by the spirits shows an obvious symptomatology: he becomes extremely nervous and withdrawn, begins to act strangely, unpredictable. Writers such as Thomas Szasz and R. D. Laing have both pointed out that in a shamanistic culture an individual suffering "an excessively labile nervous system" would be called on to grow with the condition; his condition would not be seen as a degenerate or pathological state, but as an invitation to shamanize.

The shaman clearly has access to dimensions of consciousness unavailable to the common man. In our culture, his condition is regarded invariably as a symptom of a psychotic episode. Yet the shaman is not psychotic; he is fully functional and most often the most intelligent and creative person within his community as well as the most sensitive. Because he had suffered psychic maiming and was able to transcend it, the shaman was now in a position to cure any of the tribe afflicted by the same condition.

In our society, we have no older shaman to help us through our traumas, our sufferings. We have no initiation rites to adulthood; we have psychiatrists who, at best, treat the symptoms and do so only on a logical, rational level when what is called for is a truer, more magical, natural healing process. Which is what the shaman does with his ability to invoke trance through dance, song, and drumming.

The difference between the Indian demonstrating psychological disturbances in his time and place and a teenage kid behaving in a similar way in the Western world today is that the culture in which the shaman resides accepts the behavior as sacred and special. It is different and as such it is rare and valuable. We reject the same behavior for the same reason: because it is different. Where they revere, we ostracize. In Indian society, the mad became shamans. In our society, they become mental cases or addicts or sometimes, if they're really lucky, rock stars. And the few that do become rock stars, such as Jerry Lee Lewis, Iggy Pop, Jimi Hendrix, Axl Rose, and Jim Morrison, became successful to the degree they do for the same reason that the shaman becomes the leader of his tribe. They express a symbolism with a vocabulary that is at one with their followers and that the rest of the world usually scorns, or at best tolerates.

As capable of sublime trancendence as they sometimes are, I can't think of a more negative or destructive hero than Axl Rose and the boys in the band. I furthermore can't think of anything more ritualistic than the American young getting fucked up and going to see Guns N' Roses in concert. The turning to drugs, en masse, along with a simultaneous participation in the rock 'n' roll brotherhood is a disorderly and desperate expression of the need for ritual with meaning.

During the reign of fascism, the destructive hero as a subject of negation was often pictured surrounded by skulls and images of death, as was Shiva, as the god of destruction, or the goddess Kali, on her throne of bone. The imagery of the cross, representing the juncture of life and death, physical and spiritual, along with the skull are ancient and powerful symbols, capable of evoking old, dark, strange and wonderful responses. The negative, or outlaw, image is not new nor is our worship at the altar of violence and sin, be it via Rimbaud, Byron, Jesse James, Al Capone, Marlon Brando, James Dean,

Jim Morrison, or Axl Rose. And we identify with them because we are all in exile, locked out of the garden.

In lieu of a functioning, attractive, and relevant mythology, the world of rock has provided its own Olympus, its own gods. Axl Rose is this age's Trickster (all that's missing is the diamond jacquard print on his tights—a baseball cap and head scarf replace the tasseled skull stocking), the Jester, the Holy Fool—if you like, an innocent who believes in Paradise (City) on earth, who knows not why he does what he does, only that he has to.

> Capable of channeling the "straight talk of the unconscious without the fear or shame that inhibits most," the trickster appears to be untamed, unpredictable, innocent, destructive, galumphing through life unmindful of past or future, good or evil. Such a type is "always improvising, uncaring of responsibilities or consequences, he may be dangerous and many of his experiments blow up in his face" (the *Trickster* by Paul Radin).

Axl thinks he's just a singer, a rock star, when in reality he is the transmitter between the electrical gods and the gods we seek, a psychicly fractured, highly sensitive, emotionally volatile rock shaman, a genuine technician of the sacred to his tribe of followers (of the profane to the outside world), a pied piper leading millions of young and old alike, American and European, back to our true nature, with risk but relevance as well.

There is a simple story, a short poignant tale, a fairy tale, that seems perfect and appropriate for the end of a book on a band, and a singer, still so young. It is a story about a boy condemned to hang for a wrongdoing no one can remember, whose mere presence and character inflames the lawmakers and those in authority. But in the end, the boy makes everyone, from the hangman to the king, dance again, and finally he is pardoned.

The dance may be forgotten, but it cannot be destroyed, and when seen, it will always be recognized for what it is: the sound of our own heartbeat made manifest.

This is why we will forgive a hero like Axl Rose or Elvis Presley or Jim Morrison—they connect us with a part of ourselves with which we have lost contact and in gratitude, for doing for us what we could not do for ourselves, we forgive them of any wrongdoing.

EPILOGUE

So in the end, it appears Mick Jagger was not too far from the mark when he compared Guns N' Roses to the Clash, who in their heyday, of course, were also compared to the Stones. All three of these groups initially wrote songs from a socially impoverished point of view. We all know how the Stones metamorphized when the big bucks rolled in. Jagger went from a street fighting man to a jet-setting man of luxury and we all know what happened to Keith Richards. What happened to the Clash when the money started rolling in? Their previous perspective was no longer valid; their street credibility was destroyed by the infusion of cash and fame, and they were unable to come up with a new vision to replace or even extend the original one. Now, the same challenge confronts Guns N' Roses—how do millionaires retain street credibility? Will they be able to develop and grow into their new circumstances with the same verve and heartfelt honesty they originally exhibited and expressed?

In the end, the Clash could articulate no vision to carry them forward and they disbanded. Internal strife helped tear the group apart as well, plus the fact that rock stardom is not synonymous with being a revolutionary. The Clash weren't onto something as new or as original as they would have liked to think, either. The antecedents for the nihilism of Guns N' Roses and the destructive cynical element of both bands goes all the way back to 1886 when the decadent movement published their first manifesto, declaring they were born from the despairing philosophy of Schopenhauer and their mission on earth was not to found something, but rather to destroy and to eliminate all the old banalities of tradition—religion, social customs, justice. They viewed society at large with a jaundiced, pessimistic eye. The nihilists said no to the established, rigid values of the day, and yes to the passions that fueled the impulse to escape from those values, until ultimately those passions destroyed their possessor or glutted that being to the point of disenchantment.

Guns N' Roses are apolitical, despite "Civil War," a single the band donated to the Romanian Angel project, an album produced by the Beatles' wives, whose sole purpose was to benefit the Romanian orphans. Politics doesn't enter into the picture. That they chose to give away such a potentially valuable (previously unreleased) song speaks more for a newfound maturity and generosity (and perhaps tax standing) than it does any actual political stand, other than "what's so civil about war anyway?" A sentiment most would be hard-pressed with which to disagree.

They express no political ideology that is anti-this government or anti-that policy. They carry no specific ideological cartel; they don't propose anything utopian, either. Yet, they share with the Clash the impulse to destroy, to tear down, to distrust and to view with pessimism all that the establishment stands for, if for no reason other than in GNR's case the government makes them criminals by virtue of their behavior. In doing so, society prejudges them and their lifestyle negatively. Drug taking is against the law: if you take drugs, you are a criminal. Axl's been rousted and harassed and been brought up on both bogus and real charges and jailed enough to be wary of the law, yet for all this, Guns N' Roses are not a political band by any stretch of the imagination. The only political promise that interests these guys is the one that asserts the right to life, liberty, and the pursuit of happiness.

Jagger may have been right, in a way, when he remarked on the danger Guns N' Roses faced being similar to the situation that brought down the Clash—what Jagger calls a "built-in obsolescence factor." Guns N' Roses do have a big something the Clash never had, that Jagger should have recognized had he not been blinded by the truth—Guns N' Roses have Axl Rose.

Guns N' Roses share much more with the Doors, or at least Axl with Morrison. Both group's singers share the common dilemma: what do you do once you've broken through? What do you do once you're where you want to be? Where do you go? How do you get there from here? The ultimate breakthrough is death. It worked for the Sex Pistols and it worked for Morrison. After achieving the hard-earned, dreamed-of success and living beyond the rock 'n' roll mortally fatal age of twenty-seven, then what? If you don't die at that relatively young age as expectedly predetermined by your excesses, what next? Where do you go from there?

What's his encore? His greatest fears have been vanquished. He made it on his own terms, was successful and didn't compromise; his dreams have been realized. Where's the motivation now? Money won't do it. Success? He has that. Freedom? He has that too. Or does he? Achieving freedom is one thing, maintaining it is another. Now what? It's Christ-in-the-desert time. It's a freedom so complete it terrifies. You can't stay where you are because your conscience won't let you and you can't just jump because it's too life threatening.

What are you going to do? Give into these new temptations or resist them? What direction do you have; what initiative do you have on your own, all by yourself; what else do you have to say now that you've gotten to where you wanted to be? Now that we've climbed the tree of life and gone out onto the limb of knowledge, now what? Just sit there? Wait? For what? Or, saw it off and make a glorious crash landing and end it all nice and neat by doing what everyone expects you to do? It's Hamlet all over again: "To be, or not to be" is precisely the question.

The poet Theodore Roethke lived at the edge of the abyss, tormented and threatened by madness from the same manic-depression that Axl suffers from. Roethke, too, complicated his problem with excessive drinking. Roethke wrote poetry from the depths of his suffering. His images arose from the madness he summoned forth, revealing truths of creation. The creative act was what held him together. From his "dark time" he gave expression to the alienation of human beings everywhere and he also wrote of the pain of the loss of personal communion with the divine.

In the first stanza of another poem called "The Abyss," Roethke stands at the edge of crisis, anticipating the downward spiral.

> Is the stair here?
> Where's the stair?
> The stair's right there.
> But, it goes nowhere.
> And the abyss? The abyss?
> The abyss you can't miss.

Before his spiritual rebirth in *The Brothers Karamazov*, one of the brothers, Ivan, declares in the dark hole of his personal hell the familiar morality at the heart of so much excessive behavior—"Everything is permitted." Dostoyevski knew all too well the pit stops on the route to freedom. He, too, was on intimate terms with the abyss and fought his way through his addictions before finally triumphing. It was this urge to live intensely on the edge of the abyss and to push beyond all limits that also drove him to surpass himself creatively. The very struggle with fate at the edge of the precipice that he experienced at the roulette table and at the bar was the same force that fed his creativity. The same thing that made him great almost killed him and he knew it. "I have an overly passionate nature," he admitted. "In everything I do, I drive myself to the ultimate limit—all my life I've been stepping over the lines."

Jim Morrison referred to the same lines and limits when he said that "I was just interested to see what would happen—testing the bounds of reality, that's all it was, just curiosity." The exact phrase of Jim's Axl copied down in an early journal. Axl Rose is constantly stepping over the same limits, fueled by the same drive that caused him to tell the *Los Angeles Times*, "I want to take it as far as I can." That is the appetite that consumes his life even as it drives him to produce and create.

R. D. Laing devoted his life to discovering what drives people crazy and to do things that are insane. In his research, Laing was first gripped and then devastated by the discovery that the behavior he considered "mad" was found not so much in his "insane" patients, but with the so-called "normal" individuals he studied.

Toward the end of his studies, Laing said something that holds special relevance for us here—stuck out on the limb with Axl Rose, teetering on the edge of the abyss—and relevant also for not only the other members of the band, but all bands and artists that aspire to survive.

> It's just what Kierkegaard called a "leap of faith," of just taking the risk to go for love and truth . . . throw ourselves into the abyss. I don't see how we can get out of it because we are hallucinating the abyss, but the leap of faith is that that abyss is perfect freedom. That it doesn't lead to self-annihilation or destruction, but the exact opposite. [R. D. Laing from *The Divided Self*]

Laing continues, "It's a source of all one's unhappiness and suffering and attachments and needs. Don't you want to get rid of your self?" This is exactly what the appetite for destruction is; it *is* a misinformed desire, a true hunger, the result of real spiritual malnourishment. When everything we gorge ourselves on fails to satiate, we get stuck, out on the limb. What can you do?

You can't run, and you can't hide; you can't go back to sleep, and you can't wake up. The drugs don't work anymore, your old behavior you can't even let yourself get away with anymore—you're damned if you do, and you're damned if you don't. What can you do about it? About the *fear*?

We need our artists to go there, wherever "there" is, stake out the territory, map out the terrain for us all to benefit— to go down and dig deep and to report back their findings to enrich us, to enable us all to continue on our own paths. But, we need that artist to come back to us—to show us not only the way, but to show that it can be done—to demonstrate and prove to us irrevocably that someone can get out alive. Following that leap of faith, at the bottom of the abyss, there is land, or God's hand, or some damn thing, because it just no longer benefits us at all merely to receive the correspondences one sends us from out there; we need more than that. That's been done before. We need evidence. We need the artist, our hero, to return in person, so we can see it can be done, that faith is not a childish wish, or a self-serving delusion justified by fear, an unrealistic expression to a realistic setting, but just the opposite—a realistic response to an unrealistic world.

As the fall of 1990 began and summer slipped away, an uncharacteristic silence surrounded the usually tumultuous Guns N' Roses camp. Then a few words began to filter back regarding the tardy new LP. From industry insiders or privileged attendants to the sessions, everyone agreed on one thing—the record is a masterpiece, and it should not be surprising—it has been well over three years since *Appetite for Destruction*—to hear how much the band has grown.

As the cold nights stretched longer into the Los Angeles crisp clear mornings, and the Christmas 1990 season loomed near, Slash, after a prolonged absence from the media, emerged in a smattering of cover stories to clear up a few misconceptions.

Looking back on the Donnington tragedy he said: "We brought back that whole element of danger, along with a few other bands—which was severely lacking. And I like that energy. But then you have to stop the show for people to settle down, or else the casualty tent is filled with all these injuries. So now I have to change my music, so people don't get killed?" The last line is clearly rhetorical and it's obvious Slash has given serious thought to the dilemma of how to make thrilling live music and at the same time avoid mortalities.

"It seems to me that maybe our audience is getting a little more civilized," he noted optimistically. "I've noticed that they can sit back and actually listen to what's going on, as opposed to ranting and raving the whole show." Slash talked about placing a few more acoustic tracks than usual to give the audience a chance to "chill out."

Donnington wasn't the only controversy from which Slash was still feeling the aftershocks. Regarding the "One in a Million" issue where Axl Rose sang the self-penned lyrics mentioning "niggers" and "faggots," Slash, who's half black, finally said: "I knew where Axl was coming from.

"Everybody on the black side of my family was like, 'What's your problem?' My old girlfriend said, 'You could have stopped it.' What am I supposed to say?" Slash queried the journalist in a near plea for understanding. "Axl and I don't stop each other from doing things. Hopefully, if something is really bad, you stop it yourself.

"It was something he really wanted to put out to explain his story, which was what the song is about. Axl is a naive white boy from Indiana who came to Hollywood; he was brought up in a totally Caucasian society, and it was his way of saying how scared he was and this and that." Slash doesn't appear to be excusing or defending or accusing. Just the facts, as he sees them. "Maybe somewhere in there he does harbor some sort of [bigoted] feelings because of the way he was brought up. At the same time, it wasn't malicious.

"I can't sit here with a clear conscience and say, 'It's okay it came out.' I don't condone it. But it happened, and now Axl is being condemned for it, and he takes it really personally. All I can say, really, is that it's a lesson learned."

Learning lessons and growing up in public seemed to be

a topic on both Slash and Axl's mind—is maturity a reasonable expectation from a band that prides itself on irreverent behavior?

"A little perspective doesn't hurt. I just turned twenty-five and something went off in my head. When I started this I was nineteen and at that age there's nothing to stop you, so far as you can see. And then as you get older—not to say I'm old now," he defended himself, "but you do change a little and see things differently. It's pretty natural. Some people are a little luckier than others as far as living through it. Because there are extremes. When you're twenty-two and on the road with access to excess—well, you can get in trouble."

Slash came across, with everything being relative, fairly secure, if not outright stable as the impending tour and new LP loomed large. He told the journalist that he hadn't used any drugs since he weaned himself off them "over a year ago." Yet in the same piece, he admits he was still using when Guns N' Roses opened for the Stones, as of that time, not nine months ago. . . . The lead guitarist has been with the same woman for eight months and he even allows for the patently mature possibility of being a father. A daughter, at least: "I don't need another one of me."

Slash went on to talk about being happy with the new album, feeling gratified by the hard work he'd put into it, looking forward to going back out on the road. "I know I have a lot more patience, and we're better musicians now, tighter. . . ."

Then he laughed, as if the sound of a responsible Slash is still awkward, even at twenty-five: "But then when we go out there, we'll all go fucking crazy. And those plans'll go right out the window."

The once constantly breaking news items regarding Axl had been strangely absent for several months, from late spring to early fall. Then arrived an item providing an encouraging bit of evidence indicating that the singer-songwriter was journeying in a right and positive direction. The news was good. It indicated he hadn't sacrificed spirit for perspective.

Axl had filed a complaint against his neighborhood cops following what he felt was an unwarranted raid on his apartment, claiming police harassment and heavy-handed intimidation.

"My wife, Erin, and my friend [Sebastian Bach, singer for Skid Row] and I were sitting there on the balcony having dinner and my wife suddenly saw about seven to nine police cars pulling up below," Axl said after the incident.

> She thought someone had been killed. It took some thirteen or fourteen cops about forty minutes to organize downstairs in the lobby. They [the cops] thought they were pulling some big sneak attack or something. My wife couldn't see through the eye hole to see who was knocking, so she opened the door, and there they were, and they said to me, "Step out," and I said, "Yeah, right." I don't know if they're out to get me, but they [the cops] hate my guts, and I don't know why. Maybe it's because if you're working the [Sunset] Strip and you saw long-haired guys with earrings who have no socially redeeming qualities going out with these girls you wished you had, it might tend to piss you off after a few years.

And of his tumultuous marriage to Erin Everly? The dramatic love-hate relationship he compared to Jim and Pamela Morrison's? Axl was able to take the oath of commitment, the leap of faith Morrison never did. Not only did they get married; Axl and Erin remained married longer than anyone was willing to guess. In the fall of 1990, Axl issued his last word on marriage, "Our marriage is good when we're communicating. Then it opens up a lot of doors and things of hope that I really didn't see or believe in before and just read about in books. Being married is more a part of me. The 'institution' of marriage itself is mumbo-jumbo paperwork, but the union of two people when you get that involved just blows me away."

When asked about potential fatherhood, Axl responded, "I'm looking forward to it. We already have the children named."

Not exactly the words of one intent on dying young.

But it was not to be.

Two months later, Axl Rose was back in the news. This time on television, the six o'clock evening news, with an item more in keeping with the character we know, yet still strangely reassuring nevertheless. Again the location is his apartment building, again it involves loud music and an irate neighbor and the local police.

As the story was initially reported, Axl was arguing with his female neighbor in the twelfth-story hallway of their apartment building when Rose allegedly took the lady's car keys, threw them out the sliding glass door and over the balcony down to the ground below, poured out the wine from the bottle the lady held and proceeded to bop her over the head with it.

According to Rose, however, a different and more believable version emerges. Axl said the complaint that arose was just the latest installment in a long-standing feud between the two that's been going on since he moved into the building. Also, the woman was, according to Axl an overzealous fan, who had been causing some late-night noise herself.

Axl also stated that at 1:00 A.M. on Tuesday, October 30, 1990, he heard his neighbor yelling just outside his front door. He stuck his head into the hallway and yelled at the lady to "Shut up!" She didn't. Instead he said she retaliated by swinging the bottle of wine at him. When he took the bottle away, she flung her car keys into his apartment, trying to get into his living area before he had a chance to close the door in her face. That's when Axl dispatched the key over the side. She proceeded to pound on the door for twenty minutes during which time Axl called the Sheriff's division, the same folks against whom Axl previously filed a police harrassment charge. Not surprisingly, the deputies did not respond to Axl's call for assistance.

According to Axl, "If she has any bruises, it's because she was throwing herself against the door; she was doing it to herself."

A short and quiet half hour later, the police deputies did show up, at the request of the lady neighbor who had called sometime after Axl. As the evening news reported it, "Axl klonked her over the head with a wine bottle. She was taken to the hospital. He was taken to jail."

Axl Rose was released after posting $5,000 in bail, sporting a shit-eating grin for the cameras, with his hands over his head as if to proclaim "Ah, freedom!" Axl later revealed to MTV's Kurt Loder that his wife, Erin, had miscarried the day before, possibly prompting an impatient response from him to his erratic next-door neighbor's harrassment.

All charges were dropped after Axl took a lie-detector test. Results indicated that Axl was telling the truth; which is what so many surmised from the very start.

Within a few weeks he declared his freedom official when he bought himself a house in the Hollywood Hills, presumably to get away from his pesky neighbors. He hadn't even moved in when he proceeded to wreak an estimated $80,000 in damage.

"Just because I'm making a lot of money doesn't mean I have to be a lonely rock star living all alone in the Hollywood Hills."

In one of the last conversations Axl had with the press before the end of 1990, Axl commented on a time in his life not so long ago when he was so frustrated and depressed he tried to kill himself with an overdose of pills. The interviewer looked at the Axl Rose before him, a clear eyed, soft-spoken, sensitive, articulate, gentle man, and asked the singer, "So how did you make it from where you were to where you are now?"

Axl laughed. "You mean, what comes after 'everything all the time'?" Axl said, quoting a line from an old Eagles song. The writer laughed too, at the absurdity of hard rock's most outrageous singer paraphrasing one of the most laid-back bands of all time.

"Yeah," the writer said, "How did you do it?"

"I was lucky," Axl answered. "And it's tricky" Axl admitted, "very, very tricky."

On New Years Eve, during a jam at *RIP* magazine's annual end of the year bash, Axl dove from the lip of the stage into the audience, headfirst, over and over again, as if to demonstrate tangible proof that maturation is not necessarily at odds with an insane, trancendent performance.

Unfortunately, despite providing such hopeful sentiments and uplifting demonstrations, Axl's relationship with Erin ultimately fell apart. Rose and Everly's marriage was officially annulled in the first month of the new year.

In an affidavit, Axl stated that "I am an artist and performer, and I sincerely believed that Erin was my greatest inspiration," Axl continued. "I was in a severe state of fear and depression that unless I married Erin at the time, she would leave me and I would therefore lose the person whom I believed to be my greatest inspiration."

Axl needn't have worried. In barely six months, Guns N' Roses would be back, with a vengeance, in the news, on the road, and despite all given odds, on the charts with two albums worth of new material, over thirty songs adding up to more than two hours worth of what the critics called the best one-two hard rock punch since *Exile On Main Street* at its very best or perhaps the Clash's two LP set *London Calling* at the very least.

POSTSCRIPT

PART I *USE YOUR ILLUSION*

"What do I think of Guns N' Roses chances of surviving? Hey, it's not my gig to weigh up other people's chances of living or dying, baby—that's what people do to me! I used to be number one on the list of the next guy to turn into a zero, so I wouldn't dream of doing it to them. I ain't gonna judge 'em. I wish 'em all the luck in the world. They're good guys. What can I say? I really feel for those guys right now 'cos it ain't the Baby Doll Lounge they're playing anymore. Where they're dealing from, it's like *Jaws* out there every night."

—Keith Richard

t is standard record industry wisdom to commence a concert tour in approximate conjunction with, or slightly after the release of a new LP so the attendant publicity generated by such a release will spur ticket sales, with the concert itself producing further interest in the record. Ideally a sort of synergy occurs, with airplay and sales spurring concert attendance and concert attendees turning around and buying the new release. Usually, an established band will wait a month or so after the record's hit the racks before touring in order to give the new songs a chance to be heard, since no one wants to listen, in concert, to songs they've never heard before. Much better, industry tradition has it, to become familiar with the new material on the new album first and then go see the show.

To tour a month or so in front of a new release is considered a risky move and although this occasionally happens, it is usually only the most established and successful bands that have a following large and devoted enough to pull it off without playing to less than capacity crowds.

To book a young band's first headline tour, in the biggest venues around the world, no new LP yet in the racks, sending this band out on tour during the worst concert season in years, with only a hope and a prayer and blind faith that if you play they will come anyway, has to be considered the height of commercial ignorance and is probably indicative of a subconscious career death wish. In the unwritten rock n' roll professional rule book, it just isn't done.

But, of course, this is Guns N' Roses and they aren't concerned with appearing to be professionals and they don't play by the rules. Not playing by the rules is part of the reason why the people came anyway, making the Guns N' Roses' tour, against all reason, the most successful tour of the 1991 summer-fall season.

Originally, both Geffen Records and the Gunners intended to have the long-overdue *Use Your Illusion I* and *II* LP's and the world tour coincide in the customary fashion. The tour dates were booked well in advance, anticipating a spring release for the albums, and for a while there it looked like everything would go according to plan. *Use Your Illusion I* and *II* would be in the stores, fans wouldn't have to listen to as many as ten songs in concert they hadn't heard before, radio would be all over them, and the record would be high on the bestseller charts before the road work began.

Then, depending on whose version you believe, the expected or the unexpected happened. *Use Your Illusion* was pushed back for the umpteenth time as it became clear the record would not be finished in time for the record to be released in front of the tour. At which point someone had to make the decision: postpone the tour, cancel the dates, and reschedule for a later date sometime after the release of the album; or, to hell with what's expected, so what if we've never headlined, so what if the record isn't in the stores, we're going out anyway, to hell with the safety net.

To the casual observer, it appeared the band had fucked up yet again and to the fans it began to look like the new albums might never come out.

As far as Axl Rose was concerned, however, the records weren't late and they weren't delayed, they simply weren't completed. "There wasn't any delay," Axl said, "the record just hasn't been fucking finished. It's done when I say it's done." The previously announced release dates were nothing more than wishful thinking on the part of record company personnel, many of whose future depended on the success of the new Guns N' Roses record.

Life on the rim has not been easy for Guns N' Roses.

As the musicians—Slash, Izzy, Duff, new drummer Matt Sorum, and latest addition keyboardist Dizzy Reed—moved from the recording studio to the rehearsal to prepare for the impending tour, Axl Rose moved into the recording studio, bringing only his exercycle and his sheaf of lyrics, and then stayed there for a month, laying down his vocal tracks and perfecting the lyrics. Speculation was that the band couldn't even get it together to record and rehearse as a full band when the reality of the situation was Axl wasn't too keen on the idea of rehearsing in the first place, believing such repetitious work would sour the spontaneity of later performance and as far as he was concerned, everything was working out just fine—perhaps even for the best.

Even after the vocal parts were recorded, the final mix refused to jell in the alloted time. A new producer was brought in. At each stage of the recording process, Geffen would optimistically announce a new release date, much to the band's chagrin, only to see the date come and go with no new Guns N' Roses record any closer to release. It seemed not only Geffen, but the entire retail music business was anxious to get this record. Record sales, in general, were down. Guns N' Roses were being counted on, as The Eagles and Fleetwood Mac had been in previous eras, to bring the industry out of its slump.

"People want something and they want it as soon as they can get it," Axl said, adding it was an impulse with which he was familiar. "I'm like that too, but I want this record to be right—I don't want it to be half-assed. Since we did *Appetite for Destruction*, I've watched a lot of bands put out two to four albums and who cares? They went out, they did a big tour, they were rock stars for that period of time and that's what everybody is used to now. So what? The record companies push for that. We weren't just throwing something together to be rock stars. We wanted to put something together that means *everything* to us."

And judging from the reaction of their fans and the media, they succeeded.

Geffen would have preferred to have gotten the new Guns N' Roses LP's with a group photo on the front or, at the very least, on the back cover. But no such desire to cooperate was forthcoming from the band's quarters. As he had chosen the artwork for the first LP, once again Axl had stumbled on a drawing that elegiacally captured the dual nature at the heart of both him and his band. A striking, almost deceptively simple drawing. In the background, a haggard figure, either deadly tired, or perhaps immersed in bone-crunching melancholia, while in the foreground is a smaller figure, an androgynous cherub caught in the midst of the act of creating, appearing to be writing and dancing simultaneously. Axl seemed to be saying: I used my illusion, by writing and dancing, to get to where I am, so can you. Yet, be aware, be prepared for the sadness and despair always lurking in the background ... these two figures are inseparable.

Not only was Geffen given artwork that looked more like an eighteenth-century Renaissance painting than the cover of a hard rock record, but they were being instructed to place the same photograph on both of the records and then to ship them together, apart. There was a flurry of meetings seeking to dissuade the band, and when that failed, more meetings were held to discern the best way to proceed with the situation as it was. Then, there were contract renegotiations and more delays.

Finally, after months of speculation, rumor, hearsay, aborted release dates, scheduled and aborted again, only to be reset and postponed once more, the *Use Your Illusion* LP's were at long last confirmed for release on Tuesday, September 17, 1991.

In an unprecedented industry coup, *Use Your Illusion I* entered at No. 1 and its companion, *Use Your Illusion II*, entered at No. 2 on *Billboard* magazine's top 200 album chart. The feat marked the first time in history that two albums by a band, or artist, simultaneously entered the chart at its apex. During the first week, more than 1.5 million units were sold worldwide. The two LP's shipped a total of 7.3 million units and reorders at the end of the first week totaled over 800,000. Retailers reported the best business they'd done in years.

Geffen Records had enforced a ban on any sales commencing before the September 17 release date, and for the first time in entertainment history, record stores around the country either kept open or reopened their doors at midnight. As the calendar turned from Monday, September 16, to the next day, the faithful turned out, lining up as early as dusk. By midnight, news cameras on the East Coast were broadcasting the phenomenon to the West Coast three hours behind, its own lines growing longer by the minute. The presentation was ominous, as well as celebratory—lines stretched down and around the blocks, lines of fans three and four deep, security guards defending the record store doors.

In an attempt to get a handle on what was happening, why this was happening, news reporters questioned the attendees relentlessly. "What's so great about this band?"

"They're just so cool."

"They're honest."

"Who else is there?"

"No one else compares."

"There's no one else who does what they do."

But what is that? The reporters wanted to know. "What is it that this band does so well?" the questioning persisted. "What's so special about a record that would make you wait up until midnight to buy it?"

"Because they're the best!"

It was not exactly the answer the news wanted. So, they reported on the tangible.

People by the tens of thousands lined up and waited to buy two albums rather than wait nine hours until morning. From New York City to Los Angeles, no one had ever seen anything like it. Camelot Music, a chain of 300 stores, sold 80,000 records within twenty-four hours. Dallas-based Sound Warehouse sold 15,000 units on the night of release. Tower Records sold 23,000 in one night.

Use Your Illusion also entered the No. 1 and No. 2 chart positions in the UK, Australia, New Zealand, and Japan. In Sweden, Germany, Austria, Norway, Spain, and Switzerland, it entered on the Top Five.

"Most international territories," reported Mel Posner, who heads up Geffen's international department, "achieved their nine-month sales projections in less than a week after the albums' release."

For the first time in a long time, the critics agreed with the hard rock buyers, almost unanimously giving the LP's an unqualified thumbs up.

Four years ago, no one seemed sure whether or not this band would survive to record their follow-up LP, so no one debated the unlikely prospect of whether they would improve and grow and by how much and in what directions. Not only have they survived, relatively intact, they have grown stronger and matured without sacrificing their bite, their lip, or their wit. Becoming millionaires has not eliminated their outsider stance, they're still pissed off, angry, confused, scared, vulnerable, arrogant, out on the edge, up front, and over the top, with hope and innocence running like a quicksilver stream throughout.

"Rose does not discriminate," *Rolling Stone* declared. "Guns N' Roses fire on all comers and take no prisoners. Was *Use Your Illusion* worth the wait, the traumas and the onstage tantrums? Yes."

Of *Use Your Illusion, Billboard* magazine raved: "Guns N' Roses' readily anticipated double-barreled studio opus is remarkable in nearly every way. Astonishingly rich." The trade bible wrote: "Artistic verdict: A brillant vindication of America's top hard rock band."

Billboard's review seemed to sum up the prevailing sentiment to the double set that many had secretly felt would prove to be too pretentious, too overloaded with inferior material, too inflated with songs better left out from a band who lack all sense of critical objectivity, better off as a single album. Others chose to believe Guns N' Roses simply recorded two albums in three and a half years—what's so indulgent about that?

Melody Maker declared, "Flawed, but majestic . . . revealing that Rose is seriously fucked up, but it also suggests he's grasping towards healing, towards a life without regressive crutches. Transgression, transcendence, tragedy; the fact is that Guns N' Roses are playing with perennial underground rock themes on the biggest imaginable stage."

Even *Time* magazine explored this ignoble, unignorable phenomenon: "Rock n' roll has always been filled with sexist, violent bands, but very few of them sell 14 million copies the first time out of the chute. What sets the Gunners apart is that they are a genuinely electrifying band that neither looks nor sounds like the interchangeable Whitesnakes, Poisons, and Bon Jovi's. . . . Anyone who can get past the offensive lyrics will be buying one of the best rock albums of the year. Or two of them."

Not all the news, however, was as glowing and good. There are some people who it would appear could not even get past the offensive lyrics.

Even with the grim economic state of the music business,

previously thought to be recession proof, there are those who would rather perish than appear to be promoting or endorsing Guns N' Roses.

According to Geffen sales chief, Eddie Gilbreath, there are many distributors and outlets that gave a flat no-go from the start. "They would prefer to lose all the revenue based on the fear of complaint from one parent. They're doing a censorship job before they ever find out if anyone even has a problem with it."

Anticipating objections from the outlets, Geffen planned to sticker the albums with not one, but two advisories. Early CD jewel boxes were branded with the warning: "This album contains language which some listeners may find objectionable. They can F?!* OFF and buy something from the New Age section instead." Elsewhere, the conventional RIAA parental advisory warning was tagged on.

No sooner was the record on the charts than it was pulled from some shelves and never even stocked on others. Neither *Illusion* package was, nor will be, sold by two of the nation's largest mass merchandisers, Wal-Mart and K-Mart.

Of course, the controversy surrounding the release of *Use Your Illusion I* and *II* is minor compared to the uproar generated by that other Guns N' Roses event, the one that wasn't postponed, the dates that could not be so easily moved about or arbitrarily rescheduled. . . .

PART II *THE TOUR*

A lot of people don't like it when someone calls Axl Rose a hero. What's that guy done, they ask, besides throw out obscene epithets with a remarkably ignorant consistency and indulge in childish tantrums in public? Just think of all the *good* he could do . . . the guy's the worst role model since Jim Morrison or Alice Cooper, take your pick. Besides, what's he got to be so pissed off about? He's making millions. You'd think the least he could do is show up on time to collect all that money.

Axl Rose makes people either applaud or shake their heads. A lot of people just don't get it. A lot of other people don't want to get it. But Axl gets them anyway. He's either a hero or an asshole, depending on whom you speak to. What the nay-sayers fail to realize is that there just isn't a whole lot of difference between the two.

Author James Redfield, in the introduction to a book titled *The Best of the Achaeans*, described the hero Achilles this way: "The hero, after all, is not a model for imitation, but rather a figure who cannot be ignored."

So Axl Rose isn't only an anti-hero but to many, a real hero, and like Achilles, prone to being childish, petulant, and demanding—and, like Achilles. He is capable of provoking great devotion or severe criticism and, as we learned during the summer of 1991, when the Guns N' Roses show featuring Axl Rose almost singlehandedly saved a failing concert season, usually both. Guns N' Roses went on their first tour as headliners and all hell broke loose.

The "Get in the Ring, Motherfucker" tour kicked off with three select club dates (unannounced until the very last minute), starting May 9 at the Warfield in San Francisco, proceeding to Los Angeles where they played at the Pantages Theater, and on to a May 19 New York City engagement at the Ritz where, by all accounts, they performed a stellar high-energy show during which Axl leapt from a speaker cabinet and tore ligaments in his left heel. I'll avoid the obvious Achilles analogy here.

From the injury onward, Rose was making news, making enemies, thrilling concert audiences, and baffling just about everybody else.

During a July 2 concert in St. Louis, Missouri, the press reported that an irate, impulsive, irresponsible Axl Rose dove into his audience to wrest away a video camera from a biker by the name of Stump. Actually, it was only after Axl had repeatedly requested security intervention that he did so. Guns N' Roses' contract rider specifically bans bottles, cameras, and recorders—a clause of which security was no doubt well aware. Following his tussle with the audience, Axl returned briefly to the stage to further berate the unresponsive security staff before storming off, the rest of Guns N' Roses trailing in his wake.

The crowd stomped, clapped, and shouted "bullshit!" for ten minutes, at which time the house lights came up and the audience rebelled, rioted, destroying over $200,000 worth of the band's equipment. More than 500 police were called to the scene. Dozens of fans were taken to the hospital, bleeding, injured, shocked, angry. . . .

All fingers pointed to Axl. The promoter blamed Axl. The press blamed Axl. Other musicians blamed Axl. Ted Nugent told the press: "If I was as ugly as Rose I'd be pissed off about cameras going off in my face too." Nugent invited fans to bring cameras to any of his band's concerts. Vince Neil of Mötley Crüe, whom Rose referred to as "plastic-faced, pussy-assed" and chooses off in the song "Get in the Ring," went beyond criticism and accepted Rose's challenge live on MTV.

Spin magazine publisher, Bob Guiccione Jr., whom Axl also attacked, by name, and invited to suck his private part, announced he was willing to meet Axl in the ring as well.

Even some of his own fans blamed Rose. Nikki Ward from Louisburg, Missouri, asked, "Is it so unusual for fans to want pictures of their rockers? I think Axl's a big crybaby. What he did in St. Louis was bogus."

Due to lost equipment damaged during the riot, shows in Chicago, Illinois and Bonner Springs, Kansas were cancelled. Rose blamed the promoters and their security staff. If they'd been doing their job, he reasoned, he wouldn't have needed to go into the audience in the first place. What he did wasn't irresponsible, just the opposite—he was doing their job for them. If the promoters would have let the band go back on stage before the riot started, none of this would have happened. The promoter claimed the band refused to go back on stage. What came out in the aftermath supported Axl's version, but did not prevent him from taking the brunt of the blame.

For the next show in Dallas, Texas, Axl, who was understandably upset over the riot and somewhat reluctant about facing 20,000 drunken, stoned fans who'd heard nothing else other than the riot news, showed up about two hours late.

It should become clear to anyone closely watching this band that here is a singer who simply cannot walk on stage at a designated time and automatically put on an act, or merely entertain. Here is a man not interested in what the clock says, or what his obligations are, or what's expected of him—if it's not real, he's not interested. Whether he is genuine or an asshole depends on you—and Axl doesn't care what you think.

When he finally did get on the stage at the Starplex Amphitheater, Axl Rose decided to get some things off his chest. This is what he told the audience: "It's hard to figure out why we get up on stage to do this, because at some times it's fun but other times it takes all the physical fucking energy we've got to get up here and do what we do for a living.

"For the last few days, I'm watching CNN and reading this shit in the St. Louis papers about how I incited a riot and they're talking about . . . 'and the band, they have a recovering heroin addict'. . .—what the *fuck* does that have to do with St. Louis?

"And I had to realize that no matter what we did tonight and how good or bad we played there'd probably be one person in the press here that for some reason didn't dig it, and he'd write about something else and write some lies.

"Now at the same time that won't have an effect on Dallas, and it shouldn't affect me, it fucks with the entire thing called rock n' roll in general. Because who are the main people that watch these news things and read this shit? They're all in their forties to fifties, sittin' there eatin' their bran flakes and drinking their coffee.

"I ain't knockin' getting old. It's a fact of life, unless you die before you get there, you're gonna get old. But just because you're old doesn't mean you have to deny young people their humanity. And so now, there's a lot of people reading these negative things about Guns N' Roses and if their kid likes Guns N' Roses, he's gonna get smacked upside the head or something because some paper said it was an evil thing.

"And that really makes me go, 'Fuck, what's the point?' But I'll tell you what the point is. We're up here and what we are doing is something that is dying in America—it usually stays at an underground level and doesn't get as successful as Guns N' Roses—and that's freedom of expression. And, basically that's all we are. Guns N' Roses are just a prime fucking example of freedom of expression."

The monologue was the highlight of a show that had no shortage of high points, all of which the press duly neglected to report.

The controversy continued apace. At the Nassau Coliseum concert in Uniondale, New York, long after Skid Row had finished their set, after two hours of "bullshit!" chants and shots of topless female fans on the video screens, Guns N' Roses eventually showed up.

"I'm sorry I'm late," Rose told the packed audience after climbing out of a helicopter that brought him to the show.

"I know it sucks, and if you think it sucks, why don't you write a letter to Geffen Records and tell them to get the fuck out of my ass!"

Then, after one song, he launches into the media.

"There's a *Rolling Stone* coming out with us on the cover. Do me a favor, don't buy it. Steal it!"

On a roll, Axl goes after a photographer and before the end of the night will have harangued *The Village Voice*, a rock writer from *The New York Times*, and a Philadelphia newsman who praised Guns N' Roses but slagged co-billed Skid Row. Just for good measure, he also laid into bootleggers and fans who throw things. It was an awesome display of bad temper run amok, but it also made for dramatic, riveting theater.

In Knoxville, Tennessee, the band repeated its Nassau Coliseum stunt, keeping fans waiting for almost two hours before taking the stage.

In Denver, Colorado, Guns N' Roses were barely into their fifth song when trouble erupted. Axl halted the show midsong and demanded that a security guard remove a front-row spectator who'd been flipping the bird all during the show. Fearing a repeat of St. Louis, the guards ejected the offender immediately.

During a Guns N' Roses set in Sarasota Springs, New York, Axl informed the audience of the group Poison's disintegration, voice dripping with irony and remorse.

"This is a very sad occasion. You know, sometimes people just can't get along. Poor little Bret and Bobby and C.C. have apparently called it quits."

Axl has now insulted or offended two out of three of the biggest Southern California hard rock bands.

As usual, Axl Rose was saying what was on his mind, when it mattered to him. Controversy follows this band everywhere, in the studio, behind the scenes, on the stage, on the road, and even at home.

In his hometown of Lafayette, Indiana, upset about a county curfew, he stormed on stage and began with a five minute tirade against the local authorities. He mentioned that only in Indiana would there be a 10:30 P.M. curfew.

"I grew up in this state, and it seems to me there are a lot of scared old people in this fucking state, and basically for two-thirds of my life they tried to keep my ass down." He paused here, relishing the moment before addressing the fans directly, many of the same people who are in the same position he was in not so very long before. "I got a lot of cool prisoners here in Auschwitz."

Following the show, the band was fined $5,000 for breaking curfew and the next day Axl's "Auschwitz" comment made headlines. Again, very few reporters interpreted Axl's words as he intended.

"I wanted to tell them that they could break away, too," he later said.

After the media torpedoed him for the St. Louis incident the Lafayette monologue, and his frequent tardiness Rose, under fire, quipped, "A lot less pressure killed Jim Morrison."

In the meantime, Steven Adler had filed a lawsuit against his former band. According to the band's official version, Adler had been forewarned—it was time to record the new album and he had to kick the drugs on which he'd become dependent. He promised he would. He didn't. He was warned again. Again, he promised and again he failed.

"He just had a lot of difficulty doing drugs and playing drums at the same time," Axl told a writer just before going out on the road. "He wasn't a very good junkie. He would go out to get a pack of cigarettes or a beer for five minutes and come back two and a half hours later." When he wasn't going out to score, there were a lot of stranger (than usual) characters hanging around, bringing the goods to him.

Steven admitted that at the time he was fired he had a habit, but so did practically everyone else in the band. Adler complained to anyone who would listen: Izzy and Slash were still getting high, using heroin, they weren't thrown out of the band.

"They needed a scapegoat," Adler said in an exclusive interview. "They fired me to make themselves look good because the record company was getting on their case." If anyone was responsible for the delay of the new albums, Adler said, it was Rose.

Adler said he was ready, eager, and willing to work. Slash and Duff, his closest friends in the band, were intimidated by Axl's tactics.

"He scared everybody," Adler remembered. "If someone in his view looked at Axl funny, he was fired. We had Axl get his own bus because we couldn't stand being on the bus with him. Izzy wouldn't even hang out with him anymore, he doesn't even like Axl anymore. I hear he's got his own tour bus."

According to this version, Adler was the one to confront Rose because everyone else refused to.

"I'd say, 'What are you doing?' And he would kick me in the balls, which he'd done before. The first week I knew Axl, he kicked me in the balls! Out of nowhere! It was over some girl he was fucking with and I said, 'Leave the chick alone!' "

Of course, Steven is far from feeling complimentary toward his former bandmates since the split. Steven Adler's lawsuit against his former band members seeks unspecified damages, demands royalties for Adler's contribution to the *Illusion* LP's, and accuses the band of defamation of character.

"Defamation?" Adler retorted. "It was destroyed! I had an offer to play with AC/DC. Then Axl went on MTV and said I was an addict, I was fucked up and I couldn't play drums anymore. So AC/DC said, 'No way.' "

The drummer wasn't the only person ordered to leave the

Guns N' Roses organization. In February 1991, the brash and obnoxious Alan Niven was asked to step down and make room for Doug Goldstein, the more capable, even-tempered, and personable road manager.

Niven, unlike Adler, negotiated a settlement arrangement.

According to Adler, the really tragic thing about his dismissal was that it came just as he was actually quitting heroin. In March, Goldstein (whom Adler refers to as "Dougie") escorted him to a doctor for withdrawal medication. It was at this juncture, one week before Guns N' Roses were to play at Farm Aid IV, that the others moved in for the slaughter, waving a contract in his face that justified discharge as a consequence of continued drug abuse. Adler signed. But according to his lawyer, Elliot Abelson, the contract served no such purpose.

"In the agreement," Elliot says, "Steven gave up any interest in Guns N' Roses, including the music he'd already written. He agreed not to play with anyone else, and also not to speak about Guns N' Roses in the future. He basically gave up everything that he could give up legally."

"They said 'sign this paper,'" Adler remembered, 'or you're not going to be at Farm Aid with us.' It was all a matter of seconds so I had no choice."

For two weeks, the band tried to record "Civil War." Nearly two weeks into his medication, Adler was still apparently suffering from its side effects, which he alleged took three weeks to dissipate. Research has not revealed any drug used to allay the withdrawal effects of heroin that would incapacitate a patient for so long. Methadone detox continues for twenty-one days but after the first two or three, the dose proceeds to be lowered and any intoxicating effects are shortly dissipated. Darvon, Valium, Clonodine, and Buprinex all have side effects, but after the critical period of withdrawal has passed (seventy-two hours), the dose is lowered and side effects become minimized as the need for the medication becomes less and less.

Nevertheless, fourteen days into the so-called cure, Adler begged the band, "Can't we wait until the next weekend when I wouldn't be so sick?"

Steven says the band wouldn't budge and no compassion was offered. "They gave me such a hard time. They kept accusing me—saying I was high—and they knew I was sick from medicine I got from the doctor."

It was Slash, Steven's boyhood chum, who delivered the bad news about the dismissal.

"He told me that I suck, that I can't play anymore and it was the biggest waste of time."

Doug Goldstein then had the thankless task of making it official. "He called me up and said I was out of the band." Adler says.

Over the ensuing weeks, as his anxiety and panic rose, Adler attempted several times to contact other band members. None of his calls were returned. After months of unanswered calls, Adler claims, he showed up at Duff's front door off Mulholland Drive, "just to wish him a happy birthday." He did the same for Slash on July 23.

"They would not let me in. I left their birthday gifts on the porches of their houses. I felt totally betrayed."

Steven didn't see Slash again until the two crossed paths while out on the town one night at the Rainbow Bar & Grill.

Slash nonchalantly asked the drummer, "So, you're suing us?"

"Yeah," Adler said.

To which Slash allegedly said, "Well, Axl's going to kick your fucking ass."

Adler supposedly drove around for weeks terrorized that Axl would emerge from a shadow, or out from a car door, from anywhere, to "kick my ass."

Guns N' Roses have responded with the following: "All of the statements attributed to Steven Adler are categorically denied."

When Axl Rose had stood on stage at that Rolling Stones co-bill in Los Angeles more than a year previous and confronted the rest of his band about their substance abuse and threatened to quit unless they got their act together, no one really expected much to come of it.

Then Adler was fired for drug abuse.

Next Slash came out of the darkness into the media spotlight and candidly admitted: Yes, I used to be a junkie, but I'm not a junkie anymore. No references were made during this period of press accessibility about his problem with alcohol.

Not long after that Duff announced, just before the warm-up dates commenced, that he had not taken a drink of alcohol for sixty days, giving credence to the presumption held by so many that his previous drinking was more compulsive than social, as he had often insisted.

Regarding Guns N' Roses own "invisible man," as Axl calls his friend, Izzy Stradlin, nothing new was known. The Mexican children in the William Burroughs tome *Junky* also referred to the main character, who possesses the knack of not being seen, as the "invisible hombre." Playing Keith to Axl's Jagger, Stradlin wore junkie archetypes like a well-worn pair of black boots. Stradlin wasn't only not to be seen, he wasn't to be heard from either. He did not appear during the band roll call at the end of the "You Could Be Mine" video, which went so far as to introduce the two new band members, Matt and Dizzy. No Izzy. In the next video, "Don't Cry" Stradlin does not appear at all, only the flash of a card asking "Where's Izzy?" Rumors circulated that the guitarist was too strung out to even bother showing up. But the assumption had always been, and the facts also indicated, that Izzy could do what Adler could not, that is, not only show up but maintain a drug habit and fulfill his professional obligations at the same time. But, if that was true, why didn't he show up for the video shoots? Why the rumors of him touring in a separate bus and going so far as to check into a different hotel than the rest of the band?

The last person anybody expected to clean up was Stradlin. But Stradlin wasn't talking.

Three months into the tour, the chemical intake update was not surprising: Duff had begun to drink again and had begun to bloat and discolor. Slash had also resumed his relationship with the bottle, assuming for the moment he had given it up. He still needed his wake-up pull on the bottle to keep his hands certain and still enough to pull out the necessary chords and notes. Even new member Matt Sorum has admitted to feeling right at home with the heady nonstop party atmosphere surrounding the world's most popular and dangerous rock n' roll band.

It has become increasingly clear that Axl Rose doesn't need any extraneous chemicals to alter his consciousness or to affect his behavior—he has his own internal pharmaceutical biosynthesis laboratory bubbling over, percolating away, flooding and ebbing, generating its own barrage of substances independent of its host's will. Axl's aware of this erratic biological production, referring in the song "My World" to a "bent configuration" and having to live with a "misfired synapse." No one seems eager or able to contradict his analysis.

Then Izzy granted a rare interview, his second with the same reporter whom he had spoken to almost two years before while he had been strung out and traveling in Europe. Backstage at the Shoreline Amphitheatre in San Jose, California, Stradlin sat with his large Alsatian dog, Treader, isolated and away from the rest of his band, listening to Thin Lizzy play from a mini-system, ready and willing to speak. He lit one of a steady stream of cigarettes and, after a brief silence, the only drug- and alcohol-free Guns N' Roses member decided to pull the sheets on everyone.

"We've just gotten to the point where everyone's back and finally coherent enough to be able to play together. That's what the deal is here. It's been such a trip from having no money and notoriety to having all this money, notoriety, all these drug connections. . . .

"Axl, I think . . . now he's pretty much . . . he understands responsibility a lot more than he used to. Before, he used to be one of those guys who, if he even thought someone was looking at him weird, would just haul off and smack 'em. And, sometimes, the people he went for weren't even looking at him to begin with. . . .

"Slash? Well, let's just say he can pronounce his syllables better now. He was pretty bad though . . . . Fuck. He was a mess. He's a great guy an' all but he can't monitor his own intake, with the result that he's always fuckin' up big time. Like leaving dope hanging out on the table when the police come to call; nodding out into his food ... shit like that. I love the guy a lot but the fact is, man, Slash is not what you'd call your thinkin' man's drug user. He's real careless, doing really shitty things like OD-ing a lot in other people's apartments. A lot.

"Fuck, I sometimes wonder how the other guys get away with some of the shit they pull with the police and everything. Slash got pulled over in L.A. for drunk driving and this was when he was using a lot of heroin, right? Anyway, I was staying in a hotel in Venice and he showed up at four in the morning, fucked out of his mind. How he managed to drive from Laurel Canyon [where he lives] out to the beach will always remain a mystery to me! So, I let him spend the night. The next morning, I find two rigs [syringes] hidden in my closet. I had to tell him: Listen, fucker, I got problems and I just can't have this shit around, cos I was on probation for six months at the time and I had to do drug testing ... fucking involuntary piss-tests almost every day for about a month as well."

A dirty test or being caught with drug paraphernalia would have landed Izzy in jail.

Izzy continued. "Right now Slash is a lot better. But, these guys, they still drink, they still party. Probably way too much for their own good. Fuck, these guys like to trash the fuck out of themselves." Izzy shakes his head and gives a soft laugh. "They really haven't changed that much."

Stradlin wasn't happy with Rose's decision to send former manager Niven packing. "I felt bad about it," Stradlin said. "But Axl and he finally had too much of a clash of personalities. Alan has his way of doing things which is more a military strategy. Axl wants to do stuff his way, at his pace, in his time." As Niven was given his marching orders, Goldstein took over and now "He's the guy who gets to go over to Axl's at six in the morning when his piano is hanging out the window of his new house. Shit like that. Now we get these fuckin' calls—'You hear what happened?' No, what now? 'Axl just smashed his $50,000 grand piano out the fuckin' picture window of his new house.' That nice, Dougie. You just take care of it. Call me when it's all over."

When Stradlin and the English journalist interviewing him

previously spoke in Europe, Izzy was trying to come to grips with the difficult business of the second album. Three months had been wasted in Chicago. Izzy had told him about how he hoped the recording could be completed without any one of the group's lives being turned into "absolute shit." Not very long thereafter, Adler's life was all but devastated.

But Stradlin, by some miracle, managed to get clean and stay straight, even when touring with the most dangerous band in the land, where excess always has access and indulgence is the norm. He not only looks clean, he sounds it too.

"I've been straight for a year and half now. No booze, no weed, no nothing. I just stopped cold. I said, 'Fuck, I should give this a shot.' At first it was real hard. When I finally stopped and then started going out, just riding around on a fuckin' bicycle, I thought, 'Wow, this is really cool. How did I forget all this simple shit?'"

The last drink he took was a special occasion—the night he and Axl lived out their mutual childhood dream of performing a song on stage in Atlantic City with their quintessential bad-boy heroes, the Rolling Stones. It seems a forgiveable transgression.

The two groups had already performed together in Los Angeles months earlier. "It was the biggest thrill I ever had, working with that band, but it was also pretty nerve-wracking, 'cause we did four gigs in L.A., right? At six A.M. the morning of the first show Axl calls me up, completely hammered, and tells me, 'I'm quitting.' I told the other guys, 'It's gonna be a long four days, fellas.'"

Then, of course, Axl went onstage and announced he was quitting in front of 80,000 people unless certain people quit "dancing with Mr. Brownstone."

"That's typical of Axl's style. Here's a guy who knows how to go the whole nine yards!" Stradlin commented.

"How we managed to get through those Rolling Stone gigs, I'll never know," Izzy said. "There was so much shit raining down on us. Axl wanting to quit, the drug problems, the Steven problem, the whole 'One in a Million' controversy—plus I had a court date the morning after the last Stones' date, at eight in the morning for pissing in a trash can on an airplane, and I was facing six months in jail because I had a prior arrest for drug possession [later dropped]. So that was a fuckin' major psycho-time."

Another outbreak of psycho time was during an evening performance in San Jose, California. Axl went on a veritable rampage, working himself into a frenzy. Crazed and stalking the stage, he deliberately destroyed one microphone stand after another, first one, then another, and then another, all within the space of one song. His personal roadie, whose main job it is to make sure that Axl has everything and to ensure the best possible performance, was making quick, short runs, trying his damnedest to keep pace with Axl. He frantically scurried to and fro attempting to repair and erect, or replace each twisted microphone stand as quickly as possible. By the time he got one back on its feet, another mangled corpse would leave Axl's hands. After the third one was rebuilt and erected, Axl decided he didn't want them put right—he wanted them where he left them, and he didn't want his roadie running around the stage every time he broke a microphone stand. So he kicked the roadie bending over to pick up the latest mangled stand. Hard. Not hard enough to send him ass over ankle but hard enough to humiliate the roadie if not hurt him.

"I said, *don't pick that mike stand up, motherfucker!*" Axl accosted the guy, who hadn't caught on yet to Axl's displeasure. The roadie froze on the spot, on the stage, stone still. The audience began cheering. In the wake of all the press reports about the riots and misdeeds and outrageous episodes, many people were hopeful that this night's performance would also be a memorable one.

Axl then announced "Hey, check it out—I'm having one of those 'irrational temper tantrums' you keep reading about in the press," and then he laughed: "You know you fuckers shouldn't encourage this sort of shit."

When the band launched into the next song, Axl picked up the most recently erected telephone stand and hurled it like a javelin at the frightened and humiliated roadie, who ducked just in time. The audience was transfixed. The aggression unleashed, the sudden eruption of violence, was galvanizing. Suddenly, in a room of twenty thousand, nobody was safe anymore.

Later Axl, referring to the incident, grinned his boyishly charming smile and said to the crowd: "Well, as you can see, being a fuckin' psycho basket like me does have its advantages."

Backstage, as the record company delegation ran around trying to obtain a firm and realistic release date for the *Illusion* LP's, Stradlin, who usually "shows up just a half an hour before the gig, plays, then says good-bye, goes back to a different hotel and gets some sleep," was still ready to talk.

The writer asked him if it was hard to be surrounded by such wild and crazy guys and still maintain his sobriety.

Stradlin answers: "Not really. When I see these guys doing whatever, I know that first they're going to get that rush, that euphoria, and then tomorrow they're going to wake up and feel like shit."

New member Matt Sorum, in due course, commented: "Izzy just doesn't dig it all anymore. He don't dig the drinking, even. Me? I like to party. . . . I guess sometimes I go overboard. Every night's a fuckin' party, man. Chicks, beer, you name it . . . take anything you want, man. It's just like being a kid in a candy store."

Izzy, who had his girlfriend, Anneka, along for the first half of the tour, had other things on his mind. "After this tour's finished, I'd like to go hang out in Europe, preferably somewhere near the ocean, and just keep writing songs . . . ."

Then the most silent band member, the one they call the "invisible man," expounds with an almost eerie sense of perspective.

"I think Guns N' Roses will take its natural course. Even though it could end tomorrow night. Still, I think we'll take a long break and then come back and do it again. That's what it feels like could happen. But, then again, two years ago I never really thought this tour could happen. Frankly, I didn't think any of us could have this much of a future."

Two months later, Izzy Stradlin threatened to leave the

band unless a list of his demands were met. The rest of the band had been sequestered in meetings around Los Angeles for almost ten days before final word was announced: Founding member and Axl Rose's long-time friend, Izzy Stradlin has left Guns N' Roses. Guitarist Gilby Clarke of the Los Angeles band, Kills for Thrills, has been named as his salaried replacement.

After the announcement, Slash wasted no time and immediately rushed the new line-up into a crash rehearsal period to prepare for the remaining dates on their world tour.

The future of Guns N' Roses, as always, is on the edge. Right where they belong.

ACKNOWL-EDGMENTS

Working on this book provided a fascinating and life-affirming experience for me, not just because of the intellectual fodder that was discovered, but because of the way it united my life with the Doors' music and philosophy with my life as a writer and with what that life means. Accordingly, my first thanks go to Ray Manzarek, John Densmore, and Robby Krieger for their patience, support, and trust. Especially Ray, who has been at various times my father, my teacher, my mentor, my partner, and my best friend. And to Jim Morrison, for getting me started (on writing and reading and more), for the blessings (as well as the curses), and without whom this book, or even life as I know it, could not be; my eternal gratitude.

I don't care what anyone thinks of agents; I have been blessed with two of the best, Jim Stein and David Goldman. Since the undertaking of this project, I have also learned that they are even more valuable as friends. For their faith, their professional acumen, but primarily for their friendship, all my thanks are due.

Rosemary Carroll, for being my lawyer, confidant, and long-suffering friend . . . I hope it's getting better for you, too. And John Branca, for old and good reasons, thanks is due.

My editor, Jim Fitzgerald, for (1) his faith in this project; (2) being a real editor; and (3) letting me try to be a real writer. Thanks, gratitude, and respect. Additional thanks to Alex Kuczynski. And Brian Diamond, for being like a brother.

Lynette Phillipson, for her diligence, loyalty, and help, special thanks. Monika Mayo, for rescue at the computer, thank you.

Floyd Peluce, Connie Medford, and Robin White for handling everything that no one else knows how to do, or does as well, so I can concentrate on writing and staying alive in a somewhat constructive manner, my gratitude and respect is, once again, overdue and in abundance.

To my friends who are writers, for confirmation and brotherhood—Michael Talbot, Phillip Cousineaux, Tim Leary, Wallace Fowley, Buddy Arnold, Kurt Loder, James Grauerholz and William Burroughs, Jim Carroll, Pamela Des Barres, Cameron Crowe, Jim Ladd, and Ian Astbury, I appreciate and thank you all.

Thanks, too, to Don Epstein and the guys at G.T.N., for all their efforts and skills. To Oliver Stone, for his vote of confidence, and friendship; all my appreciation is accorded.

To my mother, brothers Joe and Chip, and my sister Nan, all my love and thanks.

Thanks also to Tom Zutaut, for his vision and sense of fair play, and Dr. H. Karkus, for his expertise, knowledge, and unflagging support.

To Josh Richman, for his friendship and support, The Henry Kissinger of the Hollywood Hills award.

And Axl Rose, because he cares, because he's unique, because he has the intelligence to investigate prior to judgment and the guts to base his conclusions on the outcome of that investigation. And because I hated the proposition of writing about an object of so much affection when the object of that affection didn't seem to want it done. For letting me know I was wrong about that, and for more than I can say, a very heartfelt thanks.

Honorable Mention to Mark Rowlands for his invaluable contribution to this book. Ditto, Rob Tannenbaum, Lisa B., and Kim Fowley.

And lastly, to Fawn—for reasons good and true.

INDEX

Abyss, The, 197
"Abyss, The," 218
AC/DC, 136
Ackerman, Diane, 40
Adler, Steven, 61, 64, 70, 135
  background, 51–52, 60
  drugs/alcohol and, 52–54,
    109, 120, 136–37, 139,
    155–56, 158, 159
  Rose on, 69
  Slash on, 139, 159
  Stradlin on, 155–56
Aerosmith, 8, 11, 49, 61,
  76–77
  GNR compared to, 80
  GNR tour, 134, 136–38
Afternoon of a Faun, 196
"Ain't Goin' Down," 116

Alcoholics Anonymous (AA),
  43, 160
Allman, Duane, 120
Allman, Greg, 120
Anslinger, Harry, 122
Appetite for Destruction, 22,
  34, 69, 75, 104, 117–18,
  133, 220
  success of, 28, 100, 155,
    158
"Are You Experienced?", 96
Aristotle, 95
Arken, Wes, 162
Arnold, Buddy, 121
Artaud, Antonin, 93, 96
Astbury, Ian, 195
Asylum Records, 73
Avalon, Frankie, 80

"Back Off Bitch," 116
"Bad Apples," 116
Bailey, L. Stephen, 58
Bailey, Sharon, 58
Bailey, Stuart, 134
Baker, Chet, 121
Baker, Ginger, 120
Balzac, Honoré de, 124
Barbiero, Michael, 82
Barrett, Sid, 120
Basil, St., 190
Baudelaire, Charles, 41, 46, 92, 94, 124–27, 131, 132, 197
Baudelaire: A Biography, 130
Beard, W., 129–30
Beatles, the, 28, 38–39, 80, 93, 203, 206, 216
Beethoven, Ludwig van, 198
Beggar's Banquet, 104
Berry, Chuck, 94, 184
Billboard, 28, 82
Birth of a Tragedy Out of the Spirit of Music, The, 45–46, 169, 191
Black, J. R., 56
Black Rock Coalition, 9
Black Sheep, 61
Blake, William, 105
Blakely, Art, 121
Bloom, Allan, 46
Bloomfield, Mike, 120
Blue Oyster Cult, 195
Bolan, Marc, 122
Bonham, John, 11
Bon Jovi, 137
Bono, 195
Boone, Pat, 80
Brando, Marlon, 211
Brixx, Mandy, 137
Brothers Karamazov, The, 218

Brown, James, 181, 187
Browne, Jackson, 73
Buckley, Tim, 120
Buffalo Springfield, 70
Burroughs, William, 55, 96, 131
Bush, George, 29, 209
Butterfield, Paul, 120
Byrds, the, 70, 116
Byron, George Gordon, Lord, 28, 94, 123, 211

Calhoun, Will, 11
Campbell, Joseph, 50, 118, 194, 195, 203, 208
"Can't Kick the Habit," 121
Capone, Al, 211
Capote, Truman, 140, 162
Carroll, Jim, 120, 131, 195
Cathouse, the, 85
Charles, Ray, 121
Chatterton, Thomas, 139
Cheap Trick, 135
Cheever, John, 123
Chicago (group), 82
Cicero, 178
Cincinnati Lancet, The, 56
Cinderella, 136
Circus, 92
"Civil War," 216–17
Clapton, Eric, 120
Clark, Dick, 160
Clash, the, 14, 215–16
Clink, Mike, 82
Closing of the American Mind, The, 46
Cocteau, Jean, 41, 129
Coleridge, Samuel Taylor, 124–25, 134–35
Collins, Tim, 76–77, 138
Columbia Records, 9
"Coma," 116

"Communication Breakdown," 134
Confessions of an Opium Eater, 125
Confucius, 79
Conrad, Joseph, 179
Conversations with Kafka, 140
Cooper, Alice, 18, 136, 159
Cosineau, Phil, 50
Costello, Elvis, 206
Coury, Fred, 136
Crabbe, William, 124
Crane, Hart, 123
Crash, Darby, 120, 152
Crew, Todd, 116
Crosby, David, 120
Cruddup, Arthur, 186
Cult, the, 8, 53, 137, 162, 195
Curtis, Ian, 120

Danielou, Alain, 173–74
Dante Alighieri, 190, 196, 198
Davis, Miles, 120
Days of Thunder, 116
Dead Pool, The, 82–83
Dean, James, 100, 211
Decline of Western Civilization, The: The Metal Years, 136
Degas, Edgar, 129
De Quincy, Thomas, 124–25
Devil, The: Perceptions of Evil from Antiquity to Christianity, 176
Diary of an Unknown, 129
Dick, Alan, 33–34
Diddley, Bo, 118
Dionysus and Shiva, 173–74
Dionysus—Myth and Cult, 42, 174

Dionysus: The God of Ecstasy, 175
Divided Self, The, 43, 166, 219
Divine Comedy, 198
Dixon, Willie, 186
"Don't Cry," 116
Doors, the, 26, 34, 70, 192, 206
    GNR compared to, 28, 80, 216–17
Doors of Perception, The, 113
Dostoyevski, Fëdor, 91, 94, 119, 218
"Downbeat Effects of Rock Music on an Upbeat Generation, The," 47
"Down on the Farm," 116
Dreams of Decadence, 94
Drugs, 165–66
Durell, Henry Edward, 183
Durual, Akron, 175
Dylan, Bob, 116

Eagles, the, 80, 225
Eastwood, Clint, 82
Eastwood, Kyle, 82
Echo and the Bunnymen, 195
Elektra Records, 70, 71, 73, 77
Eliot, T. S., 80
"End, The," 80, 115
Ensenat, Teresa, 82, 83
Europe (group), 82
Evans, Arthur, 176
Everly, Don, 101
Everly, Erin, 101, 223–25
Exile on Main Street, 49

Faith No More, 148
Family Physician, The, 129–30

Farmer, Frances, 147
Faster Pussycat, 135
Faulkner, William, 123–24
Fiedler, Leslie, 123
Fitzgerald, F. Scott, 123, 124,
    139
Flux and Reflux:
    Ambivalence in the
    Poems of Arthur
    Rimbaud, 132
Fowley, Kim, 69–71
Frances, 147–48
Franklin, Aretha, 181
Freud, Sigmund, 43, 108, 207

Garcia, Jerry, 120
Gautier, Théophile, 124
Gazzari's, 85
Geffen, David, 73–74
Geffen Records, 29, 100, 104,
    117
GNR's first contract (1986),
    58, 74–78, 133
George, Boy, 120
George, Lowell, 120
Germs, the, 152
Getz, Stan, 120
Ginsberg, Allen, 96
Glass, Philip, 148
GNR Lies, 115, 116,
    success of, 28, 104–5
Goat's Head Soup, 49
Goethe, Johann Wolfgang
    von, 198
Goldstein, Doug, 134, 135
Gore, Tipper, 46
Grand Funk Railroad, 73
Grateful Dead, the, 59
Great White, 77
Gregory Nazianzen, St., 190
Guns N' Roses (GNR), 3
    Aerosmith compared to, 80

Aerosmith tour, 134,
    136–38
Beatles compared to,
    38–39
Byrds compared to, 116
Clash compared to, 14,
    215–17
Cooper tour, 136, 159
critics' views of, 9, 21, 24,
    25, 28, 91
dance and, 187, 191
Dead Pool, The, and,
    82–83
Donnington concert
    (1988), 33–36, 102, 221
Doors compared to, 28, 80,
    217–18
drugs/alcohol and, 11–12,
    21, 53–54, 63, 64, 66, 67,
    74–75, 77, 89, 106–7,
    118, 120, 133–39, 142–
    44, 146, 151–61, 162–64,
    192, 211, 217
early days of, 51, 60–78,
    158, 193
at Farm Aid Spring, 116
first gig (1985), 61–62
first record (1986), 75
first record contract
    (1986), 58, 74–78, 133
future of, 104–5, 106–7,
    108, 115–17, 192–93,
    200, 215–17, 220, 221–
    22, 225
Geffen Records and, 29,
    58, 74–78, 100, 104, 117,
    133
Hamilton on, 75
Iron Maiden Tour, 137
Jagger on, 14–15, 215, 217
money and, 6, 8, 64–66,
    74, 75, 77, 137–38, 155

Mötley Crüe compared to, 71, 74, 116, 117
Mötley Crüe tour, 134, 136
New York Dolls compared to, 80
as out-of-control/vulgar/ unpredictable/self- destructive, 14, 17–18, 21–22, 24–30, 33, 36, 38–40, 46, 47, 59, 69–70, 74, 77–80, 85, 89–92, 96–100, 102, 105–8, 110, 118, 134–35, 156, 159– 60, 163, 170, 207, 212, 216, 217, 220–22
Poison compared to, 117
Rolling Stones compared to, 5, 6, 9, 14–15, 24, 25, 28, 79–80, 184–85, 215
Rolling Stones 1989 L.A. concert, 4–6, 8–9, 11–15
Rolling Stones 1990 Atlantic City concert, 161, 222
at Roxy, 69
Sex Pistols compared to, 14, 24, 25, 28, 80, 217
as shaman, 208
success of, 8, 17, 21–22, 24–30, 35, 39, 68–69, 75, 80, 83–87, 89–91, 97, 100–105, 137–38, 156, 158, 162–63, 194
at Troubadour, 61–62, 68
U2 compared to, 117
Warner Brothers Records and, 117–18
at Whisky A Go-Go, 69, 161
See also Adler, Steven; McKagan, Duff; Rose, Axl; Slash; Stradlin, Izzy

Guns N' Roses, music of
"Ain't Goin' Down," 116
Appetite for Destruction, 22, 28, 34, 69, 75, 100, 104, 117–18, 133, 155, 158, 220
"Back Off Bitch," 116
"Bad Apples," 116
"Civil War," 216–17
"Coma," 116
Days of Thunder, 116
Decline of Western Civilization, The: The Metal Years, 136
"Don't Cry," 116
"Down on the Farm," 116
GNR Lies, 28, 104–5, 115, 116
"It's So Easy," 92
Live?! Like a Suicide,* 75, 104
"Ma Ma Kin," 137
"Mr. Brownstone," 4, 13, 89, 118
"Nice Boys," 90
"Night Train," 13
"November Rain," 115
"One in a Million," 3, 9, 221
"Out ta Get Me," 118
"Paradise City," 4, 34, 99, 101–4, 118
"Patience," 12, 104–5
"Rocket Queen," 99
"Sweet Child o' Mine," 40, 76, 100–102, 118
"Under My Wheels," 136
Use Your Illusion, 115
"Welcome to the Jungle," 40, 80, 82–87, 96, 100–2, 118, 175

Haggis, 137
Hamilton, Vicky, 74
  on GNR, 75
  on Rose, 148
  Rose on, 69
  Slash on, 69
Hancock, Butch, 186
Hanoi Rocks, 161
Harrison, Jane, 189
Hawes, Hampton, 120–21
Hayter, Althea, 125
"Hear That Long Black Snake
  Moan," 180
Heart, 82
Heidegger, Martin, 196
Hemingway, Ernest, 124
Hendrix, Jimi, 96, 120
  Rose compared to, 26,
  139, 211
Henley, Don, 52
Heroin Solution, The, 56,
  121
Hero with a Thousand Faces,
  The, 194–95
Hiatt, John, 139
Hilburn, Robert, 4, 13, 16
History of Secret Societies,
  175
Holliday, Billie, 120
Hollywood Rose, 60–61
Homer, 121, 123
"Honky Tonk Woman," 134
Hooker, John Lee, 186
Horace, 25
"Hotel California," 80
Hudson, Ola, 54
Huxley, Aldous, 113

Iceman Cometh, The, 139
Idiot, The, 119
Idol, Billy, 195
Igjugarjuk, 110

Illuminations, 130
Intoxication, 40–41
Iron Maiden, 137
"It's So Easy," 92

Jagger, Mick, 9, 10, 34, 49,
  59, 92, 152
  on GNR, 14–15, 215, 217
  Rose compared to, 14, 26,
  79–80, 208–9
James, Jesse, 211
James, William, 196
Janouch, Gustav, 140
Jesus Christ, 196, 205, 206
John, Elton, 73, 148, 207
John Barleycorn Must Die,
  94
John of the Cross, St., 196
Johnson, Don, 209
Jones, Brian, 120
  Rose compared to, 139–40
Joplin, Janis, 11, 120, 181,
  184
  Rose compared to, 139–
  40, 187
Jullian, Philippe, 94
Jung, Carl, 32, 43, 44, 96,
  140, 143, 195, 207

Kafka, Franz, 140, 143
Keats, John, 124
Kenevan, Phillis, 197
Kerrang!, 21
Kierkegaard, Søren, 219
Kiss, 73, 82
"Knocking on Heaven's
  Door," 18, 116

"La Chambre Double," 132
L.A. Guns, 60, 61
Laing, R. D., 43, 166, 210,
  219

Lame Flames, the, 137
Larson, Stephan, 209–10
Last Judgment, The, 205
Laurie, Peter, 166
"Layla," 115
Led Zeppelin, 61, 160, 206
Lefebure, Molly, 133
Lennon, John, 73, 115, 120, 203
Les Paradis artificiels, 125
"Let It Be," 93
Let It Bleed, 93
Letters from the Earth, 205
Lewis, Jerry Lee, 95, 120, 184, 186–87, 211
Little Richard, 94, 120, 181, 184, 186–87
"Live and Let Die," 115
Live?!* Like a Suicide, 75, 104
Living Colour, 9–11, 15
Loder, Kurt, 160, 225
London, Jack, 94, 123, 124
Long Day's Journey into Night, 139
Longhair Professor, 186
Lords of the New Church, The, 195
Los Angeles Times, 4, 9, 110, 219
Lucian, 190
Lydon, Johnny, 26
Lynryd Skynryd, 101

McCartney, Paul, 115
McGuiness, Paul, 90–91
McKagan, Duff, 70, 135
    background, 53, 60–61
    Brixx and, 137
    on Donnington concert, 33
    drugs/alcohol and, 53, 66, 120, 158–59
    on GNR, 66, 67, 77, 89, 101
    marriage of, 159
    on the music, 67, 101
    Rose on, 69
    on Slash, 101
    Slash on, 159
    Stradlin on, 62
Mailer, Norman, 149–50
"Ma Ma Kin," 137
Man and World, 197
Manet, Edouard, 129
Martin, Dean, 59
May, Rollo, 44
Metallica, 148
Metraux, Alfred, 181–82
Mezzrow, Mezz, 120
Michaels, Mark, 135
"Mr. Brownstone," 4, 13, 89, 118
Mitchell, A., 166
Mitchell, Joni, 148
Money, Eddie, 82
Monroe, Michael, 161
Moon, Keith, 120
Morrison, Jim, 70, 91–94, 96, 106, 120, 175, 187
    death of, 57, 192–95, 217
    Rose compared to, 4, 13, 26, 57, 80, 87, 101, 108, 139–40, 146–47, 187, 192–94, 208–09, 211–13, 217, 219, 222–23
Morrison, Pamela, 101, 223
Moses, 44
Mötley Crüe, 8, 71–73, 80, 151
    GNR compared to, 71, 74, 116–17
    GNR tour, 134, 136
Motorhead, 158

MTV, 83, 99, 100, 136, 160, 162, 225
Murphy, Eddie, 209
Music Connection, 60
Music Journal, 27

Napoléon, 79
National Committee on Music, The, 47
Natural History of the Senses, 40
Navarro, Fats, 120
Nelson, Ricky, 80
Neumann, Erich, 143–44, 197, 206
Nevison, Ron, 82
New York Dolls, 80
"Nice Boys," 90
Nielsen, Rick, 135
Nietzsche, Friedrich, 26, 32, 46, 79, 89, 95, 108, 115, 169–70, 196–98, 205
"Night Train," 13
Nijinsky, Vaslaw, 96, 191
Niven, Alan, 77–78
No One Here Gets Out Alive, 192
Notes from the Underground, 91–92
"November Rain," 115

"Ode to a Nightingale," 124
Odyssey, The, 121
O'Neill, Eugene, 123–24, 137
"One in a Million," 3, 9, 221
"Only Women Bleed," 18
Opium and the Romantic Imagination, 125, 128
Opium Diary of a Cure, 41
Osbourne, Ozzy, 82
Otto, Walter F., 41, 42, 173
"Out ta Get Me," 118

"Pains of Sleep, The," 133
Paradise, 190
"Paradise City," 4, 34, 99, 101–4, 118
Parents Musical Resource Committee (PMRC), 46
Parker, Charlie, 120, 150
Parsons, Gram, 104
Pater, Walter, 27
"Patience," 12, 104–5
Paul, St., 43, 185
Pearls, Frederick, 32
Pennsylvania Medical Journal, 142
Pepper, Art, 120
Perkins, Carl, 186
Perry, Joe, 49–50, 77, 120
Peschel, Enid Rhodes, 132
Phillips, John, 120
Picasso, Pablo, 26, 129
"Pipe Dream Blues," 121
Place of Creation, The, 144, 197, 206
Plato, 90, 95
Poe, Edgar Allan, 16, 96, 124–27
Poison, 117
Politics, 95
Polo, Marco, 131–33
Pop, Iggy, 8, 92, 120, 195
    Rose compared to, 211
"Poppy, The," 124
Portable Coleridge, The, 133
Presley, Elvis, 11, 80, 120, 170, 184
    Rose compared to, 26, 186–87, 209, 213
Prince, 8, 186–87
Proffer, Spencer, 76

Rainbow Bar & Grill, the, 66, 85

Ramones, the, 207
Rasmussen, Knud, 110
Reagan, Ronald, 29
Reid, Vernon, 9–11, 16
Republic, 95
Richards, Keith, 15, 49–50,
    59, 120, 138, 152, 156
Richards, A. A., 133
Rimbaud, Arthur, 27, 94, 96,
    105, 106, 197, 211
"Rime of the Ancient
    Mariner," 132–33
RIP, 225
Road Crew, 60, 61
"Rocket Queen," 99
Rock Lives, 95, 96
Rock Stars, 91
Roethke, Theodore, 218
Rogers, Will, 90
Rolling Stone, 137, 139, 146
Rolling Stones, the, 26, 59,
    93, 97, 104, 166, 170,
    206
  GNR compared to, 5, 6, 9,
    14–15, 24, 25, 28, 79–80,
    184–85, 215
  GNR 1989 L.A. concert, 4–
    6, 8–9, 11–15
  GNR 1990 Atlantic City
    concert, 161, 222
Ronstadt, Linda, 73
Rose, Axl, 18, 36, 62, 65, 75,
    82, 83, 96, 98, 117–18,
    135–36, 158, 167–68
  on Adler, 69
  background, 51, 58–59, 61,
    148, 181–82, 184–85, 221
  Brown compared to, 186–
    87
  critics' views of, 4, 13
  dance and, 185, 186–87,
    190–91

Dionysian duality of, 40,
    57, 80
  on Donnington concert,
    33, 35
  drugs/alcohol and, 4, 11–
    12, 53, 54, 57, 58, 63, 67,
    89, 120, 133–34, 137,
    139–40, 142–44, 146–
    48, 151–55, 159–63, 167,
    192–95, 200, 211–12,
    216–18
  Everly (Erin) and, 101,
    223–24
  family and, 12–13, 58–59,
    86, 134, 155, 192–94
  Farmer compared to, 147–
    48
  Fowley, letter to, 69–71
  future of, 104–5, 192–95,
    200, 216–19, 221–26
  on GNR, 6, 11, 33, 35, 53,
    63–64, 67–69, 76, 99–
    101, 108–10, 117, 135,
    137, 155–56, 162–63
  on Hamilton, 69
  Hamilton on, 148
  Hendrix compared to, 26,
    139–40, 211
  Jagger compared to, 14,
    26, 57, 79–80, 208–9
  Jones compared to, 139–
    40
  Joplin compared to, 139–
    40, 187
  as larger-than-life figure,
    85–87, 89, 90, 92–95,
    106–8, 139–40, 208–9,
    210–13, 216–17
  Lewis compared to, 186–
    87, 211
  Little Richard compared to,
    186–87

Rose, Axl (*cont.*)
  Lydon compared to, 26
  on McKagan, 69
  marriage of, 101, 159,
    223–26
  money and, 6, 155, 225
  Morrison compared to, 4,
    13, 26, 57, 80, 87, 101,
    106, 139–40, 186–87,
    192–95, 208–9, 211–13,
    217, 219, 223
  on the music, 3–4, 6, 11,
    13, 16, 76, 84–85, 99–
    102, 115–17, 155, 192
  Pop compared to, 211
  Presley compared to, 26,
    186–87, 209, 213
  Prince compared to,
    186–87
  racism and, 3–4, 10–11,
    13, 15–17, 221–22
  rehabilitation of, 144, 146–
    48, 161
  as shaman, 208–9, 211–12
  on Slash, 53, 59, 69, 101,
    162
  Slash on, 61, 134, 146,
    148, 159, 167, 220–21
  on Stanley, 76
  on Stradlin, 69, 101, 153
  Stradlin on, 51, 148, 155
  Turner (Tina) compared
    to, 186–87
Roth, David Lee, 11, 135–36
Roxy, the, 66, 69
Ruskin, John, 25–28
Russell, Jeffery, 176

Sabbah, Hassan I., 131–32
*Sacred and Profane Beauty:
  The Holy in Art,* 178,
  189, 190

*Samuel Taylor Coleridge/
  Bondage to Opium,* 133
Saturday Night Live, 59
Schep, Archie, 120
Schiele, Egon, 93–94
Schopenhauer, Arthur, 94,
  216
Scott, Bon, 120
Sex and Drugs, 164
Sex Pistols, the, 59, 98, 206
  GNR compared to, 14, 24,
    25, 28, 80, 217
Shaman's Doorway, The, 210
Shapiro, Harry, 150
Shelley, Percy Bysshe, 26–28,
  93, 139
Siggers, Landon, 33–34
"Silly Love Song," 115
Slash, 15, 16, 18, 70, 75–76,
  84, 115
  on Adler, 139, 159
  background, 54–55, 60–61
  on Donnington concert,
    34–35, 220–21
  drugs/alcohol and, 11–12,
    22, 53–58, 64–65, 77, 89,
    120, 134, 135, 137, 139,
    152, 155, 157–60, 162–
    63, 166–69, 221–22
  on GNR, 22, 34–35, 51,
    53–54, 60, 62–67, 75–
    77, 82, 97–101, 103–4,
    134, 136–39, 157–59,
    220–22
  on Hamilton, 69
  on McKagan on, 159
  McKagan on, 101
  on the music, 53, 61, 63,
    64, 67, 76, 98–101, 103–
    4, 116, 158, 221–22
  rehabilitation of, 159,
    167–69

on Rose, 61, 134, 146, 148,
   159, 167, 221–22
Rose on, 53, 59, 69, 101,
   162
on Stanley, 76
on Stradlin, 61, 158
Stradlin on, 155
Slick, Grace, 120
Smith, Patti, 131, 195
Some Girls, 15
Sorum, Matt, 53
Spheeris, Penelope, 136
Spin, 152
Springsteen, Bruce, 181
"Stairway to Heaven,"
   115
Stanley, Paul, 75–76
Starkey, Enid, 130
Starr, Ringo, 120, 167
Stevens, Cat, 61
Stone, Sly, 120
Stradlin, Izzy, 59, 98, 116
   on Adler, 155–56
   background, 49–51, 61
   drugs/alcohol and, 50–51,
      54, 64–65, 118, 120, 152,
      153, 155–60
   Fowley, letter to, 69–71
   on GNR, 62–63, 69, 76,
      77, 118, 134, 135, 138,
      155–57
   on McKagan, 62
   on the music, 76, 118
   on Rose, 51, 148, 155
   Rose on, 69, 101, 153
   on Slash on, 155
   Slash on, 61, 157–58
Stravinsky, Igor, 191
Stravinsky brothers, 8
Sullivan, Ed, 186
"Sweet Child o' Mine," 40,
   76, 100–2, 118

Swinburne, Algernon Charles,
   124
"Sympathy for the Devil," 34
Szasz, Thomas, 210

Tannenbaum, Rob, 137
Taylor, Dallas, 120
Tennyson, Alfred, Lord, 26
Theater and Its Double, The,
   93
Thompson, Francis, 124
Thompson, Steve, 82
Thus Spake Zarathustra, 95
Townsend, Pete, 120
Trebach, A. S., 121
Troubadour, the, 61–62, 68
Turner, Big Joe, 186
Turner, Ike, 8
Turner, Tina, 8, 186–87
Twain, Mark, 205
Twilight of the Idols, 115
2 Live Crew, 37
Tyler, Steve, 49, 76, 77, 120

"Under My Wheels," 136
Use Your Illusion, 115
U2, 90, 117
Uzi-Suicide label, 75, 104

Van der Leeuw, Gerardus,
   189–90
Van Eyck, Jan, 205
Van Gogh, Vincent, 26, 94,
   96
Van Halen, 11, 80, 151
*Varieties of Religious
   Experience, The,* 196
Ventura, Michael, 180, 183–
   84, 186–87
Verlaine, Paul, 123–24, 129–
   30

Vicious, Sid, 120
Voodoo in Haiti, 181–82

Wagner, Richard, 170
Waiting for the Man, 150
Warner Brothers Records, 117–18
Waste Land, The, 80
Waters, Muddy, 186
Watts, Alan, 204–5
"Welcome to the Jungle," 40, 80, 86–87, 96, 118, 175
success of, 82–85, 100–2
Wells, H. G., 113
Western Mythology, 204
"When the Music's Over," 34, 96
Whisky A Go-Go, the, 66, 69, 70, 85, 161

White, Tim, 91, 95, 96
Whitten, Danny, 120
Who, the, 34
Wilde, Oscar, 26, 27, 96, 105–6, 110
Williamson, Sonny Boy, 186
Willis, Bruce, 209
Will There Really Be a Morning?, 147–48
Wilson, Bill, 43
Wilson, Brian, 120
Wilson, Robert Anton, 164
Wonder, Stevie, 8
Woodman, Marion, 43

Zodiac Mindwarp, 137
Zutaut, Tom, 73–74, 76, 82